ENVIRONMENTAL EDUCATION

ENVIRONMENTAL EDUCATION

DR. ARCHANA TOMAR

PUBLICATIONS

KALPAZ PUBLICATIONS

DELHI-110052

Environmental Education

Rs. 175

ISBN: 9788178354835

Published in 2007 in India by
Kalpaz Publications
C-30, Satyawati Nagar,
Delhi-110052
E-mail: kalpaz@hotmail.com

Lasser TypeSetting by: Rudra Computer Graphics, Delhi
Printed at: Salasar Imaging System, Delhi

Contents

Foreword

It is not hard to imagine how more fertilizers; more people and more industries with inadequate pollution controls over the past two decades have resulted in local pollution problems expanding to transboundary and regional proportions of almost every continent. As a result human health is jeopardized; the flora and fauna are gradually becoming extinct. Severe climate change is an event experienced throughout the globe. Regardless of the severity, it is clear that developing countries are more vulnerable and will be the first to suffer from global warming. The emissions are increasing at a rate of 4-5 percent as a result of industrialization and improved standards of living.

Local, national and global environmental problems have the same underlying policies and practices, and inadequate policies concerning natural resources and the environment. The challenge in dealing with the complex nexus of global environment and development is to reform these policies and to bring environmental considerations into the mainstream of economic decision making. This challenge can best be addressed through sustainable development actions at the country level.

Whether in the long run developing countries will become deeply engaged with issues like global climate change depends on a clear understanding of the risks of business as usual to their own citizens and future generations. Current scientific knowledge and global modeling exercises have yet to pinpoint regional impacts, let alone national impacts, of most global environmental issues. Yet these problems cannot be resolved without local capacity to analyze and define specific impacts on individual nations. Local scientists must be in a strategic position to provide their policymakers with the advice they need to formulate strategic directions and process for their adoption. Otherwise, there can be little progress toward sustainable development and environmental improvement.

Man in addition to the natural process has himself been responsible in changing the climate. The rapidly increasing contribution of nuclear energy for generation of electricity, industrialization, volatile organic compounds and particles in the air change the heat and balance of atmosphere. Establishment of large hydroelectric power plants required for constructions of dams on rivers, regulation of rivers and diversion of some rivers. All this has influence on climatic change.

Population, poverty and pollution are the three major problems now facing the country. These three are interlinked with each other thus forming a problem web. Besides pollution over exploitation of natural resources also disturb the recharging capacity of the natural system thereby minimizing the protective cover. Our activities should always aim at sustainable development.

None of us live on islands. Interdependence means that all of us, whatever the stage of our development, are travelling in the same boat, floating and sinking together. All of us must be partners in the global venture to implement the best blueprints brought forward by governments, international organizations and conventions, civil society, including the scientific community, and the private sector.

Thus environmental education has to extend to all: Teachers, students, housewives, policy makers, planners, workers, industrialists etc. All the efforts should be made to make this earth more habitable and congenial free of health hazards due to environment.

When gradually the awareness to save the planet earth is increasing and Supreme court has decided to make its education compulsory for schools and colleges. This book will be valuable for teachers to educate the students about nature and scope of environmental education. It will educate the teachers and students about various approaches that can be used to make environmental education interesting and live. The knowledge should be broad based and as far as possible in an integrated and interdisciplinary manner.

Dr. Archana Tomar has written the book on environmental education, which will be a good resource material for the teacher educators and B. Ed students. It covers number of things from objectives, history, basic concepts, environmental problems, curriculum for environment, role of NGOs, role of media, various methods of teaching environmental education and value analysis model for developing proper attitude towards environment. It will be useful for the researchers in the area of classroom instruction. I congratulate Dr. Archana Tomar for her contribution in the field of Education.

Prof. K. C. Upadhyay
Former Vice Chancellor
The Maharaja Sayajirao University of Baroda
Baroda.

Preface

Environmental Education is a process to promote the awareness and understanding of the environment, its relationship with man and his activities. Environmental education is both a style and subject matter of education. Style means approach of teaching environmental education and subject means the content matter of environmental education. This book focuses on both the style and subject of environmental education.

First unit focuses on need and importance of environmental education. Why do we need to give environmental education? What are the ways of dealing with environment? What has gone wrong with environment? It also highlights goals, objectives and guiding principles of environmental education.

The first unit is followed by the history of environmental education. This unit highlights environmental education in modern and ancient times of India. How was environment worshipped this is followed by values and philosophy of environmental education?

In the third unit knowledge base related to environmental education are given. It talks about ecosystem and its components. The biotic and abiotic factors and bio geo chemical cycles and their importance are highlighted in this chapter.

Fourth unit deals with the problems related to environment. Problems like deforestation, energy crisis, ecological degradation, population explosion, air pollution, green house effect, acid rains etc., in the end a sample of its teaching and assignment is given.

The fifth chapter focuses on the Role of Non Governmental Organization in developing citizens with values related to environment. This unit is followed by role of non-governmental organization. Environment is facing so many problems these problems need to be tackled through different approaches and many angles here NGOs play a vital role because of their specialized structure. It deals with various organizations working in the field of environmental education at international, national and local level, the activities that they carry out and there objectives.

The next unit deals with Conservation its concept, forest conservation, soil conservation, water conservation, conservation of biodiversity, national parks and sanctuaries, various projects involved with the improvement of environment.

Next unit deals with sustainable development, its concept, why do we need sustainable development, how can we achieve the objective of sustainable development? What are the strategies for sustainable development? Etc.

Followed by sustainable development is the unit on Environment laws and policies it deals with various acts brought about from time to time to improve the condition of environment, it also deals with drawback and problems in legislation.

Curriculum of environmental education the characteristics and types of curriculum are given, which is followed by framework for environmental education. It discusses various styles of curriculum development.

Having discussed the knowledge base, curriculum and the efforts made by NGOs in imparting values pertaining to environmental education. In this unit various methods of teaching environmental education are discussed like exhibition, debate, quiz, project, games, puppets, etc. etc.

Next unit deals with the Role of Media in popularizing and bringing awareness regarding environmental education; it talks about various types of media available and how to select from the various media? The media can play a major role in inculcating values related to environment.

The unit on role of media is followed by Value Analysis Model. There are numerous issues that talk about environment and development they are contradictory. What should we do when such contradictions arise? How should we reach a decision? Here value analysis model comes to our rescue. It is a small unit, which discusses value analysis model there are many dilemmatic situations, which requires clarification and proper analysis to integrate them in real life.

From the various units it clearly emerges that environment education has to be managed properly as it is concern and need of all the citizens of the country be it rural or urban, young or old, school going or college going, developed, developing etc.

Finally a glossary is given at the end and various days that are celebrated for imparting environmental education.

Dr. Archana Tomar

Acknowledgements

I take this opportunity to thank all my teachers who introduced me to this fascinating world and its environment. They continuously gave the input, humans are not the only inhabitants of the planet earth. I am thankful to Dr. Diwakara Rao who inspired me to write the book on environmental education, so that it can reach out to many more people.

I am thankful to Professor D. R. Goel for institutionalizing this course in the Department of Education, Faculty of Education and Psychology as Head CASE. I heartily thank you Professor Sneha Joshi for guiding me in my Ph. D work on environmental education. Madam you were always there whenever I needed your help on any matter be it related to book, personal or professional thank you Mam.

I would like to express a deep sense of gratitude to Professor K. C. Upadhyay Vice Chancellor Maharaja Sayajirao University of Baroda, Vadodara for writing the Foreword of my book.

I am thankful to all my students who gave some wonderful ideas during discussions related to environmental problems. I am indebted to the trustees of Navrachana College of Education for giving me all the needed support. I am thankful to Dr. Xavier Principal, Navrachana College of Education Baroda and the faculty members for inspiring me to complete this book.

I would like to thank my father, mother and brother who constantly supported me in this endeavor. My acknowledgement will be incomplete if I do not thank my father in law for looking after all the routine responsibilities of mine. I am greatly indebted to my husband and my daughter Muskan, who had to live without me on many evenings. Above all I would like to thank almighty for creating such a wonderful universe and making me a part of it.

Finally I thank the publishers for timely printing the book and bringing it in the market.

Dr. Archana Tomar

1

Environmental Education

The life on the planet earth has evolved to the present stage through millions of years of interaction between the organism and its environment. It therefore goes without saying that the very existence, survival and progress of man on earth depends on the quality of environment. The thinking man, Homo sapiens is a product of his environment. The History of human civilization is a unique contradiction of strange paradoxes. On the one hand, we have developed agriculture, medicine, and industry, and on the other oblivious consequences. We have tempered with the environment, we live in and have overused it to an extent that today the whole human civilization is in peril. Misuse or overuse of nature and natural environment by the primitive man has made man more and more victim of this contradiction. His psychosocial heritage has not been strong enough to keep him from his self-destructive process. The demand for the supply of material resources has never dwindled. The use of resources is increasing exponentially not only because we are too many, but also because so few of us are demanding too much from the fragile biosphere. In the 21st century the land has become more urban and more developed. Large and middle-sized communities have evolved a large percentage of population stays in smaller percentage of land surface. Consequently the independent rural oriented living that once characterized our social and political heritage is no longer a dominating influence in most of our lives. Therefore we have community environmental problems, such as air, water, and noise pollution, traffic congestion, urban decay, environmental health problems, indiscriminate use of pesticides, housing problems.

Since, the world population is doubling every 35 years at present the rate of growth, the need for resources, by a naïve estimate, is doubling in the same period. It has been called a naïve estimate because the actual rate at which the demand is increasing is many times more than the one mentioned above. In the next 30 years or so, keeping in mind the present rate of demand, it is estimated that the energy use will increase 500% in certain parts of the world. The hazard, to the global environment are increasing at an equally alarming rate – carbon dioxide in the atmosphere, waste, heat, industrial waste in the sea, oxygen depletion, radioactivity – all these are threatening human health and life span. War and preparation for war are demanding more material resources than are used for bettering the life of the human species. The population is facing the scarcity of freshwater; recently the fight for water and scarce resources is commonly evident in many parts of the world. Similarly the changing climatic patterns are also an evident threat for the very survival of different life forms on earth. All this tends to suggest, as if the desire to live in a habitable environment and a safe world has totally disappeared. Whether the menacing by-products of our technology based civilization should be dealt with a better technology or by an alternative approach to life and living is a debatable issue. The consciousness and the desire and efforts to improve existing environmental situation as well as to create a new global ethos that would sustain the planet for a better tomorrow have been reflected in the societal thoughts almost in every part of the globe. This is nowhere near suggesting that it has, in any major way, diverted the trends that are steadily leading to a silent catastrophe but a greater number of us are more convinced today than before that our future is not what it was thought to be. Environmental protection is assuming ever-increasing importance all over the world. More than one hundred years back, Fredrick Engles displayed remarkable foresight when he wrote. " Let us not..............Flatter ourselves overmuch on account of human victories over nature. For each victory on nature takes its revenge on us. Each victory, it is true, in the first place brings the results unforeseen effects which only too often cancel the first. It is just like continuously removing stones from a concrete structure, the continuous removal of the stones will on a day lead to collapse of the structure. Compared to the structure environment is more resilient still we must not try to test its patience, as it could be disastrous for life on planet earth. Harmony between man and his environment is the essence of life and growth. Since the needs and aspirations of the society are reflected on the educational superstructure, the UNESCO UNEP International Environment education program was put into action at the UNESCO secretariat in Paris in 1975. This program was a direct outcome of Stockholm Sweden, 1972, which stated that" it is recommended that the secretary general of the organization of the united nations system especially UNESCO and the other international agencies concerned should after consultation and agreement, take the necessary steps to establish an international program in environmental education interdisciplinary in approach, in school and out of school, encompassing all levels of education and directed towards the general public, in particular the ordinary citizen with a view to educating him as to the simple steps he might take within his means to manage and control his environment. With this background let us understand what is the importance of environmental education?

Importance of Environmental Education

Borders bind the countries, but when it comes to the natural environment it is found to be global. Any change in the climate or vegetation or ocean current brings a substantial change in the subcontinent and world over. As we share the same natural resources throughout the world, we need to develop world citizenry who can think globally and act locally. After all environment is affected by the actions of people both individually and collectively. We overuse the environment for our selfish purposes without realizing the ill effects. Environmental education will help in developing various values, attitudes, skills necessary for solving environmental crises. The people will be able to cast their votes on environmental issues to bring about proper policies. People can boycott a product and campaign for others. They can ask questions.

The foundation for strong environmental action rests to a large degree, on what happens in our homes, schools, youth program, community, media and interest groups. Each of these has a particular role to play in the education of the individual. Today's youth will soon be the citizen and voters whose decisions will affect not only the immediate environment in which they live, but also that there nation and other parts of the world. They will make the choices and directly or indirectly by their behavior cast the votes about recreation, transportation, and beautification, water needs and control of air and water pollution. Therefore, it is imperative that our education systems develop comprehensive environmental education programs so that our youth and adult become aware about the environmental problems; they develop skill to solve environmental problems. They are equipped with the skills to reduce the emerging challenges of environment. People must understand the importance of relating ecological, economic, social, technological and political information when working towards the solution of environmental problems. Now let us know what is environmental education?

What is Environmental Education?

The term environmental education is made of two term "environment" and education. Environment is defined as " The sum total of all conditions and influences affecting the life and development of organisms" Education is " Forming desirable attitudes, values, skills, understanding and interest about the environment so as to preserve it and improve it for survival of the present and future mankind. The conditions and influences can be biotic or abiotic that is living or non living. As we all know that all living beings are directly or indirectly dependent on nature. So, it becomes pre-requisite that, we should be aware about the extent to which the homeostasis of nature works. Beyond equilibrium there are backlashes, which certainly are undesirable. Our main goal should be sustainable development. To understand the meaning of Environmental Education, its three major aspects are to be considered. They are:

1. Education about Environment. Environment as the subject of investigation.

2. Education through Environment and where the environment is a medium for education, the use of real life situation as the basis of inquiry
3. Education for Environment. Education for conserving and improving the environment. A study of environmental problem and working towards their solutions. (Praharaj 1987)

These three aspects in short specify that education should be about environment by making environment as a subject of investigation. Education through environment means where environment should be used as a medium of study using real life situations. Education is for conserving and improving the environment and finding solutions to the problems related to it.

According to UNESCO "Environmental Education is the process of recognizing values and clarifying concepts in order to develop skills and attitudes necessary to understand and appreciate the inter relatedness among man, his culture and his bio physical surroundings. Environmental Education also entails practice in decision making and concerning environmental quality" International Union for Conservation of Nature and Natural resources commission of education, International working meeting on environmental education in the school curriculum, Paris UNESCO. (1970)

Environmental values contribute to public well being and concern itself with the survival of the human species. Its force should reside mainly in the initiative of the learners and their involvement in action and both immediate and future subjects of concern should guide it. (Final report of the Tbilisi Conference1977)

According to United States Environmental Education Act (1970): "Environmental Education is an integrated process which deals with man's interrelationship with his nature, population growth, pollution, resource allocation, technology and urban and rural planning to the total human environment"

Allen A Schmieder (1974) states that: "Environmental education is concerned with dynamic interaction between humanity and nature and it is directed at the improvement of the quality and existence for all living things."

UNESCO report (1976) defines: "Environmental Education as the outcome of reorientation and devoting of the various discipline and of different educational experiences making it possible to achieve and integrate perception of the environment and to act towards it, it is a way that is more rational and corresponds to social needs."

William Stapes "Environmental Education is a process aimed at developing a world population that is aware of and concerned about the total environment and its associated problems, which has knowledge, attitudes, motivations, commitments and skills to work individually and collectively toward solutions of current problems and the prevention of new ones".

We need to identify and develop educational programs that focus on the causes of environmental crises, rather than just the symptoms. It is apparent that we will be facing today's environment problems in the future, and breeding new ones, until we identify the causes of our environmental crisis and develop comprehensive action programs to resolve them. We will have to create awareness about the various environmental problems and their complexity. Awareness alone is not sufficient, so we will have to provide with adequate knowledge and skills regarding the environment and its allied problems along with skills to handle these problems. Finally at the stage of internalization we have to bring about the change in behavior and attitude and develop alternate and ecologically friendly behavior so that we can move towards a more sustainable development.

Goals of Environmental Education

1. To Foster clear awareness of, and concern about, economic, social, political and ecological interdependence in urban and rural areas.
2. To provide every person with opportunities to acquire knowledge, values, attitudes, commitment and skills needed to protect and improve the environment.
3. To create new patterns of behavior of individuals groups and society as a whole towards the environment.

Objectives of Environmental Education

The objectives of Environmental Education are as follows:

1. **Awareness:** To help individuals and social groups acquire an awareness of and sensitivity to the total environment and it's allied problems.
2. **Knowledge:** To help individuals and social groups acquire basic understanding of the total environment, its associated problems and humanity's critically responsible presence and role in it.
3. **Attitude:** To help individuals and social groups acquire values, strong feelings of concern for the environment and the motivation for actively participating in its protection and improvement.
4. **Skills:** To help individuals and social groups acquire the skills for solving environmental problems.
5. **Evaluation ability:** To help individuals and social groups evaluate environmental measures and education programs in terms of ecological, political, social, aesthetic and education factors.
6. **Participation:** To help individuals and social groups develop a sense of responsibility and urgency regarding environmental problems to ensure appropriate action to solve their problems.

Guiding Principles of Environmental Education

1. Consider the environment in its totality – natural and built, technological and social (economic, political, technological, cultural- historical, moral, aesthetic) ;
2. Be a continuous lifelong process, beginning at the pre school level and continuing through all formal and non formal stages;
3. Be interdisciplinary in its approach, drawing on the specific content of each discipline in making possible a holistic and balanced perspective;
4. Examine major environmental issues from local, national, regional and international point of view so that students receive insights into environmental conditions in other regional areas;

5. Focus on current and potential environmental situations, while taking into account the historical perspective;
6. Promote the value and necessity of local, national and international cooperation in the prevention and solution of environmental problems.
7. Explicitly consider environmental aspects in plan for development and growth.
8. Enable learners to have a role in planning their learning experiences and provide an opportunity for making decisions and accepting their consequences.
9. Relate environmental sensitivity, knowledge, problem solving skills and value clarification to every age, but with special emphasis to the learner's own community in early years.
10. Help learners discover the symptoms and real causes of environmental problems.
11. Emphasize the complexity of environmental problems and thus the need to develop critical thinking and problem solving skills.
12. Utilize diverse learning environments and a broad array of educational approaches to teaching/learning about and from the environment with due stress on practical activities and first hand experience.

Environment is important for the healthy survival of living organism and they have to be educated about it. When and how did we realize about it?

Some Questions

1. State the meaning of environment?
2. State the meaning of environmental education?
3. State the objectives of environmental education also suggest two activities to achieve them. (At school level).
4. Explain the need and importance of environmental education.
5. Explain any five guiding principles of environmental education in your own terms.

2

History of Environmental Education

In 1948, International Union for the Conservation of Nature and Natural Resources (IUCN) was established. During the same period, International Youth Federation for Conservation (IYF) was formed. In the 50's and 60's there were wide spread catastrophic events like London Smog, Minamata tragedy, New York Smog. Acid rains etc. got widespread publicity and forced people to think seriously about the state of global environment. Carson (1962) through his well-known title "Silent Springs" drew the attention of world towards the chemical poisoning of environment. It was considered that the publication of this was the beginning of environmental movement. In 1968, Club of Rome was established. In 1969, the publication of "Journal of Environmental Education" started. The decade of 70's is remembered in the history of mankind as the decade of environmental revolution. The International Council of Scientific Union (ICSU) with United Nation's Scientific and Cultural Organization (UNESCO) launched the "Man and Biosphere" program, which led to a series of International meetings and discussions.

Since 1970, there has been a growing effort and activity on the educational front devoted to environmental problems and to environmental education. The United Nations reflected the global nature of this awareness in 1972; it organized the first international conference on Human Environment in Stockholm, Sweden. The conference revealed a widening interest in the environmental problems it also exposed a lack of wide spread experience in tackling the problems. Perhaps the most outstanding achievement of the conference was the establishment of the UNEP United Nations Environment Program in January 1975. In 1975, this program held an International Environmental Education workshop in Belgrade, Yugoslavia. A major outcome of this workshop was the Belgrade Charter. This Charter recognized the urgent need of environmental education to develop a global understanding or perspective of the ecological, economic and moral considerations. Belgrade Charter (1972) states the goal of Environmental Education is to develop a world population that is aware of and concerned about the environment and its concerned problems and which has the knowledge, skills, attitudes, motivations and commitment to work individually and collectively towards solutions and current problems of the prevention of new ones' The charter further said the goal of environmental education is "to improve all ecological relationships including the relationship of humanity with nature and people with each other".

1970 - April 22nd Earth Day was observed. The US Environmental Act defined the goal of Environmental Education. The IUCN Sponsored International Conference on Environmental Education in school curriculum", at Nevada.

1972 - UN sponsored "Conference on Human Environment" at Stockholm, Sweden. In October United Nation Environment Program (UNEP) was established with its head quarters at Nairobi, Kenya.

1975- UNESCO in cooperation with UNEP launched the UNESCO_UNEP International Environmental Education Program (IEEP) Paris.

In October under IEEP and "International Environmental Education Workshop" was held in Belgrade, Yugoslavia, which led to Belgrade Charter" Formation.

1976-1977- Many meetings were held in Africa Arab states, Asia pacific, Europe, North America, Latin America and Caribbean region.

1977- The International Conference on Environmental Education was organized in October in Tbilisi, Georgia, USSR that resulted in formation of "The Tbilisi Declaration". USSR 1977 report on inter governmental conference on environmental education has summarized the ultimate aims of environmental education.

- To enable human beings to understand the complex nature of the environment as this results from the interaction of its biological, physical, racial and cultural aspects.
- To provide the individual and the community with the means of interpreting the interdependence of these various elements in the environment so as to create a greater sense of awareness of their place in the environment.
- To provide a more considered and cautious use of the universe to satisfy the present and future material and spiritual needs of mankind.
- To contribute to the development of a national awareness of the importance of the environment in the economic, social, cultural processes.
- To provide a clear awareness of the economic, social, cultural political interdependence of the modern world and develop a spirit of responsibility and of solidarity between countries and regions.

1987-An "UNESCO_UNEP International Congress of Environmental Education and Training" was held at Moscow, USSR.

1992-In June "The Next Earth Summit" was held in Rio De Janeiro Brazil, South America.

1995 – On April 7th, the UN Climate conference in Berlin adopted a mandate on strengthening the 1992 Rio Climate Treaty.

Apart from the above international summits, there were few regional summits held for the purpose of protecting the environment. Simultaneously in India also awareness regarding environment was there right from ancient period when people used to worship nature and protect her. Apart from this the Government of India has also imposed certain Articles and Acts.

1972 - The Government of India Passed a Wildlife Protection Act.

1976 - Under the leadership of Mrs. Indira Gandhi the 42nd constitutional Amendment was passed and provisions regarding the protection of environment were incorporated in it.

1980 - The forest (Conservation) Act amended in 1988.

1981 - On the basis of these two Articles, The water (prevention and Control of Pollution act) Act 1974 and The Air (prevention and control of pollution) act 1981 were passed.

1985 - The Ministry of Environment and Forests was established in the Center.

1986 - The Environment (Protection) Act. In our country, the National concern was reflected in the National policy on Education-1986" document. The Document observed:

"There is a paramount need to create a consciousness in the environment. It must permeate all ages and all sections of the society beginning with the child. Environmental consciousness should inform teaching in schools and colleges. This aspect will be integrated in the entire educational process".

The Parliament was thus forced to enact a comprehensive legislation called Environment (Protection) Act, 1986 along with rules.

1987 - The national sentiment and concern for environment was echoed further by late Sri Rajiv Gandhi, The Prime Minister of India during a keynote address to the UN General Assembly in September.

This was followed up by mooting the idea of "Planet Protection Fund" where each country was to donate certain percentage of its Gross National Product for conservation of environment to a globally established fund in the Belgrade non-aligned meeting of nations.

Many institutions have also been established in the country for imparting environmental education. It can be said that environmental education has emerged as a pragmatic response to the problems of human environment. Is the concern for environment a recent phenomena?

Concept of Nature in Ancient India

If we look at the tradition of India, we have always revered the mother earth, for all the gifts that it has bestowed us with. We are fortunate enough to get the various blessings of Mother Nature. It nourishes us from childhood to the graveyard, and has its multifold mechanism to sustain itself in the very fascinating manner. In the Ancient India we have tales, where mountains were worshiped, we still celebrate it as Goverdhan Puja, next day of diwali, we offer prayers to the trees somwati amawash, tulsi vivah, etc., and plants, with the help of various other plants and plant products like banana, turmeric, banyan tree, tulsi, sandalwood, mango leaves, ashok leaves, beetle leaves, beetle seeds, jaw, wheat, rice and even grass. We have the tradition of worshipping the rain god, to give us better rains. We have the tradition of Worshiping River and on important festivals taking holy dip in river. The tradition of offering prayers to Sun god is also very old. On Holi festival we offer our prayers to the fire. So basically if we see, since ages we have been worshiping sun, trees, fire, earth and water. Basically, these are the constituents of our nature, which sustain the life on planet earth. River Ganga is worshiped as a holy river.

The Hindu scriptures, particularly the Veda and Upanishads, the Smritis literature, the Epics and the Puranas, have clearly laid down the rationale for practicing conservation of nature and religious sanction against indiscriminate use of natural resources. No one species has an absolute power over another, although there does exist a balance between them. Man is particularly obliged to be protector and guardian of all creatures, since man is endowed with the unique quality of consciousness which other creatures lack. The ancients believed in the theory of rebirth, which is a continuous cycle of all living species. The fact that a human being may slip into a baser form of life to dereliction of assigned ties and values and may once again come upto the status of a human being by observing the prescribed norms of conduct, places all living creatures in the same plane in a metaphysical sense, and by implication enjoins on man to be considerate and respectful to other forms of life. The Ancient Indian view of ecology emanates directly from this theory of creation.

As a result of this concern for environment, the Ancient Indians carefully observed the natural processes their scriptures abound in detail of trees, plants and other vegetation, along with the importance of their preservation for general welfare. In ancient India therefore, causing environmental pollution was considered to be a serious and punishable offence. Kautilya's Arthashastra prescribed punishment for violating norms of civil sanitation, particularly for polluting air and water, which, according to Charak Samhita, the ancient text on medicine, were responsible for causing imbalance of the five basic elements in the body and thereby disease. The Smritis prohibited killing of animals and destruction of forests. There are innumerable references in Ancient Indian texts to suggest a sensitive awareness of the importance of maintaining ecological balance, which were made operative both ideational and through actual decrees.

However, along with this attitude of nature as objects which has to be utilized for the sustenance of human life this aspects of religion. Nature had to be controlled to obtain food. Thus the earliest religious ideas of the Aryans were, naturally those of a primitive animism where the forces around them, which they could not control or understand, were invested with gods and divinity.

All of which was personification of nature in one form or another. But even among them, the atmospheric gods enjoyed a position of preeminence, particularly Indra, the rain maker and Varuna, the god of seasons. With the beginning of settled agriculture, these gods receded into background and the cult of mother goddess has of course a very ancient antiquity all over the world, and hardly requires elaboration. However, even without going into controversy of the specific needs of pastoral and agricultural economy and forms of worship in ancient India, one can easily observe that at the root of all these was obviously the desire to control nature to the advantage of the human beings.

Simultaneously existence of these two attitudes towards nature may appear somewhat contradictory but actually they were not. Ancient Indians perceived nature as an all-encompassing reality to live in. It was essential to control nature to the extent that sustenance was ensured but not to a degree which threatened the very existence of nature as environment. Therefore, in the level of production organization there was a pragmatic attempt to control nature, not by means of indiscriminate exploitation but through persuasion as it were granting nature autonomy of its own. But in a much wider sense, both functionally and metaphorically, nature was meant to be preserved and nurtured. Human and nature dualism never formed a part of ancient Indian attitude towards the problem of how to strike a balance between these two contrary tendencies, in fact, nature to imply oneness with it. This attitude found its expression in ancient period, particularly with Kalidasa. Kalidasa endowed nature with consciousness, so humans became an extension of nature and therefore comparable with each other. (Moonis Raza 1988).

Philosophy of Environmental Education

Philosophy is interpreted in many ways and is defined accordingly. The dictionary meaning of philosophy is "Pursuit of wisdom", "Study of realities and general principles" "System of theories on nature of things or on conduct" and "Calmness of mind."

The philosophy of environmental education can be described in terms of relationship between human and nature. The relationship will hold well only when there is right value orientation. There are three aspects of value orientation, viz., submission, domination and mutuality.

People who believe in submission consider themselves quite powerless before nature and other forces. During ancient period, these types of people were there who did not know the ways the nature worked to the full extent. So they began to worship any form of nature. For example, if there was flood, then they thought nature was against them. So, they began worshipping water and thought that by doing so Nature would forgive them. Domination emphasizes the welfare of self at the expense of others including nature.

This view is predominant in western culture and even some say it has Biblical sanction, in Genesis of the old testament of which says "God blessed them" said to the "Have many children fill the earth and take control of it. Rule over the fish in the sea and birds in the air, rule over every living that moves on the earth"

Mutuality is such a value orientation, which is almost related with Indian culture. It is nothing but commonness in-groups, where a type of symbiotic relationship between man and nature is seen. It aims at welfare of both. It considers non-living on the same platform as living beings as they also have some worth. But this does not mean that the use of resources of nature is avoided but it is used to certain extent from where there is return. This sort of utilization is not exploitation to the point of no return. This concept of mutuality is seen in an episode of Mahabharata. It says that when the Pandavas were given exile to live in forest, they were told not to live in a particular forest for a longer time as there would be exploitation of resources rather than utilization. So, the Pandavas moved from one forest to another and completed their exile.

In Buddhism also such relation is seen. In Karniya mett stutt, it says that any living organism whether it is small or large or medium, micro or macro visible or invisible, far or near, born or not born should be in harmony. For this we should protect them and that too by developing concern for them just like mother protects her only son by sacrificing everything.

From researches it has been found that in today's world also we see such examples, like the tribal people of Andaman, Bastar, (M.P) and Bishnoi community of Rajasthan (Praharaj 1991)

The environmental philosophy also tells about the three R'S viz. Reduction, reuse and recycling of waste in daily life which is supposed to be the golden rule for survival of mankind on earth.

The philosophy of environmental education aims at inculcation of environmental awareness on one hand and environmental ethics on the other amongst humans by asking them to live in communion with nature. Environmental ethics is a code of behavior, which ensures progress, without harming the environment. We must learn to live in harmony with both nature and fellow beings. To live, to let live and to be able to live together in peace and harmony is the basic "ethics of all ethics" this is the main foundation and goal of environmental ethics. The above idea is presented in the Vedas. A verse from Rig-Veda (R. V. 160.2, 6.5.1.5) states that:

"The sky is like father, the earth is like mother and the space as their son. The universe consisting of the three is like a family, and any kind of damage done to any of the three throws the universe out of balance".

Yajur Veda (6.33) warns us not to poison water and not to harm trees or cut trees. Kautilya was very particular about maintaining proper sanitation. Atharva Veda states that plants and herbs destroy poisons.

The Charak Samhita (5th C.BC) also warned that "when air, water and other elements of nature are spoiled (which in today's time is stated as polluted); seasons start working against the routines, vegetation gradually begins to ruin which is now said as global warming) ......So long as the earth is all of nature (forests, lakes, rivers and mountains) human race is going to flourish".

The unifying ethical principle of reverence for nature and its creations is reflected in almost all the major religions of the world. Quran states (44:11-12);

"Then watch for the day when a ball of smoke will appear in sky and envelop the people".

The day has come, and now we see "smog's" in the sky everywhere. Buddha said, "Water must never be misused". But because of the misuse of water, the water shortage is being experienced all over the world. Jainism emphasized on protection of flora and fauna.

According to shikhism "man's need and greed has exploited to the maximum extent" (Laxmi Sree, 200)

An eminent philosopher Cicero (1972) believed that there should be harmony and balance between man and nature. There was a purpose behind the existence of everything. He also said that those who do not live for the wellbeing of the world. Every person must remember that nature is older than culture, i.e. it is the mother and culture rests on Nature. But now, it seems doubtful whether nature can continue to support culture, or not as modern science and technology is acting like a parasite which is about to destroy its host. Humanity can be sustained if we put a check on exploitation and over use of nature. In short, it can be said that humans can enjoy the richness, gift and generosity of nature by giving up greed to destroy nature. The best way to be happy as ancient sages and rishis had said that it is not to add to one's richness but by taking away someone's wishes.

In the past, great emperors of India like Ashoka and Shahjahan had great concern for environment. In 20th century great personalities are associated with environmental issues. Sunderlal Bahuguna (Chipko Activist). Medha Patkar (Narmada Bachao Andolan), Maneka Gandhi (Crusader against cruelty done to animals and Former Environment Minister), Vasant Kanibera (from Andhra Pradesh), K. B. Annasahab Hazare (from Ahmednagar), Panduranga Hegde (Appiko Activist), Prof. Veera Badra Mishra (crusader against Ganga pollution in Varanasi) and M. C. Mehta (champion of environmental law in India and for introducing environmental education in school and colleges) and many more in the world are serving hard to save the Mother Earth from the clutches of man's unethical deeds. It can be said that environmental ethics calls for personal feeling, thinking and acting towards saving environment from greed of humans.

Value System in Environmental Education

Dictionary meaning of value is "worth" or "price" of something, which can be, exchanged by money. But here, value is a belief of what is good or desirable needed for peaceful co-existence, which helps in self-evaluation and self drive. Values are made visible through behavior. Values determine decisions in the face of difficult choices.

The fundamental value is the human and social survival. Another fundamental value is preservation or improvement of human health and safety, which is, supported by cleanliness from the personal, family and community standpoints. Some of the ecological principles which carry moral implications for society are as follows

(a) Interrelatedness of nature i.e. what happens in one part of the web of nature ultimately affects every other part.

(a) Systematic and holistic thinking

(c) Appreciation for global and international values from the biophysical reality of the planetary biosphere, from the reality of the ecological web that ties every man to man in this planet; and from the common threat to mankind posed by harming the biosphere.

(d) Man is part of nature, hurting the natural ecosystem will eventually hurt man. Respect for nature and responsibility for its protection. This responsibility must be socially shared rather than pursued by few people.

(e) Attitude of harmony and balance towards nature, rather than conquest and mastery.

(f) Diversity of species leads to stability or monoculture leads to vulnerability

(g) Conservation is necessary for the sake of future generation.

(h) Maintenance of stability and productivity of an ecosystem, avoiding harvesting more than the sustainable yield.

(i) Minimizing stress on the ecosystem such as dumping industrial waste and destroying habitat.

Environmental education is needed in order to establish Harmony with environment. At present the need for agricultural land is increasing forests are declining either due to rapid industrialization or due to rapid population explosion. To meet the needs of people, so many big and small industries are coming up. These industries cause a lot of pollution both of air and water. Science and technology has developed in all the fields that is petroleum, deadly weapons etc. also create pollution and biologically non degradable waste.

As a matter of fact to gain something we have to loose something we have paid heavy prices for development. The Bhopal Gas tragedy, Chernobyl accident and Smog incident, Gulf War, oil spills and flash floods have taken a heavy toll. Industrialization has given rise to slums, which are certainly unhygienic. For healthy development of a country or state its people should have hygienic and healthy living conditions. Science and Technology has also created lot of biologically non-degradable waste, which keeps on accumulating and makes environment unhealthy for all.

Environmental education is important for sustainable development which means whatever exists today on planet earth should be used very judiciously in a prudent manner, so that whatever we have today should also persist in future. The development cannot be stopped, but certainly alternatives can be chalked out. Thus we can say history indicates;

Environmental education is must for :

1. Sustainable development
2. Conservation of bio diversity and natural resources
3. Control of pollution in air, water and sound
4. Population stabilization
5. Recycling of waste for developing environmentally friendly products.

Before studying various problems and its impact on environment, let us study about basic concepts of environment.

Some Questions

1. Why is it important to know the history of environmental education?
2. Give five reasons why environmental education should be taught at school level looking at its history?
3. Explain the concept of nature in ancient India.
4. a). Write a short note on philosophy of environmental education.

   b). Write a short note on Value System of environment education.
5. Match A with B

	A	B
1.	Earth day	a. 1986
2.	1972	b. 1975
3.	Belgrade Charter	c. 22nd April
4.	Tiblisi Declaration	d. Stockholm Conference
5.	Environment Protection Act	e. 1977
		f. 1980
		g. 1985

3

Basic Concepts of Environment

From first unit it is clear that everything that surrounds an individual is his environment. It includes the physical and biological components. The physical components of the environment are soil, water, air, light, and temperature. These are termed as biotic and abiotic components. The plants and animals including human beings are referred to as biotic components. All these components of the environment work together, interact and modify the effect of each other. Our planet earth is the only planet, which has life on it. It consists of three components: the land (lithosphere), water (hydrosphere) and air (atmosphere). It is because of this unique combination that life originated, and is still sustaining on this planet. This life-supporting zone of earth, where atmosphere, hydrosphere and lithosphere meet, interact and make life possible is known as Biosphere.

Lithosphere or outer layer (crust) of earth hydrosphere or all water sources above and underground and atmosphere or air (a mixture of gases) comprises abiotic or non- – living components of the environment. Among the biotic or living components all sorts of living organisms like plants, animals and microbes living on earth are included. A constant interaction between living and non living components of the biosphere results in the transfer of food and energy, which makes it a dynamic but stable system. The biosphere is the biggest functional ecosystem but, in fact, it consists of smaller functional units known as ecosystems or ecological systems.

Ecosystem

Ecosystem is a self sustaining, structural and functional unit of biosphere. It is an open system and depends upon solar energy from outside as its energy source.

Ecosystems can be small or large and are placed in nature contiguously. Between adjoining ecosystems there is frequent exchange of material and energy. Thus they are all interconnected and hence interrelated. The vast network of all interconnected ecosystems constitutes the biosphere.

Ecosystems are mostly natural systems, but these can be artificial too. The natural systems are terrestrial (land) as well as aquatic. The common examples of land ecosystems are a forest, grassland or a meadow, a desert or a hillside. A pond, a lake, a river, a seacoast and an ocean are the examples of aquatic ecosystem. Artificial systems created by man are a cropland, a garden, a park, a kitchen garden, or an aquarium.

Structure of Ecosystem:

An ecosystem consists of two major components: abiotic and biotic.

Biotic part	Abiotic part
1. Producers	1. Climatic factors
(a) green plants	(i) Light
(b) photosynthetic bacteria	(ii) Temperature
(c) chemosynthetic bacteria	(iii) Precipitation
	(iv) Atmosphere and wind
2. Consumers	2. Edaphic factors
(i) Herbivores	(i) Nutrients content
(ii) Carnivores	(ii) Acidity
(iii) Omnivores	(iii) Moisture content
(iv) Detrivores	
3. Decomposers	3. Topographic factors
(i) Bacteria	(i) Aspect
(ii) Fungi	(ii) Angle of slope
	(iii) Altitude

Abiotic Components: The abiotic components are inorganic and organic substances and climatic factors such as air, water, soil and sunlight.

Light: All the energy in an ecosystem originates as radiation from the sun or solar radiation consisting of Electro magnetic waves of wide range in length. Solar radiation reaching the earth's' surface or the biosphere however consists of wavelengths measuring between 300 and 700 (MU), visible (to the human eye) radiation lying between 390-760 mu infra red or thermal radiation is above 760 mu and ultra violet is below 390 mu. Light has three aspects, which influence the biotic community in the ecosystem: intensity or energy content; quality or wavelength composition; and morphological processes of plants and animals.

For instance light intensity and quality, to a high degree, determine the rates of photosynthesis in both terrestrial and aquatic habitats. Day length or photoperiod influences the initiation of flowering, dormancy and leaf fall in higher plants as well as the onset of migration, hibernation, nesting and even changes in coat colors of animals.

Temperature: The radiant energy from the sun absorbed by molecules of gases, liquids or solids raises the temperature of the absorbing substance. Temperature differences cause the flow of energy in the form of heat from warmer substances or sites to colder substances or places. Temperature, then, is essentially a measure of the tendency of a substance to release heat. There are two important aspects of temperatures absolute and relative. Temperature of the environment directly influences the functioning of the organisms by controlling their body chemistry. It directly affects the status of other environmental factors, e.g. evaporation. Most living forms function within a temperature range of 0-50 degrees C.

Water: Water constitutes the bulk of the living tissues of plants and animals. Most physiological and biochemical processes occur in an aqueous matrix. Water is the medium of life for aquatic habitats, the rain forest and the desert provide an adequate picture for relationship of water and the vegetation. Differences in precipitation and solar radiation largely account for the variations in water supply, which basically determines the functioning of terrestrial habitats.

Atmosphere: It contains mainly nitrogen and the vital gas oxygen and carbon dioxide. It is a vast gaseous reservoir that permeates the whole surface of the earth and its biotic habitats. The atmosphere in motion is the wind. Strong winds may directly induce physical damage or cause malformation on plant structure in terrestrial communities. Wind action may accelerate the process of transpiration.

Edaphic factors Edaphaic Factors : Edaphic factors are environmental controls that are dependent on the soil, the upper weathered layer of the earth's crust is influenced by plants and animals. It harbors biotic communities, which include, among others but especially, bacteria, fungi and other organisms that fix atmospheric nitrogen decompose organic matter and incorporate it with mineral matter. In terrestrial habitats, the soil serves as a medium for plant growth. Soil acidity and pH, determines the solubility and availability or the fixation and non availability of inorganic salts in the soil solutions.

Topography: Topography or surface relief tends to modify the climatic factors in the environment that may change vegetation types. The aspect or slope orientation of a particular habitat determines the amount of solar energy received at the surface, especially at middle or high latitudes. Slopes directly facing the sun are warmer and hence, more productive than those under shade conditions. Hence marked differences in population distribution between slopes of a contrast and surface ability

(a) Biotic Components: These are discussed below:

I. Producers are the chlorophyll bearing plants such as algae, grass and trees. The green plants, ranging in size from microscopic phytoplankton of aquatic habitats to the gigantic trees of the tropical rain forest, are the main producers in the ecosystem. They convert solar energy into chemical energy during photosynthesis. This is the source of food for many organisms. The green plants are also called autotrophs as they synthesize their own food, which is in the form of carbohydrates. Carbohydrates are basically the building blocks from which foodstuffs, such as protein and fats, are made in living organisms.

II **Consumers** are the organisms, which obtain food by consuming other plants or animals. They are referred to as heterotrophs (consumers). These are mostly animals. Those who feed directly on plants (autotrophs) are called herbivores (grasshopper, rabbit, goat, and sheep) .The animals who feed on the herbivores are called carnivores. (Lion, tiger). The organisms that feed on almost any organism or any thing are omnivores (cockroaches, fox, and human). Detrivores consume dead and decayed plants and animals (Pigs, crows, vultures). Consumers convert the ingested food into new protoplasm. The ultimate source of the food energy obtained and used by consumers is the organic matter produced by autotrophs in any ecosystem

III **Decomposers** are microorganisms, notably the so-called bacteria and fungi of decay that breaks down the complex organic molecules of the litter, wastes and remains of both producers and consumers. Decomposition leads to the release of simple inorganic substances that can be reused by green plants. In terrestrial ecosystem bacteria generally act on plants. By digesting the dead tissue through enzyme secretion on it, the basic elements are made available for re use to the producers. Decomposers are as essential a part of the ecosystem as producers and consumers; in their absence, the basic elements of life would remain locked in the complex molecules of the wastes and remains of other living forms, rendering them unavailable to the producers to the production in the ecosystem.

Food Chains and Food Webs

We have seen above that the food prepared by green plants is consumed by a series of consumers (herbivores and carnivores)

and finally decomposed by decomposers in nature. This process of food transfer from the source in plants through a series of organisms, with repeated eating and being eaten, is called a food chain. At each transfer a lot of energy from food is lost as heat. Therefore, the number of steps in any food chain is limited to four or five. The shorter the food chain, the greater is the available energy. A simple generalized food chain (arranged in a linear manner) may be presented as

Producers ⟶ herbivores ⟶ Carnivores or taking organisms as example, a simple land food chain may be ⟶

Grass ⟶ Deer ⟶ Tiger

Grass ⟶ Grasshopper ⟶ Frog ⟶ Snake ⟶ Eagle

A food chain does not ever work in isolation. Often several food chains are interconnected under natural conditions. One animal based on its food habit may be linked in more than one food chain. This network of food chains is called a food web. For example, grass may be eaten by grasshoppers as well as rabbits or cattle, and each of these herbivores, such as frog, snake, bird, or tiger depending on their food habits.

Trophic levels: The different steps or levels in a food chain form different trophic levels. The green plants (autotrophs or the producers) are the first trophic level which fix up the solar energy (producers) and make it available for others (consumers). Herbivores (primary consumers insect, rabbit, rodents, deer, cattle, etc) who feed on plants, are second trophic levels. The animals that feed on the herbivores are called secondary consumers or carnivores (frog, small fish), make the third trophic level. Still larger carnivores (tertiary consumers, lion or tiger), which make the fourth trophic level eat these up.

Functions of Ecosystem

By now it is clear that in an ecosystem the two processes of energy movement (energy flow) and nutrient movement (biogeochemical cycle) proceed side by side. The energy movement is in a single direction and non-cyclic (food chain). While the movement of nutrient is cyclic. (Any mineral cycle).

1.Energy flow: The sun energy is transformed by plant (producers) into chemical energy (carbohydrates) by the process of photosynthesis. In herbivores and carnivores this energy is then transferred further at various trophic levels. In these animals this chemical energy is transformed mostly into mechanical energy (work done) and heat. Heat part is lost to the atmosphere at each trophic level. Some energy is utilized in respiration (metabolism) by the organisms, and some energy, which remains unutilized, also goes waste. It is estimated that like this about 90% of the energy is used up at each trophic level. As a result, at the last (decomposer) trophic level no energy is left for recycling. Hence energy flows from sun through producers, to consumers in a single direction only. Fast decreasing energy level at each step sets the limit of trophic levels only to 4-5 at the maximum.

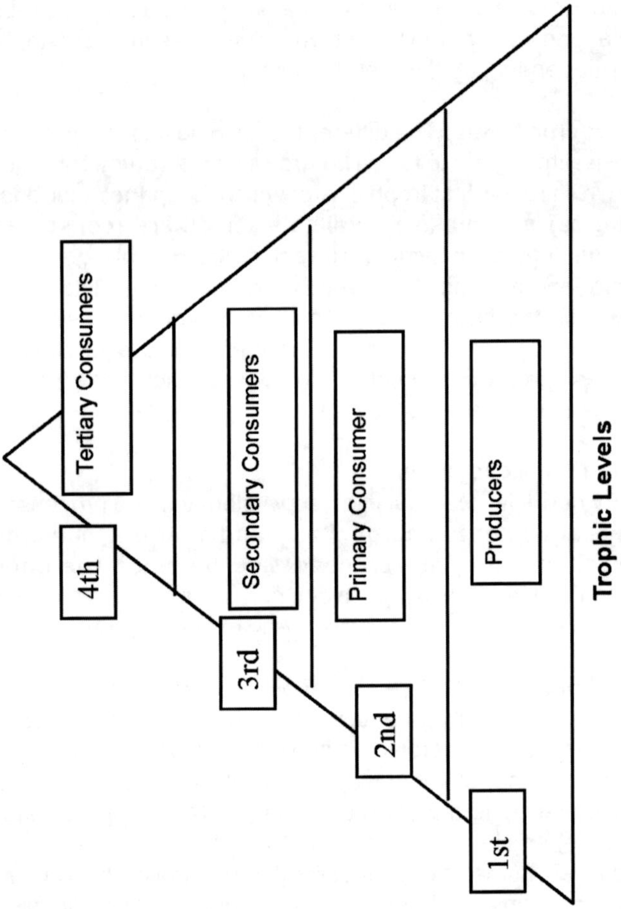
Tertiary Consumers
4th
Secondary Consumers
3rd
Primary Consumer
2nd
Producers
1st
Trophic Levels

We find that there is maximum energy at the producer (plant) level and as you go further and further the energy in food goes on decreasing. Therefore, the herbivores (or vegetarians) at second level have maximum energy.

Biogeochemical Cycles

You have noticed that some energy is lost at every trophic level but there is no such loss of nutrients. When finally the dead animal body is subjected to decomposition by decomposers, the nutrients are released to the environment. There they are again available for reuse and for recycling.

The cyclic flow of nutrients between non living environment (soil rocks, air, water) and living organisms is known as biogeochemical cycle. The major nutrient elements, i.e. carbon, hydrogen, oxygen and nitrogen, which form about 95% mass of the living organism, are cycled again and again between living and non living components of the ecosystem.

Chart Carbon Cycle

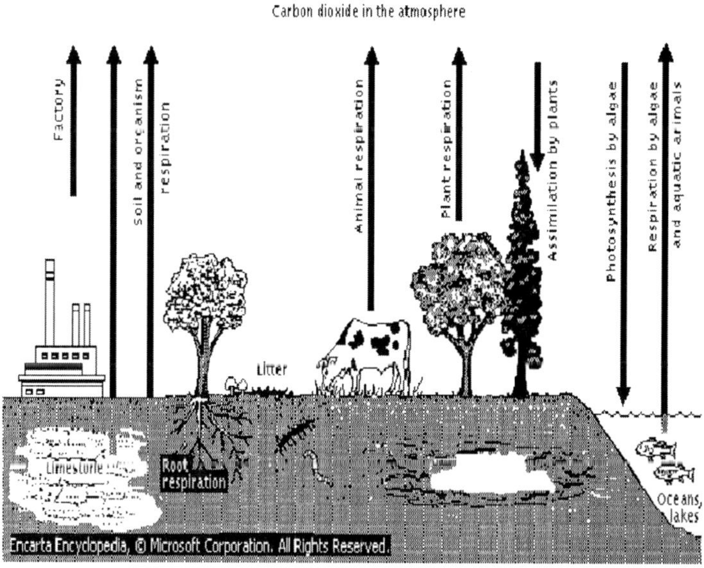

A. Carbon Cycle: From where does the carbon come? There are three main reservoirs. i. Atmosphere, ii. Oceans and iii. Carbonate rocks. Atmospheric carbon amounts to 2.3 x 10 raised to 12 tons. Ocean contains 1.3 x 10 raised to 13 tons. The atmosphere – ocean continuously exchange carbon dioxide with the biosphere and lithosphere. The producers of the biosphere borrow annually 60 x 10 raised to 9 tons of carbon dioxide for photosynthesis. A negligible amount is borrowed by chemosynthetic producers. Inside the biosphere the basic movement of carbon is through the food chains from the producers to the consumers and from both these groups to the decomposers. From the biosphere almost the same amount of carbon dioxide is annually returned through two processes i. the biological process of respiration in the producers, consumers and decomposers; and ii. The non biological process of combustion. Calcium carbonate as a by product of photosynthetic assimilation is released by a number of plants living in alkaline waters. Besides the earth releases annually about 100 millions tons of carbon dioxide by the weathering of rocks. In this chemical process rocks are changed to carbonate rocks. Hot springs and volcanic activity involving deposits of fossil fuels and carbonate rocks pour about 100 million tons of carbon dioxide back into atmosphere. About 40,000 x 10 raised to 9 tons of carbon dioxide from the atmosphere of the past geological sphere now lies buried as fossil fuels. Man now returns six billion tons of carbon dioxide each year by burning these fossil fuels in homes and factories.

B. Carbon is the most significant element. The basic movement of carbon is from atmospheric reservoir (0.032% concentration) to producers, to consumers and then to decomposers. Other reservoirs for carbon are water, fossil fuel and sedimentary rocks.

Plant utilizes the atmospheric carbon dioxide in photosynthesis to produce carbohydrates. Plant food is taken by herbivores and then passes through small and large carnivores. The respiratory activities at each level help in returning CO_2 is returned to the atmosphere by various activities such as respiration, decomposition of dead organic material, burning of fossil fuels and volcanic activities

C. Nitrogen Cycle: Nitrogen is another important element required by organisms for synthesizing proteins. Atmosphere is the reservoir (78% approximately) for free nitrogen. But the nitrogen in the element form cannot be used by living system. First it has to be converted into nitrates for the use of plants. This can be done either by industrial nitrogen fixation or by some nitrogen fixing bacteria (Azobacter and Rhizobium) convert the atmospheric nitrogen into nitrates, which are soluble in water. The process is called nitrogen fixation. These are absorbed by plants into their system and utilized for making organic matter (proteins) etc.

Organic matter of plant and animal origin is decomposed to ammonia and amino acids by microorganisms in soil. The ammonia may escape to atmosphere or be retained in the soil, and is sometimes oxidized to nitrates. The process of ammonia formation is called ammonification. Some microorganisms convert ammonia into nitrates. The process is called nitrification. Finally there are some other bacteria (decomposers) which reduce nitrates back to nitrogen or to ammonia or to some other oxides. The process is called denitrification. Free nitrogen returns to atmospheric pool and plants take up oxides.

Nitrogen Cycle:

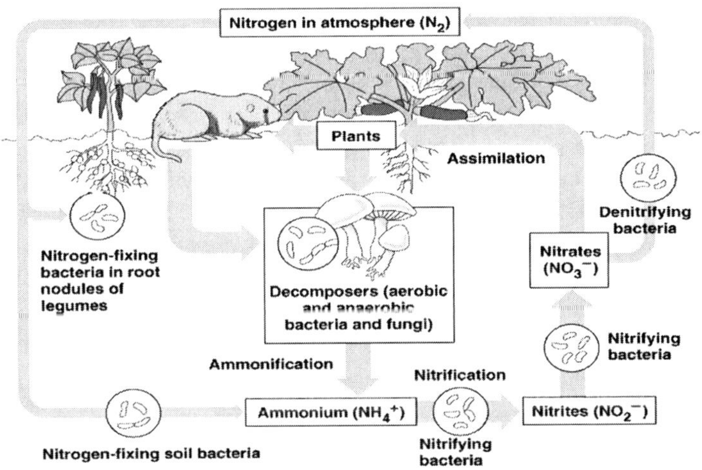

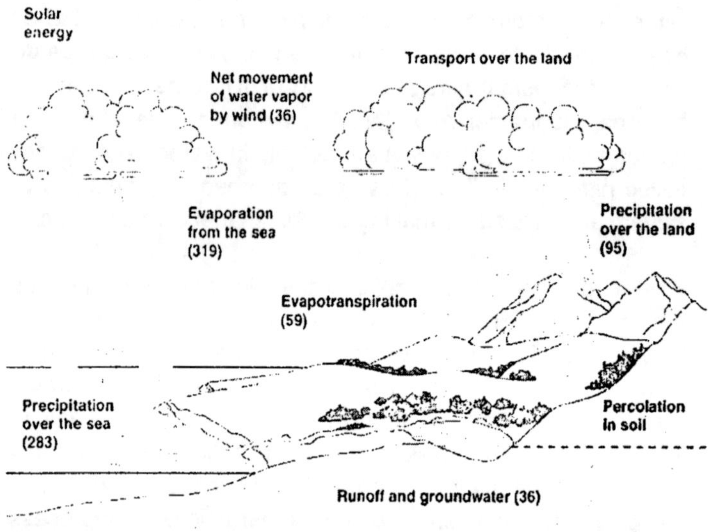

Water Cycle: Look at the diagram and understand the water cycle.

Hydrogen Cycle: The only source of hydrogen is the hydrosphere as a constituent of water molecules. Hydrogen enters the living world through photosynthesis. In photosynthesis the water molecules are split into oxygen and hydrogen. Hydrogen enters into the composition of sugar molecule. Through glucose it moves to various organic components that are constructed directly In indirectly from glucose and becomes part of living matter. The respiration the glucose molecule is broken down and the hydrog atoms are oxidized to form water. Likewise the organic compounds of waste and dead organisms undergo the process of decomposition in which the hydrogen atoms are oxidized to form water again. Carbon, oxygen and hydrogen cycles are inseparably related with one another.

Oxygen Cycle: Twenty percent of atmospheric air is free oxygen, being a constituent of water molecule; the hydrosphere which is dissolved in water is used for respiration by aquatic life forms. In the course of respiration oxygen combines with hydrogen and forms water. Oxygen serves as a raw material in photosynthesis. Oxygen enters the structural components of living matter remains within the organisms until death after death through decaying action it returns to the environment.

Types of Ecosystem: Broadly there are two main types of ecosystems, namely terrestrial and aquatic. Each ecosystem has its unique combination of a variety of organisms and physical conditions. In terrestrial ecosystem, based on the dominant vegetation (grass, tree, etc,) and other climatic factors several further types are recognized, such as grassland, forest, desert, man made etc. Aquatic ecosystem also can be distinguished into several types depending upon the salt content of water. There can be fresh water ecosystem, (like pond ecosystem, river ecosystems etc.) and marine ecosystems.

Biodiversity: The boundless diversity in living forms is the most distinguished characteristic of life. The term biological diversity or bio diversity refers to the extent of variation of living organisms on earth. It is the total living component of our biosphere. Biodiversity can be defined as the variety of all animals, plants and microorganisms found on earth. Organisms look different from each other because of differences in their genes. Hence biodiversity means diversity in the genetic make up of living organisms. Biodiversity can thus be observed at species level, genetic level.

Conservation of biodiversity is very important for the sustenance of mankind. All the components of nature are in a perfect balance. These are interwoven and interdependent. A disturbance to one type of fauna and flora can threaten the whole life support system. Human beings are also a part of this whole complex system. The loss of diversity therefore, can lead to the destruction of human species as well. Every species are also supporting and cooperating with each other directly or indirectly. Conservation of Biodiversity is discussed in detail in the unit on conservation. Before going to conservation we must see how human beings have changed the environment through their actions.

Some Questions

1. Define the following terms;
   a. Abiotic factors
   b. Biosphere
   c. Food chain
   d. Food web
2. Explain the inter relationship between various factors of environment; land, air, water temperature and its effect on biotic factors.
3. Draw and explain nitrogen cycle in your own words.
4. Analyze the components of water cycle and state their importance in maintaining hydrological balance.
5. Explain the concept, structure and function of Ecosystem with suitable illustration.

4

Genesis of Environmental Problems

Throughout history man adapted the environment, transformed, destroyed and improved it through its cultural evolution. The resulting intervention was mostly local in nature at the initial stage and people did not realize its consequence. Advent of modern science and technology combined with man's greed and caprice to exploit the resources of the earth beyond point of redemption led to the creation of environmental problems. The industrial revolution of the seventeenth century probably signaled the beginning or "pangs of modernity" a euphemism for environmental problems. The unprecedented rapid growth in human population, science, technology, modern production and consumption processes and last but not the least change in human life style have wrought serious havoc in the environment resulting in gross interference in its ecological processes and thereby endangering the health and even very survival of man on earth. Notwithstanding the heavy debate over the extent and nature of the environmental crises, it is generally agreed that the environment is in trouble and the 'planet is in peril'. To get a complete picture of the environmental problems, with their ramifications, damages and implications for humanity, few of the serious environmental problems have been discussed below.

Population Explosion

The world population crossed the five billion mark in July 1987. At the turn of the century it has nearly touched 6 to 6.5 billion. If the current population growth rate remains unaltered, India's population at that time is likely to be around one billion estimate at the prevailing rate of population growth; India will outstrip China in population around the middle of the next century. The carrying capacity of an environment in terms of population is decided by such factors as existing environmental conditions, availability of life supporting system, limits of tolerance of species inhabiting it etc.

Despite war, famine, natural disasters and diseases men by their ingenuity have overcome such natural checks and balances and continued to multiply crossing the carrying capacity. A peculiar characteristic of population explosion has been the tendency in developed countries towards zero population growth, whereas most of the developing countries register nearly three fourth of the increase in world population. The pyramidal age structure in developing countries with pre ponderance of young further accentuates the problems and accelerates the growth. About 72 per cent of people in these countries are below 35 years of age. Another characteristic of this growth has been what is often called 'population implosion' the migration of metropolis, cities and urban areas by people from countryside. The villages are gradually being depopulated and squatter settlements, slums and shantytowns, notorious for vice criminality, prostitution, squalor, poverty, insanitation and disease etc., are on the rise. Thomas Robert Malthus (1926) in his essay on the principle of population had warned that rapid population growth is the real cause of poverty among nations. Paul Ehlriich (1972) had identified population explosion to be the root cause of all forms of environmental degradation. Although his prediction of hundreds of millions of people starving to death in 1970s has not come true, humanity continues to be tormented and languished by population explosion. The UN international conference on population held at Mexico City in 1984 had called upon nations to rectify the disequilibrium between rate of change in population and changes in resources, environment and development. Solution of the crisis lies in limiting family size, improving living standards, reducing infant mortality providing social security and above all spreading population education. Changing attitudes, regarding sex of the child, abortion religious obscurantism also help in alleviating problem.

Water Pollution

Eighty per cent of all diseases in human beings can be attributed to polluted water. In India 70 per cent of available water is polluted water. (Basu 1986). Industrial effluents, sewage, garbage, bio waste, chemicals of many kinds including artificial fertilizers, pesticides, herbicides, detergents and even animal carcasses mix with water making it unsuitable for human use and disrupt aquatic ecosystems. Mining adds heavy metals and lot of particulate matter into water leading to its pollution. The mineral rich water enhances the algal growth. Lakes and rivers on receiving organic waste and chemicals containing nitrogen and phosphorus get eutrophicated when their threshold for bio degradation is crossed. Such rivers and lakes get clogged with growth of algae. These algae die and settle down at the bottom giving rise to a spurt of microbial decomposition and making heavy biological oxygen demand on water. In the process all oxygen in the river gets depleted leading to death of aquatic life. The water emanates a smell of hydrogen sulfide, indicating the death of lake/ river water is a good parameter of its water quality. In India, the Dal and Wuler lakes of Kashmir, Pushkar of Rajasthan and Lake Ooty in Tamil Nadu have been eutrophicated severely. Hussein Sagar Lake at Hyderabad is on its way to eutrophication (CSE, 1985)

With modernization of society and run towards the luxuries men have added more than a million chemicals to the biosphere. But hardly a thousand of them have been scanned through rigorous safety evaluation system. Many of these chemicals are released into water and cause water pollution. Heavy metals like cadmium lead mercury and arsenic etc. On entering tho body damages the brain and central nervous system. They can produce cancer, sterility, abnormal fetus, kidney dysfunction etc.

The tragedy that struck residents of Minamata Bay and Niigata islands during 1953 and 1965 due to consumption of fish contaminated by methyl mercury chloride is a classic example. Even DDT, which has been banned in many countries, has been detected in copious amounts in tissues of Eskimo's and in Penguins, who inhabit places where DDT was never sprayed. Pesticides residues have been detected in 20 percent of 100 random sample of breast milk in Tamil Nadu in amounts beyond maximum resistance limit. Most of the chemicals referred to above have entered man through food chain and in sizable quantities through bio magnification. Sewage effluents are continuously disrupting the ecosystem of oceans, radioactive wastes and spills from large oil tankers. In June 1989 a Maltan oil tanker, MVP on collision with another ship in Arabian Sea near Bombay spread 5,500 tons of furnace oil in covering 700 miles of Bombay coast. The Torrey canyon disaster in North Sea drew worldwide attention. Oil being highly toxic to fishes, plankton, marine birds and even hump back whale, oil spills cause colossal damage. The oil slick in the Persian Gulf near Kuwait during the Gulf war drew loud protests from environmentalists all over the world. Some measures have been taken to stop water pollution. The industries are supposed to make Effluent Treatment Plants (ETP) plants. The municipal corporations are also expected to treat sewage before releasing in the water bodies. As individuals we will have to reduce the usage of detergents to avoid water pollution.

Air Pollution

Emission from factories and industries automobiles exhaust, rail engines, airplanes, and other internal combustion engines that burn fossil fuel, thermal power plants, quarry and mining activities, nuclear fallout's, dust and particulate matter etc., pollute the air. Major air currents above the earth spread air pollutants worldwide. Breathing polluted air causes respiratory diseases like, bronchitis, allergy, tuberculosis, and emphysema and aggravates asthma. Inhalation affects hemoglobin. Some pollutants like asbestos dust etc., are even carcinogenic. Sulfur dioxide causes total destruction of plant, fluorine compounds on entering body of cattle through food chain cause them to loose weight and develops abnormal bone and teeth. Peroxyl Acetyl Nitrate (PAN) suppresses photosynthesis and causes leaves of many plants to collapse.

Leaves too becomes discoloured and curled. Air pollution causes acid rain, smog, green house effect and depletion of ozone layer and has potential for affecting global climate adversely. These effects have been described very briefly in the following paragraphs.

Pollutants	*Effects*
Sulfur dioxide	Aggravation of respiratory diseases, e,g. asthma chronic bronchitis Impairment of pulmonary function Irritation of eyes and respiratory tract Leaf injury and reduced growth in plants Corrosion of metals Deterioration of building materials, textiles.
Particulate matter	Direct toxic effects or aggravation of effects of gaseous pollutants Increase in chronic respiratory diseases impairment of visibility Alteration in incident sunlight Interference with plant photosynthesis Soils surfaces and materials Abrasion of building materials and textiles
Oxidants	Aggravation of emphysema, asthma and bronchitis impairment of cardio pulmonary function leaf injury and reduced growth if plants Deterioration of rubber, textiles
Hydrocarbons	Contribution to formation of photochemical oxidants sensory irritation
Carbon monoxide	Increased general mortality and coronary mortality rates reduced tolerance for exercise Impairment of mental function
Nitrogen dioxide	Aggravation of respiratory and cardiovascular illness Discolors

	atmosphere Damage to vegetation Fading of plant dyes
Lead	Increased storage in bodyImpairment of hemoglobin and porphyrin synthesis Impairment of learning and intelligencein school children Lethal to animals eating contaminated food.

Reference: A monograph on air pollution –Its dispersion and effects, Atkins Research development, February 1979, England.

Some efforts have been made to reduce air pollution like all vehicles need to obtain pollution under control (P.U.C) certificate. Euro II standards have been introduced for the car segment. Use of CNG has been recommended instead of petrol and diesel. In the big cities the industries running in the residential areas have been closed down. In the metropolitan cities gradually the vehicles older than eight years have been withdrawn from roads. The traffic police confiscate vehicles making use of kerosene or any other fuel-polluting environment.

Acid Rain

Air pollutants like oxides of Sulfur and Nitrogen react with water vapour and oxygen in the air to form sulphuric acid respectively. These acids fall to earth either in the wet form with rainwater and in other forms of precipitation or deposited as dry gases. Acid rain turns water in lakes and rivers acidic, thereby the size and diversity of fish population decreases. Vegetation is destroyed. It causes corrosion of outdoor equipment, building and works of art especially in urban areas. Acid rain also leaches nutrients from soil reducing its fertility. Some experts ascribe stone cancer seen on Taj Mahal to acid rain caused by Mathura refinery. Although India is not affected by acid rain many other unindustrialised countries in the tropics are experiencing it due to release of oxides of Nitrogen and hydrocarbons from forest clearance, agricultural activities and biomass burning. Because water droplets are removed from the atmosphere rapidly, acid rain is a regional or continental rather than a global phenomenon.

There are some measures to mitigate acid rain. Application of great quantities of lime to lakes and forests is one. Giving plenty of fertilizers is another. However the most simple and ultimate solution of this problem is the control of emission of pollutants

If the occurrence of this problem is limited to the border of one country, it will be controlled by the establishment of new regulating laws. The most famous one is the Helsinki protocol, which aims to decrease the So2 emission to 70 % of 1980 levels by the year 1995. Another agreement was arranged for NOx emissions. In November 1988, the Executive Body for the Convention on long-range Transboundary Air Pollution held its 6th session in Sofia, Bulgaria. Its most significant achievement was the signing by 25 countries of a new protocol to freeze NOx emission by 1994 (UNEP, Regional Bulletin of Europe, Dec. 1988)

Smog

Due to temperature and inversion effects, sometimes, smoke, sulfur dioxide and carbon monoxide and other effluents of fossil fuel combustion mix with cold fog to form smog Smog is highly toxic and harmful to life. During the 1950s some 4000 people were killed due to smog in London. Another type of smog is called photochemical smog, it is formed due to hydrocarbons and nitrogen oxides. This type of smog contains a mixture of undesirable gases like ozone and PAN have been discussed earlier.

Green House Effect

The glass of a greenhouse allows sunlight to stream in freely but blocks heat from escaping, mainly by preventing the warm air inside the greenhouse from mixing with outside air. In a similar fashion gases like carbon dioxide, methane, water vapour, oxides of nitrogen, chloroflurocarbons (CFCs) emitted from different sources on earth are transparent to incoming solar radiation but trap heat near the surface of the earth by more efficiently absorbing the longer wavelength infrared radiation released by the earth. This results in global warming up and the phenomenon is called greenhouse effect. The chief source of greenhouse gases are combustion of fossil fuels, industrial practices, rice cultivation, cattle breeding, bio mass burning, deforestation, microbial activity in municipal land fills and swamps. All these are increasing day by day resulting in greater production of these gases. Carbon dioxide concentration which was about 280 parts per million (ppm) at the end of the last century, has risen to the current level of about 350 ppm and is likely to be 380 ppm by 2000 AD. Computer simulation models show that the concentration may double by 2050AD. Similarly concentration of methane has risen 700 parts per billion (ppb) at the beginning of this century to the present level of 1700 ppb. Methane traps 20 times as much as carbon dioxide but is significantly less abundant. However, direct worldwide measurement shows that methane levels are growing more rapidly than carbon dioxide.

In the absence of clear quantitative historical record, it is difficult to tell how the doubling of carbon dioxide and other green house gases will affect us. Mathematical models show a modest increase between 3.0 degree centigrade and 5.5 degree centigrade in earth's surface temperature. Melting of Antarctica's ice rather will cause an 80 cm. rise in sea level. Melting of one per cent of the Antarctic sea cap (90 per cent of all the ice on the earth) will raise the sea level by 80 cm Change in precipitation and temperature could threaten natural ecosystems, agricultural production and human settlement patterns. Stream run off may be reduced due to speed evaporation affecting irrigation and water quality. In the resulting deluge low lying cities like Bombay, Dhaka, Calcutta and the entire Maldives may be submerged. Heat distribution profile of the earth along with wind pattern and rainfall may change, resulting in less wheat production in Europe and USSR and leading to collapse of world economy. In short, global climatic change would have economic, political and social consequences.

Several climatic models suggest that one possible result of a global warming would be to increase the volume of the ice rather than decrease it. This is because there will be increased precipitation in the Antarctica as temperature rise, resulting in higher snowfall. Thus, if temperature increases by 3 degrees C and

Antarctica precipitation rises 24 per cent, the volume of ice in the Antarctic would eventually increase by somewhat less than 1 per cent, leading to a 50 cm fall in sea level. (UNEP – GEMS, 1987)

Depletion of Ozone layer

The ozone layer in the stratosphere extending between 25-35 kms, in the atmosphere serves as a shield protecting the planet from harmful effects of ultraviolet radiations. This layer is however thinning out due to the widespread use of a group of chemicals called chloroflurocarbons (CFCs) these chemicals are used in aerosol sprays, refrigerators and room air conditioners as refrigerating liquids and in blowing of plastic foams. etc. Use of these chemicals is on the increase in the modern world. Cold vortex measurements in the Antarctic region in 1985 have indicated a 40 percent thinning in ozone layer and even an ozone hole of the size of USA has been created over Antarctica. Destruction of ozone layer and resulting exposure to ultraviolet radiation can speed aging of skin, produce skin cancer and cataracts, damage crops and phytoplankton, the basis of food chain in sea and stunt growth of many plant and marine life. Fortunately, the world community has become conscious of the problem and the Montreal protocol have been signed in 1987 in Canada aimed at reducing production of CFCs and replacing them with other harmless substitutes. Mechanism of Ozone layer Depletion CFCs are stable and cannot be easily decomposed. However, these CFCs are climbing up to the stratosphere through the troposphere taking 10 or more years. In the stratosphere CFCs

$$\begin{array}{ll} Cl + O_3 \longrightarrow ClO + O_2 & H + O_3 \longrightarrow OH + O_2 \\ Cl + O \longrightarrow Cl + O_2 & OH + O \longrightarrow H + O_2 \\ O_2 + O \longrightarrow 2O_2 & O_3 + O \longrightarrow 2O_2 \end{array}$$

$$\begin{array}{ll} Cl + O_3 \longrightarrow Cl + O_2 & \\ Br + O \longrightarrow Br + O_2 & NO + O_3 \longrightarrow NO_2 + O_2 \\ ClO + BrO \longrightarrow Cl + Br + O_2 & NO2 + O \longrightarrow NO + O_3 \\ \hline -2O_3 + O \longrightarrow 3O_2 & O_3 + O \longrightarrow 2O_2 \end{array}$$

are attacked by the radiation of UV and are decomposed, releasing atoms of chlorine. These chlorine atoms attack ozone molecules and destroy them. Some reactions to be considered occuring in the stratosphere are shown on the previous page.

Destruction of Ozone

In Addition to the regulation decided by the Montreal Protocol, the world is requesting more and complete reduction of CFCs. These requests become stricter as time passes. The latest declaration which was made at Helsinki, Finland on 2nd May 1989 on the occasion of the first Meeting of the parties to the Vienna and the Montreal Protocol agreed:

To phase out the production and the consumption of CFCs controlled by the Montreal protocol as soon as possible but not later than the year 2000 and for that purpose to tighten the timetable agreed upon in the Montreal protocol;

To both phase out halogens and control and reduce other ozone depleting substances which contribute significantly to ozone depletion as soon as feasible;

To facilitate the access of developing countries to relevant scientific information, research results and training and to seek to develop appropriate funding mechanisms to facilitate the transfer of technology and replacement of equipment at minimum cost to developing countries.

There is no argument that we need to protect the ozone layer for our health and both developed and developing countries must cooperate in solving this problem. For this purpose it is necessary that developing countries be provided with possible aid to introduce these new ideas and technologies without much difficulty.

Noise Pollution

Automobiles, trains, airplanes, industry, machinery, factory sirens, market places etc., Are the major sources of noise pollution.

A jet engine during take off produces noise pollution of highest degree. It has been observed that on exposure to rock music guinea pigs suffer loss of hearing. Continuous exposure of rock music and high sound exceeding 90 decibels results in emotional distress, rise in blood pressure, tension, increased heart beat and may lead to loss of hearing.

Radio Active Pollution

Radio active emissions like alpha, beta, gamma rays and neutrons emitted from accidents in nuclear power plants atomic explosions, nuclear testing, radio isotopes, radio active wastes of nuclear reactors, x-ray machines and even picture tubes of television and electron microscopes are sources of radioactive pollution. Exposure to radiation beyond threshold limits of 0.5 rem/ year can cause radiation sickness, cancer, leukemia, and abnormal fetus in pregnant mother and even death depending upon doses received. Chernobyl and Three-Miles island nuclear power plants accident illustrates the hazard of radioactive pollution. Nuclear waste material buried in stainless steel containers or dumped in the ocean are intensely toxic for thousands of years. If buried in seismically unstable zones such containers may burst and pollute ground water. Radiation exposure also can bring about genetic changes and mutant genes in the recipient. About one million US dollar a minute is spent in the world for armament. Over fifty thousand nuclear bombs have been stockpiled. Each one of us gets a share of 3.5 ton of explosive only from the nuclear stockpile. During the Viet Nam war from 1961 to 1973 the USA used herbicides and destroyed 44% of woodlands in South Viet Nam. As a result a carpet bombing 3 billion cubic meters of soil and subsoil had been displaced.

Pollution continues to be one of the grave environmental problems. There is a worldwide debate about the causes of pollution. It may be worth mentioning here the views of Barry Commoner, the American social scientist who holds a different perception. According to commoner pollution and resulting environmental degradation are nor due to population or affluence but the methods of production, which are polluting and energy consuming. In the similar lines Schumacher suggests to develop appropriate technology that one produces goods with minimal waste and pollution. He calls it "Technology with Human Face" in his book "Small is beautiful".

Deforestation

Forests are vital to human existence as they provide fuel, fodder, timber, food and medicine. They also check soil erosion, clean air by using up carbon dioxide in photosynthesis help in rainfall, serve as windbreakers during storm and cyclone in coastal areas, provide habitat for wild animals and above all provide recreation for mankind. National Forest Policy stipulates that on the average 33% of the land area should have forest cover. But forests are continuously being denuded to meet increasing demand of people for grazing of live stock, timber, fuel, agriculture, shifting cultivation, urbanization, mining, quarry operations and for construction of hydroelectric projects, hill roads and industries. As per photographs of earth taken from remote sensing satellites, India's forest cover is around 10%. In Orrisa, forest area has been reduced from 31% in 1975 to 25 percent in 1985. Present 1980 forest denudation in the state is roughly 2.53 per cent per year.

Under capitalism, profit motive is the sole motive of economic activity, resulting in destruction of environment at a frightening speed. 40% of the world's planet have been destroyed and deforestation continues at the rate of 20 hectares per minute. 19% of the Earth's land dessertification. Coastal wet land and shallows the support system of two third of world's fisheries are being degraded and destroyed by degrading, dumping and pollution. 53.3 million square kilometers of land on earth are already deserts, one third of the total land available.

The Chipko Movement in the foothills of the Himalayas spearheaded by Sunderlal Bahuguna and others and the APKO movement in Karnataka heralded public campaign for saving forests. Another similar movement was launched in Sambalpur district of Orrisa against the bauxite-mining project of Bharat Aluminium Company (Balco in the Gandharmardan Hills, situated on the Eastern Ghats) The program of social forestry is being undertaken on a large scale in rural areas to purify polluted air. These schemes will alleviate to certain extent the pressure on forests. Tropical rain forests covering nearly 6 percent of earth's surface contain half of the planet plant and animal species. Conservation of these forests is essential for climatic stability of the biosphere, conservation of gene pool, safeguarding watersheds, allowing evolutionary processes to continue, and providing stock of plants and animals for research and also for tourism and recreation. These forests constitute about 30 % of world's total forest. The denudation of tropical rain forests is occurring at the rate of 11-40 hectares per minute (Mabberley. 1983). At this rate the world will lose bulk of its rain forests by the year 2000AD and very little of such forests will remain in India. Social forestry and other means need to be carried out and plantation needs to be increased. The rules and punishment for cutting down the trees must be made more stringent.

Extinction of Species

As per International Union for Conservation of Nature and Natural Resources (IUCN) report India has about 45,000 species of plants and 65,000 species of animals out of nearly 5-10 billion species are required for preservation of gene pool so essential, for our survival. The economic benefits and the land argument which holds that land have to foster all living beings, not human being alone, also justify the conservation of species. Genetic and ecological diversity (species richness), safe – number within carrying capacity of an environment, tolerance threshold etc., are natural parameters that decide the viability of a species. However many species are becoming extinct or endangered due to loss of habitat on account of deforestation, pollution of habitat. Indiscriminate hunting of animals have also resulted and accelerated species extinction. The present species loss per year is 10,000 times greater than the naturally occuring background extinction rate that existed prior to the appearance of human beings. The loss is so colossal that, Moonis Raza (1988) calls this age as age of extinction. The Red data Book of IUCN and the Green Book of Botanical Survey of India enlist endangered/rare species.

Launching of Man and Biosphere Programme (MAB) and World Conservation Strategy has helped conservation of species through 'In Situ' and "ex situ" methods. Monitoring the endangered species, education and training as well as international co-operation have helped to halt species extinction to some extent. Saving the endangered American Condors and success stories of white tiger in India through captive breeding are the examples of such efforts of IUCN and the World Wide Fund (WWF). Selective hunting sometimes helps conservation, as is being done with African Elephants. Social boycott of people using fur coats, banning trade in ivory and export of frog legs are steps in right direction. Voluntary organizations like 'Beauty without cruelty' 'Green peace' etc., are doing excellent job in conservation of species. Poaching of animals should be banned by all means. Making use of animal products, which kill the animal, must also be boycotted in totality.

Depletion of Natural Resources

The Natural resources of the earth, particularly the non-renewable ones like fossil fuels and minerals are being depleted at a fast rate causing severe concern, since their regular supply is vital for sustainable development. Resource use is growing at a rate of six per cent per year. Earth is like a space ship with respect to its resources. Over burdening of this spaceship earth with waste and squandering away its precious resources may lead to its extinction. As the Meadows puts it; "A society with a high level of industrialization and resource use may be non sustainable. It may be self-extinguishing if it exhausts the natural resources on which it depends."

Natural resources are not distributed and used in proportion to population and land area, among countries/ continents. The developed countries with only one-quarter of world's population consume about 80 per cent of world resources and the developing countries with three quarters of world's resources. The pollution and resources load per person in developed countries on the world environmental system is about 10-20 times the load generated by a person in a developing country (Forrester 1983). Continuous cycling and recycling of natural resources by using waste products is absolutely essential to maintain a stable economic growth and reasonable standard of living in future. Production processes should produce more easily biodegradable products, unlike plastics to help recycling. Garbage, solid waste and effluents from factories should be recycled to retrieve minerals and other useful material. The non-renewable resources require careful and judicious utilization. Wherever possible the non-renewable resources need to be conserved for longer use. Making use of car pools can reduce the load of traffic on road and also reduce petrol from being used. Making use of public transport, use of solar gas and other alternative sources of energy can save us from pollution and also from depletion of non-renewable resources.

Land Use

Due to demographic pressure land is under stress, on account of agriculture, industrialization, urbanization, railways and high ways etc., In our country extreme imbalance in land use can be seen. In Punjab where 84 per cent of geographical area is under cultivation and only 4 per cent has forest cover (Kang 1982). Government decision to set up a National Test Range missiles at Balliapal, occupying thousands of acres of fertile agricultural land for defense purpose is against the principles of land use. The move is being resisted by natives through a voluntary organization "Gantantra Adhikar Suraksha Samiti'

Though the short video film Voices of Baliapal' by Ranjan Palit and Vasudha Joshi vividly portraying misuse of land has received international acclaim Government continues to be unconcerned. To correct imbalances in land use a national land use policy for proportioning land based on topography, soil characteristics and climate etc., for short term and long term use is urgently required.

Soil fertility is going down as a result of excessive irrigation. Apart from this problem land faces one more problem of increasing garbage. The garbage is being filed in large areas causing lot of discomfort for the people leaving around as it emanates foul smell and it could also invite diseases. For avoiding this one may have to separate out dry waste and wet waste and start with vermiculture to produce compost and manure for their garden. This will also reduce the garbage in the city. The dry garbage wherever possible it can be recycled.

Soil Erosion

About 175 million hectares of land constituting 53 per cent of India's total land area is susceptible to serious soil degradation due to desertification, salination. Alkalization, water logging, deforestation and overgrazing are some of the causes of soil erosion. The country loses about 5-6 thousand million tons of topsoil every year at a rate of 10 tons / year. At this rate the entire top soil may be lost in about 250 years (Kanwar, 1978) without top soil, which has taken several hundred years for its formation, land becomes barren and is the starting point of desertification. Proper land use planning reduces erosion to some extent. The national technology mission on wasteland development will also help to save the soil. Planting trees can control soil erosion, the trees or plants of any size bind the soil and do not allow it to fly off with air or run down with water. Wherever the flow of water is cutting away land, bunds can be made to slow down the flow of water thus avoiding the cutting down of soil.

Energy Crisis

Energy is required for cooking, transport, running industries and lighting buildings and the streets. Although per capita energy consumption is less in the developing countries as compared to the developed countries. Since these countries are seeking to industrialize to raise their living standards. The energy crisis is being felt through shortage, and increased price for fuels. The organization of petroleum exporting countries (OPEC) control 75 per cent of all crude oil reserves. The war between Iraq and Allied Nations concerning liberation of Kuwait was essentially a war to control the petroleum reserves in the gulf region. The 25 per cent hike in petrol prices in India was due to this war, the adverse balance of payment positions and the IMF loans are all manifestations of the energy crisis. Seventy five per cent of Indian population use non commercial sources like wood, animal dung and agricultural waste as fuel. A sharp rise has occurred in the price of wood and coal in the last decade. Development of alternative sources like solar, nuclear, wind and tidal and biogas holds promise for solving energy crisis.

Ecological Disruption

The subtle and fragile relationships in an ecosystem can be disrupted due to external factors like human intervention. Any change in an ecosystem that is imposed from outside often triggers off a chain of reaction that dismay sometimes be irreversible. All the environmental problems described above are cause as well as manifestation of an ecological crisis in environment. Extinction of 'Dodo' and the threat from hydro electric power projects are two classic examples that amply illustrate the ecological imbalance due to human intervention. Dodo, the flight less bird of Mauritius became extinct due to hunting by colonial rulers and the dogs that they brought with them. Calvaria majora, a species of plant whose fruit was eaten by Dodo and the hard seeds passing through its digestive tract became softened facilitating germination after excretion by the bird became nearly extinct after disappearance of the bird. Recently few seeds have been germinated after being forcibly fed to turkeys.

Largely hydroelectric projects, once considered a blessing and architectural wonder are being looked with skepticism from environment point of view. President Hosseni Mubarak once said that the challenge before Egypt Is to cope wlth Aswan dam. Such projects are ecological disasters as they submerge vast tracts of forestland, uproot people mostly tribal from their home and hearth, cause water logging and salination due to canal network, change microclimate of the area, create breeding ground for disease vectors like mosquitoes and snails etc., Dams also have potential for causing earth quake due to reservoir induced seismicity.

Despite protests by the activist groups Government of India has given green signal to such hydroelectric projects like Sardar Sarovar, Narmada Sagar and one at Tehri. Fasts undertaken by Mr. Sunderlal Bahuguna, Baba Amte have produced no effect. However, Kerala Shastra Sahitya Parishad's struggle forced government to shelve the 'Silent Valley Project'.

Introduction of high yielding cereals large-scale monoculture and introduction of wide spectrum of insecticides etc. have exacerbated the ecological crisis.

These are some of the problems faced by environment and eventually by human beings and other organisms on the planet earth. Now, if we want to teach these issues at B. Ed level how do we go about, making this piece of information into environmental education?

Topic : **Pollution**
Class : **B.Ed**
Subject : **Environmental Education**

Pollution of our environment has become a serious problem and the study of this aspect has assumed unusual significance in ecology. The air, water, light and temperature conditions, soil, mineral resources, industrial, processes, dwelling conditions, crops, grassland forests and other useful organisms constitute the human environment.

Pollution means the direct or indirect changes (usually but not always brought about by man) in one or more components of the ecosystem which are harmful to the system or atleast undesirable for man.

Environment around us exhibits number of changes if we see the climate of our own city, few years back and now. We see a lot of change, earlier people in Baroda City did not have cooler's and air conditioners no body even wore sweaters as the climate was pleasant all the Time. But today we see drastic changes; winters are extremely cold and summers are extremely hot. We will learn more about the phenomena that has brought such changes "pollution".

So, Pollution is undesirable change occurring in our environment due to increasing number of pollutants. Pollutants can be in the form of dirt, dust, particulate matter, noise leading to mental tension. Contamination of air, water, land by undesirable substances, that cannot be destroyed naturally by the earth's system is pollution.

What do you understand by pollution? What are the different types of pollutions that you observe in daily life?

(Students reply "Any undesirable change in environment which cannot be corrected by nature through its self renewal process is called pollution.)

Type of pollution

Water	Pollution
Air	Pollution
Noise	Pollution
Land/Soil	Pollution
Radio Active	Pollution

That is right! Now let us study them one by one.

Air Pollution: - The chief pollutions of air are carbon monoxide, sulphur dioxide, certain hydrocarbons and particulate matter. Sulphur dioxide is primary pollutant but after combining with atmospheric etc. it becomes secondary pollutant i.e. sulfuric acid which corrodes buildings and marble. Taj Mahal is victim of such air pollution. It has led to green house effect, depletion of ozone layer and many more problems.

Water Pollution: - Water bodies such as ponds, lakes or rivers have been used as dumps for the wastes of villages, towns and cities. These aquatic bodies have a self-regulatory mechanism for recycling these wastes quickly if the amount of sewage is small. But when the contamination level increases to such an extent that the water becomes less useful or harmful, and then we regard it as pollution. Pollution of water is sewage, organic chemicals like detergents (Washing powders) and pesticides, inorganic chemicals, harmful micro-organisms and sediments. In the sea radio active materials are also dumped. The Ganga water pollution case brought by M.C. Mehta through PIL is an important contribution. Mr. Mehta brought to the notice of Supreme court that the discharge of trade effluents by tanneries near kanpur into the municipal civil lines and ultimately in river Ganga had caused considerate damage to the life of the people who use the water of the river and to the aquatic life of the river.

Land Pollution: -Indiscriminate quarrying of the natural land is causing lot of pollution. Kinkri Devi V. State of HP held that to ensure the attainment of constitution goal of the protection and improvement of natural wealth and environment and of the safe guarding of the forests, the lakes, the rivers and the wildlife and to protect the people inhabiting the vulnerable areas from hazardous consequences of the arbitrary exercise of the power granting mining leases without due regard to their life liberty and property.

Solid Waste: - Most of our daily needs are obtained from the market in nicely packed containers made up of tin, polyethylene, plastics and glass. After the use of contents the packaging material is usually thrown out as garbage. Some of the junk is readily degradable some material can be recycled. Solid waste can be controlled by 1) Recycling 2) Burning 3) Preparing compost from the organic waste.

Radio Active Pollution:-Nuclear war materials and test explosions are principal sources of radioactive wastes in the atmosphere, soil and water. Ionizing radiations cause mutations abnormality and lethality in many organisms, including man. Cancer is commonly caused even under low level exposures. Radiation effects persist for a long period in the environment.

Noise Pollution: - Only when a sound is not liked or is unwanted we call it as noise. When the loudness of the sound is irritating or unbearable we regard it as noise pollution. Sound is measured in decibel dB. Sounds beyond 80 dB can be safely regarded as pollution for it harms our hearing ability. Sound beyond 120dB is painful. Noise pollution can cause loss of hearing, disturbs mental peace, person becomes hard of hearing, increase in the rate of heart beat sometimes damages eye sight, brain and liver.

After discussing the various types of pollution some rule will be discussed

(a) To make an assessment of the technologies available for vehicular pollution control in the world, as a result we have **PUC Checks**.

Now, take your home assignment write Environmental Problem, Effect on Health and Alternative Strategy.

You can make use of Books from library or Internet. I will give you a week's time.

Student Assignment Environment Problems and their alternatives

(1)Water Pollution and Water Scarcity	*Effect of Health*	*Alternative Strategy*
(a) Sewage and other oxygen demanding waste become water pollutant they deplete dissolved oxygen from water.	More than 7 million deaths and billions of illnesses a year attributable to pollution poor household hygiene and added by water risks caused by water scarcity.	Recycling water from industries and using for irrigation.
(b) Sewage water is carrier of bacteria microbes which produce disease in man and animals.		Recycle water and use for irrigation
(c) Sediments - Reduce sunlight for green plants.	Can't sustain aquatic life Reduce population of fish & shell fish.	Proper dilution of effluent waste.
(d) Pesticides,	Makes water unfit	Recycle of cooling

surfactants, industrial products, inorganic, minerals, water soluble compounds of Hg, Pb, As, Cd, F etc.	for drinking and industrial use.	towers Blowdown.
(e) Surfactants are bio-non degradable, inhibits oxidation of organic substances forms colloidal substances which result into stable foam in river's of several mt. high	Causes faster assimil-ation of water waste depletes oxygen affects aquatic life. Affects on sea birds penetrates feathers	Reduction in the use of deterge-nts and other surfactant is re-required
(f) Heat and oil: Water being used as coolant in plants and industries which is discharged at raised temperture oil discharged from oil tankers off shore drilling rigs.	Killls aquatic animals birds, basically it is harmful for aquatic life. Oil kills many birds and aquatic life.	Water can be cooled and used for irrigation purpose. Such accidents must be averted a surfactant should be sprayed in case an accident occurs.
2. Solid and hazardous waste.	Diseases spread by rotting garbage and	Preparation of compost.
3. Soil degradation is due to excessive use of fertilizers.	blocked drains. Localized flooding, leading to death and disease. Reduces fertitily of soil Reduces	Protect land against soil erosion. Reduction in use of biologically

	nutrition the soil become depleted. The presence of heavy metals causes kidney failure, damages,	non degradable products Reduction in use of fertilizers
4. Deforestation	Change in the climate is seen globally	Afforestation
5. Air pollution:- Presence of CO_2 CO in air (more than 100 ppm) causes increase in temperature by 1.9 C green house effect • presence of oxides of Nitrogen and SO_2 • Oxides of Nitrogen, hydrocarbon depletes Ozone layer present in troposphere. • Particulate matter consisting of fly ash, asbestos, dust, root metals metal oxide, salts hydrocarbons etc.	Presence of CO in air causes Anoxia (O_2 Starvation). Affects human respiratory system, chronic Bronchitis Bronchial Asthama, lung Cancer	75% of CO originates from gasoline fed internal combu-stion Use unleaded Gasoline & CNG Electrostatic Precipitator is used.
Ozone Depletion	Skin cancer skin diseases.	Use of Fluoro carbons should be banned.
Chemical pesticides.	Kills friendly animals. Adverse effect on fish illness among farm workers minor effects	Autocide:- Elimi-nating pests by eliminating their reproductive

	reproductive activity of animals	system, chemostrilants, sex attractants, juvenile hormones etc.
Noise Pollution;- When a sound is not liked or is unwanted it is called noise. When it is irritating or unbearable we regard it as noise pollution.	Noise interferes with communication, causes loss of hearing and disturbs mental peace. Noise also causes mental stress, increase rate of heart beat, sometimes damages, eye sight, brain and liver functioning. Fast moving jet planes leaves behing sonic booms. When these booms hit the ground they causes rattling of window panes or even damages to building structures.	Noise pollution can be controll--ed in number of ways, such as restricting unnecessary use of horns, in motor vehi--cles, use of sound absorb--ers in auditori--um, use of ear plugs in factori--es, jet planes etc.

Today in the 21st century we have achieved a lot. We have progressed in all fields say it industries, agriculture, urbanization, science, technology, nuclear weapons, economic development, modernization style of living. Almost everything around has seen a sea change.

In all these changes we have damaged the environment, which is harmful for our own existence. That is an irretrievable change, due to which we have harmed our Biosphere in which we live. We have just one planet on which life exist. The planet earth, we have not inherited it from our forefathers but we have hired it from our future generation. We have forgotten that if earth is the only living planet the resources on the spaceship earth are also limited and cannot be generated indefinitely as we want.

Therefore it is high time that we take immediate actions to reduce pollution with the help of suggested alternative strategy. After a week's time students bring the assignment as given above along with a script to be implemented in their community.

Script Pollution

(The play is set in the backdrop of a village. One day under the tree in the village common place Panchayat will be held).

(Students of my class will play village members families, 5 members will be Panch and 2 members will be doctors 2 members will be from NGO.)

SARPANCH: -Dear friends, today we have called this special panchayat to discuss number of problems that our village is facing, since last year Raman, Changan and Magan have developed skin problems, Bharatbhai's land has become barren, Rajanbhai is not having any children since last many years. Dhirenbhai said we must call the Panchayat to find why there are such problems. People are falling sick again & again our Hakim is not able to solve these problems.

Let us, listen to them – individually Raman: - My name is Raman I am a land labour, who works in the field. Initially I had some rashes which gradually spread all over my body.

Chagan: - I had same problem.

Magan: - I also had same problem.

Bharatbhai: - I am continuously monitoring the produces of my land they are getting reduced, now my land is become barren, Rajanbhai is my neighbor he has taken lot of treatment but does not have children.

Magan: - Hello! Dhirenbhai, why are you late for panchayat.

Dhirenbhai: - I was coming on my way I met my college, friends. They wanted to see panchayat so, I brought them with me.

Sarpanch: - Introduce your friends to our village friends.

Rajiv a Doctor

Renu is a Doctor

Priya is working with NGO.

Dinesh is working with NGO.

(In the meanwhile they explain whatever transpired so far in the panchayat by Chagan).

Priya says: - What has changed since last 4 years in your village?

(In the meanwhile Rajiv and Renu check Chagan, Magan and Raman)

(Bharat and Dinesh go to see the Village).

In the meanwhile villagers tell how the village had developed, people got employment, they got electricity, and they also got some water pipes.

(Renu also examines few women in the Panchayat community).

Priya: - You have really progressed and I guess the only problems were discussed earlier today. Before I say something I want you to listen to Renu.

Renu: - I have examined 3 patients with skin problems. I have also seen a number of village women suffering from asthma like disease (further investigation is required). These women are victims of the Chullah. The fire and ash create problem. The men are suffering from skin disease. It will also need further examination.

In the mean while Dinesh and Bharat come back.

Dinesh:- I guess I have the answer to all the problems discussed and focused in today's Panchayat.

Dinesh: - A new factory has come near village. The pipe passing near the farms actually is effluent treatment plants exhaust pipe. The villagers are actually using its water on land. The books say by use of such chemicals the land becomes barren, skin cancer may develop, reproductive rate may go down.

Rajiv: - Yes, I agree to what Dinesh is saying. Next Wednesday we will organize a camp and do a checkup.

Dinesh & Renu: - On same day we will also have camp for unnat Chula & Bio Gas plant, only if Sarpanchji gives permission.

Sarpanch, I am proud of our son Dhiren who brought his friends to our Panchayat and solved the problems faced in our village. I thank one in all to make this meeting a success. You have really opened our eyes.

In the above topic of pollution, I have tried to integrate lecture method by briefly describing the concept of pollution and pollutants. After that I am using a brief discussion to know various, types of pollutions based on the nature of pollutants and ask the students to do an assignment by referring books and internet. 'As a part of group project students prepare the script and perform the street play in the neighboring community plus a campaign to bring awareness.

Thus, here an attempt has been made to integrate lecture, discussion, project and fieldwork to make teaching – learning process more interesting. Along with street play students also prepare project report after collecting the opinion of people regarding the problems they are facing with regards to pollution and how useful was the street play and posters for improving the environment in their vicinity. There are many NGOs working in the field of environmental education to bring awareness in the community, let us know about them.

Some Questions

1. Explain adverse effect of pollution on health
2. Explain the source, causes and effects of air/ water/ noise pollution. (any one)
3. State five urban and rural societies' problems caused due to environmental disturbance/ imbalance.
4. Explain green house effect and its Impact on environment.
5. Write short note on (its impact on environment).

(a) Population Explosion
(b) Ozone depletion
(c) Deforestation
(d) Energy crisis
(e) Extinction of species
(f) Land use.

5

Role of Non Governmental Organizations

Development and Environment

The protection of Environment is an essential part of development. Earth Summit as is commonly known took place in Rio de Janeiro in June 1992. This summit was vastly attended by 3000 strong NGO representatives along with other delegates "Agenda 21" a comprehensive plan to guide national and international action towards sustainable development was put forth. It was this agenda that encourages the NGOs to play a more prominent role in guiding and co-coordinating environmental policies and developmental programs.

Role of Non Governmental Organization

As it has been said that Environment involves all the factors, so the study should adopt not only the interdisciplinary approach but also multidisciplinary approach as through this approach, we can obtain the holistic solution to environmental problems. The study of environment is done through many ways. The main stress is laid on including a strong dose of environmental education in both school and in university curriculum, but unfortunately this is not yet fully implemented. For solving the problem, at least the organizations be in a position to help the nation in creating awareness of environmental problems not only among the students but also among the masses.

Some of the Government organizations do participate in action oriented programs. Government has framed and introduced Laws and Acts in order to protect the wildlife, forests and natural resources, but their implementation in actual sense remains a far off reality. Government organizations functions are at the mercy of the bureaucrats who are known for their three ill marks, viz., inertia, rigidity and routine. These three are followed by red tapism, lack of innovation on the part of the office bearers. While on the other hand, a non-governmental organization plays a very vital role in carrying out certain ideas and action oriented programs. Some of the reasons may be as following.

(a) It is a socially autonomous organization.
(b) It is capable of undertaking, prescriptive, recommendatory positive attitude.

The Non Governmental Organizations are very effective agents as far as environmental education is concerned they provide a very valuable channel for feedback. They have the advantage of being in direct contact with the masses. They are with specific aims and objectives and have been working with the people and for the people for years together for the betterment of human race. These Non Governmental Organizations today have understood the need of the time and are busy channeling their energies towards environmental protection.

The problems pertaining to environment cannot be handled in a dictatorial manner as we have adopted a democratic set of polity. In democracy only way of convincing people is by making them aware and responsible for their actions, when it comes to environmental education law alone is insufficient to curb the vices faced by environment. Education has a limited scope as many are still out of the education system. So the option left is to have NGOs who can persuade the general public, educate them through various means and do their bit for the protection of environment.

The Non Government Organizations have been in existence for a long time it is only recently, that their role as well as their organizational significance is being realized. Their strengths include small size, flexibility of action, high motivation and willingness of their numbers to work with minimal returns, dynamism and the capacity of handling issues with sensitivity. Considering the variety and intensity of the societal problems we face today, one has to appreciate the fact that the government can't satisfy all the needs effectively. Beside many of our problems need personalized touch, which the government is unable to do so. NGO's with specific aims and objectives have been working with people and for the people for years together. Their concern is the betterment of the society in general. These NGO's today have understood the need of the time and are busy channelizing their energies toward environmental preservation.

NGO's are effective as far as environment education is concerned.

They provide.

- Very valuable channel for feedback.
- Direct contact with masses.
- Specific aims and objectives.

There are many NGO's working at International, National, State and even at local levels.

International

- World wildlife Fund (WWF)
- Royal Society for protection of birds
- Global Response Environmental Action Network (GREAN)
- Green Shoots
- Earth Watch
- Earth Centre
- Kelvin L Ervin Consulting Ecologist Inc.
- Man and Biosphere

National Level

(a) Nehru Center for environmental science
(b) C.P Ramaswami Iyer Institution for southern states.
(c) Rashtriya Paryavaran Jagruti Abhiyan
(d) Center for Environmental Education CEE
(e) Bombay Natural History Society (BNHS)
(f) Chipko Organization
(g) Vanrai

(h) Paryavaran Saurakshan Manch and many more.

In Gujarat

(a) Center for Environmental Development Ahmedabad
(b) Environmental planning collaborative (EPC), Ahmedabad
(c) Gramya Urja Vikas sansthan, Kheda
(d) Prayas, Rajpipla/ Narmada
(e) Kutch Fodder, Fruit and Forest Development Trust (KFFFDT) Bhuj

Many more.

In Vadodara City

(a) World Wild life Fund (WWF)
(b) Society for Clean Environment (SOCLEEN)
(c) International Society of Naturalists (INSONA)
(d) Gujarat Nature Conservation Society (GNCS)
(e) Baroda Beautiful Council and many more
(f) Heritage trust
(g) Nature Education and Environment Development School (NEEDS)
(h) Tree lover's Educational and Research foundation.
(i) United way of Baroda.

In 1984, Nehru Center for environmental studies at Ahmedabad, C.P Ramaswami Iyer Institution for southern states in 1988 and Rashtriya Paryavaran Jagruti Abhiyan 1986 were established. These institutes undertook to train, resource persons to teach government officials, people from voluntary organizations. Training was given in regional language also.

World Wild Life Fund opened its Indian chapter in 1976. This organization along with its regional sister concerns undertook the task of teaching young environmentalists. They provide information as well as material to children who ask for it. Varied youth organizations have forums to carry out awareness programs, train resource persons and carry out varied campaigns related to conservation of natural resources. These forums activated people towards becoming environment conscious. India too has a long history of the work done by the NGOs towards protection of the nature conservation of forests or wildlife.

Mass scale falling of trees to build Kosi Dam in the Terai region of Gadwal unsettled the local inhabitant there. It also disturbed the ecology there. Sunderlal Bahuguna an eminent scholar environmentalist and a staunch activist founded and headed the Chipko organization and the movement. This organization looks into the problems of the people there, rehabilitates them, and gives them means of livelihood. This organization is active in Alaknanda river valley and Tarai regions of Gadwal.

Vanrai is another such organization, which carries out multiple activities in Maharashtra with conservation of forests as its base. Sri Mohan Dharia former central minister and active environmentalist established this organization in 1986. He believes that a balance has to be maintained between man, animals and nature development. Creation of environmental awareness is one of the major activities conducted by the organization. More attention is paid to utilization of local manpower and local materials towards creating a sustainable economy with sustainable environmental preservation.

Silent people's movement of Rajasthan, Greening movement of Kerala, Paryavaran Saurakshan manch, Maharashtra has tried to combine business while stopping the environmental degradation. These activists look after work, job satisfaction and monetary gains of the local people. They are also greening their surroundings and protecting ecology.

Gyan Probodhini Pune encourages students to carryout surveys in this field. This organization was the first one to start a project Nirmalya Prakalp. Their success encouraged many others to follow suit. Baba Amte will well be remembered for his Anandvan and Medha Patkar who is single handedly fighting for Narmada Bachao Sangathan. Maneka Gandhi is another crusader who is doing her bit for the animals in collaboration with society for prevention of cruelty against animals (SPCA). Justice M. C. Mehta the Magasaysay award winner and his courts of justice have brought laws for preventing environmental degradation.

United Way of Baroda

It started in 1986 with tripartite participation of Baroda Citizens Council, United Way International and United Nations International Children's Educational Fund (UNICEF) for initial five years. It allocates funds according to the Priority and needs of time. The NGO's are aware of local language dialect, local customs traditions, folk arts etc., they can use to reach people.

NGO's can be helpful :

- To aid and advise the government
- To act as the eyes and ears of the government
- To educate the people at large and create general awareness in favor of conservation.
- NGO's have understood the need of the time they are busy in protecting nature, conservation of forests or wild life providing educational programs for school children, awareness amongst people.
- NGO's: - They are the organizations working for the betterment and development of the society and mankind. They have specific aims and objectives and work for the people and with the people.

INSONA International Society of Naturalists

It was found in 1975 keeping in mind 1972's UN Stockholm Conference its head quarter is in Baroda, Dr. G.M Oza is its General Secretary and Fatehsingrao Gaekwad is the founder President.

It stands for Harmony of Humanbeing and nature. "Conserve today and Save Tomorrow"

Objectives

- To promote appreciation and love of nature particularly among the younger generation.
- To organize various kinds of activities to popularize different branches in the field of natural science and environmental conservation.
- To publish monographs memoirs, bulletins journal and other research publication on national science and environmental conservation and to exchange the same with other such institutions etc. etc.

Programs conducted by INSONA

- Society organizes
- Earth day
- World Forestry day
- World environment Day
- Van Mahotsav
- Wildlife week
- World food day
- Environment month
- Conference
- Seminars/Talks
- Excursions,
- Essay, painting, debate
- Nursery
- Journal they bring out a journal
- Campaign: Themes "Trees as our friends"
- "Environment care for human Welfare"
- "The role of women in the protection of trees"
- Etc.

(SOCLEEN) Society for Clean Environment

It was found in 1977. The focus was on preservation and improvement in and around Vadodara and places them on the agenda of official agencies.

It works closely with civic authorities, voluntary organization, corporate bodies, students, community and media.

Objectives

- To educate citizens in the art of healthy living and make them conscious of the hazards of a polluted environment.
- To obtain assistance and cooperation of local authorities, state and central government as well as individuals, other bodies and institutions for achieving the objectives of the society.
- To recommend and pursue the introduction of suitable and necessary legislation for the control and abatement of environmental pollution.
- To organize public lectures, film shows radio talks etc., for achieving the objectives of the society.

- To collect publish and distribute literature and /or data on the subject of environmental pollution.

Programs conducted by SOCLEEN

1. Planting saplings, which are protected by tree guards, does greening of the city.
2. Fighting automobile pollution i.e. traffic planning and management.
3. Noise pollution
4. Air Pollution
5. Water Pollution
6. Garbage removal and solid waste management.
7. Creating environmental awareness especially among school children through "SOCLEEN YOUTH WING"
8. Vermiculture
9. Organizing seminars, workshops, interschool competitions, summer camps awards to focus attention on the environment.
10. It publishes a quarterly journal

Gujarat Nature Conservation Society

Indubahi Patel established this organization in 1984. It has set up "Nature Education Park" in Sindhrot e.g. for 3-6 years age group children it harbors a garden and a zoo. Here children can learn about plants and animals.

The Nature Education Park is also an example of regeneration, soil conservation, water conservation, wildlife protection etc.,

The mission of the organization is

1. Nature Conservation
2. Nature Education Conservation

Objectives

- To create love for nature and wildlife among members of public, children, youth etc.
- To impart education about nature and for this purpose to establish and maintain wildlife parks, Nature reserves, sanctuaries, bio spheres etc.,

- To make assessment of bio systems and ecosystems of the state and to prepare documentaries in the respect.
- To undertake technical development of aspects concerning nature in Gujarat.
- To Co-operate with other organizations with similar objectives.

Programs conducted by GNCS

Apart from showing 30 acre park to schoolchildren at nominal charges of which 40% goes to leprosy hospital. It also conducts a project called " The experiences" to the place according to the syllabus. The camps are organized to

Class III Nature Education Park
Class IV Jambughoda
Class V Cultural Camps Ahmedabad
Class VI Mosda Forest Camp
Class VII Sasan Gir or Kutch desert
Class VIII Mithapur – Marine Camp
The fee is charged from the students.

They also conduct street plays, slide shows, followed by feedback sessions.

Heritage Trust

It was established in 1984 to preserve culture and historical monuments in Baroda. They organize workshop, seminar, and plays, lecture series by eminent personalities.

Project preservation of fort of Champaner. (Mining effects) The archeological survey of India, world monuments watch and the trust is the leading crusaders in preserving it. People work voluntarily for the organization.

The foundation for Environmental Awareness

It was established in 1983. Its objectives are:

- To be devoted to environment for human welfare and to promote the cause of the biosphere this is our only life support system, which is already menaced.
- To carry on campaigns and actively crusade for environmental awareness.

Programs

Activities are conducted in collaboration with INSONA

Nature Education and Environmental Development School (NEEDS)

It was established in 1996 and it brings awareness by field trips.

Objectives

1. To introduce participants with joy of living with nature.
2. To develop sense of appreciation about environment.
3. To go toward the approach of self-learning as the participants are with nature.

Programs

- Programs for slum dwellers, rural and tribal people.
- Camps to sanctuaries
- Film shows
- Debates
- Quiz
- CCA
- Nadiad to Ankleshwar
- Finance is provided by the United Way of Baroda.

Tree Lovers Education and Research Foundation

It was established in 1995. The founder went to Japan where he saw a hillock was covered with trees, as it was told to him that it was not a natural forest but memory of their dead relatives. These trees were taken under care by society. Each one has to plant a tree to regain 33% of forest area.

Objectives of the organization

1. To give information about the scientific cultivation of high yielding crops to the farmers.
2. To promote social forestry
3. To co-operate with other similar organization
4. To educate women about gardening
5. To publish books, posters etc.\

Programs

- Social Forestry Saplings are given free of cost. With the help of Department of Forest
- Home Gardening and Bonsai. People are told about tree plantation and conservation of water.
- Medicinal plants
- Seminars.

From all the above NGO's their program's, activities and their objectives. We can see in their own little way they are trying to bring an impact on environment by making the people aware about the grave consequences, involving them to solve some of the problems faced at the local level. They also go from school to school with various gadgets show the programs collect the views of the students, arrange various competitions. They feel it is easy to reach out to children in developing healthy habits towards the environment. They say these young children carry the message to the adults as well.

Since the earth summit it is not possible to talk about development without thinking about environment. Many companies have adopted mission statements which include environmental statement which include environmental goals and have reformed their business to reduce waste in the production, consumption, and disposal of their products. More companies are embracing the ISO 14000. Government is willing to listen to NGO's. IUCN and WWF have awakened the world's conscience and are helping developed and developing countries to conserve their biological diversity.

We continue to loose at least three species of flora and fauna every day. International agencies are working together and manage the ocean in a holistic way. In 1996 the UN conference said by 2000 half of the world's population will stay in cities.

All this will necessitate the role of NGO's in a more profound manner to educate people about the environment and its carrying capacity. Government and Non Governmental Organization alone will not be able to do much each one of us will have to join hands to conserve the nature.

Some Questions

1. Explain the importance of NGO's in inculcating environmental values.
2. Write short note on WWF.
3. What are the objectives of NGO's in general?
4. Describe various activities carried out by the NGO's in fulfilling the set objectives?
5. In your opinion are NGO's really doing the needful to achieve the set objectives justify your answer with suitable illustrations?

6

Conservation

Conservation should not only mean the preservation of wilderness but the rational management of the biosphere so that it may yield the greatest sustainable benefit to present generation while maintaining its potential to meet the needs to the future generations. An operational or functional definition can be arrived at by considering series of conservation measures.

1. **Preservation:** is the protection of nature from commercial exploitation to prolong its use for recreation, watershed, protection and scientific study. It is familiar in the establishment and protection of parks and reserves of many kinds.

2. **Restoration:** another widely familiar conservation measures, is essentially the correction of past willful and inadvertent abuses that have impaired the productivity of the resources base. This measure is familiar in modern soil and water conservation practices applied to agricultural land.

3. **Beneficiation**: is the upgrading of the usefulness or quality of something, for instance, the utilization of ores that were formerly of uneconomic grade. Modern technology has provided many examples of this type of conservation.

4. **Maximization**: includes all measures to avoid waste and increase the quantity and quality of production and resources.

5. **Reutilization:** in industry commonly called recycling, is the reuse of waste materials as in the scrap iron in steel manufacture or of industrial water after it has been cleaned and cooled.

6. **Substitution:** An important conservation measure has two aspects: the use of a common resource instead of a rare one when it serves the same end and use of waste materials as in the use of renewable rather than nonrenewable resources when conditions permit.

7. **Allocation** concerns the strategy of use, the best use of a resource. For many resources and products from them, the market price, as determined by supply and demand established to what use a resource is put, but under certain circumstances the general welfare may dictate usage and resources may be controlled by government through the use of quotas, rationing, or outright ownership.

8. **Integration** in resources management is a conservation measure because it maximizes over a period of time the sum of goods and services that can be had from a resource or a resource complex, such as a river valley; this is preferable to maximizing certain benefits from a single resource at the expense of other. This is one of the meanings of multiple uses, and integration is a central objective of planning.

A generalized definition that fits many but not all meanings of conservation is "the maximization over time of the net social benefits in goods and services from resources". Although it is technologically based, conservation cannot escape socially determined values. There is an ethic involved in all aspects of conservation.

Why do we need conservation?

Urbanization: Industrial progress along with job opportunities led to growth and mushrooming of cities all over the world as centers of commerce, production and art culture. These also encouraged migration of rural population to cities. At the time of independence the share of urban population did not exceed 8% of total population but by 1991 it was close to 36.2 % (217 millions). The number of million plus cities increased from 3 (Percent 1947 to 23 percent by 1991).

Unplanned growth of urbanization has led to infrastructure collapse, miserable living conditions in slums. Basic amenities like housing, transport, roads, water supply sanitations etc. have got disrupted.

We have increased food production by intensive irrigation, chemicals fertilizers and pesticides. But the food grain production cannot keep pace with population explosion. As agriculture grows arithmetically population grows geometrically.

Withdrawals of ground water double the rate of aquifer recharge from rainfall. As a result water table is sinking.

Fast growth of human and livestock population has led to continuous degradation of soil due to human activities such as intensive cultivation over utilization of grazing land reckless deforestation, fuel fodder collection and road construction deforestation etc., results in losing tons of top soil, resulting in soil erosion, loss in fertility, drought and flood. Population pressure has imposed severe strain on non-renewable and intentional energy resources like fossil fuel.

Change and Manipulation done by Human beings

If we see the development of human race from stone age to the recent ICT age. Man has developed tremendously. Initially "Man" was afraid of nature and worshipped it as gods and prayed for safety. Gradually as "man" got more power developed the skills of fishing, agriculture, and cattle rearing etc., he thought he is becoming powerful and can control the environmental conditions. The changes started in the environment but as the population was small the changes were not so fast at that time. Major change came in with industrialization.

Industrial revolution leads to expansion of cities and town both in size and power. Before the advent of industrial era, man was drawing from the environment but there was not much damage because the system could come to balance in some time. The industrial era brought many changes which were difficult for system to absorb.

- **Urbanization :** development of science and technology led to industrialization. Many small and big industries came up in cities and towns. People migrated from village to cities in search of jobs. Various labor intensive industries gave the job to people but enough facilities in terms of residence was not given.

- **Migration of people from village to cities:** such migration from agrarian society to industrial society brought many changes in life and living standards.

- **Development of slums:** Due to lack of residential facilities people started living near the industries, developing slums around the industries.

- **Development of metropolitan cities:** Gradually the cities expanded by the population migration and build houses and other supportive infrastructure.

- **Increase in demand of energy:** gradually the demand for energy and fuel increased. As the population increased in the cities.

- **Resource shortage electricity, petrol:** Even today we here news of power cuts in the day time for 6- 7 hours in the cities. The price of petrol is also increasing day by day.

- **Waste disposal:** Cities are also generating a lot of biologically non degradable waste. Leading to increasing piles of junk material in the cities.

- **Water conservation:** Water supply is also affected the underground water in going down as we are unable to charge the aquifers and ground water table.

· **Clearance of forestland:** In order to develop the residential areas and agricultural land plus for development of industries the forestland is cleared which has altered the global climate.

Problems due to Environmental Degradation

When the environment is not able to support living organisms or their created problems related to health or create some kind of imbalance. We can say environment has degraded. Imbalance in environment is due to the human greed. This human greed leads to following problems.

1. Different types of pollutions increase which influence human health
2. Natural resources reduce
3. Flora and fauna becomes extinct
4. Natural calamities and their frequency increase
5. Soil fertility decreases
6. Water supply decreases
7. Global temperature rises
8. Drastic changes in the climate
9. Imbalance in nature
10. Affects overall development, mental, physical and economic.
11. Soil erosion and increase of deserts
12. Energy crisis
13. Decrease in forest cover
14. More incidents of acid rains, smog, green house effect
15. Oil spills and excess light at night also cause environmental degradation

Purpose of Conservation

1. To maintain essential ecological processes and life support systems
2. To preserve genetic diversity
3. To ensure genetic diversity
4. To ensure the sustainable utilization of species and ecosystems

Thus, conservation is positive embracing, preservation, maintenance, sustainable utilization, restoration and enhancement of the natural environment.

Conservation of Biodiversity

Biodiversity is the vast array of all the species of plants, animals, insects and the microorganisms inhabiting the earth either in the aquatic or the terrestrial habitats. Human civilization depends directly or indirectly upon this biodiversity for their basic needs of survival- food, fodder, fuel, fertilizer, timber, liquor, rubber, leather medicines and several raw materials. The vast blanket of varied biological wealth spread over the earth's realm – land, water and air.

Biodiversity exists on the earth in three different levels.

- Species diversity
- Genetic diversity
- Ecosystem diversity

Species Diversity: There are millions of species on the earth. These may be grouped into plant kingdom and animal kingdom e.g. single cell virus to multicellular plants and animals.

Genetic Diversity: It includes the genetic variations within species, both among geographically separated population and among individuals within single population.

Ecosystem Diversity: It studies variation in the biological communities in which species live, exist and interact.

Conservation of biodiversity means to protect, propagate and save the species in its natural ecosystem. Nature provides various services like agriculture, fishing, water, aesthetic importance, industry, medicine, stability, and forestry.

Loss of Biodiversity: Biodiversity is destroyed in a number of ways either by natural changes or man made changes. The loss of single species is considered as a tragedy as each form of life is a natural storehouse of irreplaceable substance. It also affects food chain/web it upsets the delicate balance between prey and predator.

Natural causes: Mutation, Isolation, Natural selection

Human caused Extinction can be of two types' direct impact and indirect impact.

Direct impact: Hunting food gathering, fishing exotic species, trade in animal products, harvesting wild plants, pet and scientific trade, and predator and pest control.

Indirect Impact: Habitat destruction by indiscriminate cutting of forest for agricultural land, pollution, genetic assimilation, ignorance and carelessness.

There is direct and indirect use of Biodiversity:

(a) **Consumptive and productive:** Food grains, vegetables, fruit, nuts, condiments, tea- coffee, tobacco, liquor, oil, meat, fish, egg, milk, honey etc.,
(b) **Others:** Medicine, fuel, timber, household, fodder, fiber, fertilizer, wool, leather, paint, resin, wax, silk, decorative items and ornamental plants.

Indirect Use: Carbon fixation, pollination, gene flow etc, maintaining water cycle, buffering from climate extreme condition such as flood and draught, soil production and protection, maintaining nutrients, absorbing and decomposing pollutants, regulating climate at micro and macro level.

Thus, conservation of natural biodiversity means preservation of selected ecosystems and representative areas of different vegetation types in the country. As well as saving extinction prone species of plants and animals

The aim and objective of wildlife management is

1. Protection of natural habitat
2. Maintenance of a viable number of species
3. Establishment of biosphere reserves
4. Protection through legislation

Conservation of biodiversity, forest, water and soil are very important and are discussed here one after the other.

Conservation of Forest

Forest lands were cleared and diverted to other uses like agriculture, industries hydroelectric projects, settlement of displaced person and foreign refugees etc., This has also resulted in diminishing wildlife due to loss of habitat. Forest plays three important roles in national economy productive, protective and as a source of accessory benefits.

Forest policy of 1988 is protection, conservation and development of forests.

Its aims are:

1. Maintenance of environment stability through preservation and restoration of ecological balance
2. Conservation of natural heritage
3. Check on soil erosion and denudation in catchments area of rivers, lakes and reservoir.
4. Check on extension of sand dunes in desert areas of Rajasthan and coastal tracks.
5. Substantial increase in forest / tree covers through social forestry.
6. Steps to meet requirements of fuel for wood, fodder, minor forest produce and soil timber of rural and tribal population
7. Increase in productivity of forest produce and optimum substitution of wood.
8. Steps to create massive people participation with involvement.

Conservation of Biodiversity as Suggested by World Conservation Strategy

Conservation of biodiversity is a serious concern today. The degradation and destruction of habitats is going on due to clearing of forests areas, valuable species are becoming extinct.

According to World Conservation Strategy Conservation of species in its natural ecosystem and man made ecosystem is the need of the day.

The measures are given as under

1. Efforts are necessary to protect and preserve the endangered species.
2. A sound planning and management in respect of the prevention of extinction is required
3. Steps to be taken to preserve and propagate varieties of food crops, fodder plants, timber trees, animals' livestock and their wild associates without disturbing ecological balance.
4. All countries should identify habitats of variety of wild life and ensure their protection
5. Habitats or biosphere where different species, feed, breed and nurse their young should be saved and protected.
6. International trade of wild plants and animals must be controlled and regulated

Thus it is our duty to protect, preserve and propagate varied natural bounty of the nation to make it worth living and pollution free. 2 per cent animal species 8 per cent plants species are on the verge of extinction.

Conservation can be done in two ways in-situ and ex-situ

In-situ: Conservation in their natural ecosystem. This is applicable to wild flora and fauna as conservation is achieved through protection of population. The concept of protected areas falls under this category, e.g., National Parks, Sanctuaries and Biosphere Reserves etc.,

Ex Situ : Away from natural habitat it includes 'gene banks' botanical gardens, zoos etc.

In Situ conservation 3 types

1. Biosphere Reserve
2. Wildlife Sanctuaries
3. National Parks

What is a Biosphere Reserve?

A biosphere reserve is a unique concept which includes one or more protected areas and surrounding lands that are managed to combine both conservation and sustainable use of natural resources.

Biosphere reserves have been described as undisturbed natural areas for scientific study as well as area in which conditions of disturbance are under control. These serve as the centre for ecological research and habitat protection. The biosphere consists of two main zones core area buffer zone 1 and buffer zone II

The objective of the program is to :

- Conserve biodiversity
- Safeguard genetic diversity
- Provide areas for basic and applied research
- Opportunity for environmental education and training
- Promote international co-operation

Promote Management of Biotic Resources

· Each biosphere reserve conserves examples of characteristic ecosystems of one of the world's natural regions, managed for their protection and study.

· It is a land and / or coastal / marine area in which people are an integral component, and which is managed for objectives ranging from complete protection to intensive yet sustainable production.

· It is a regional centre for monitoring, research, education and training on natural and managed ecosystems.

· It is a place where government decision makers, scientists, managers and local people cooperate in developing a model programme for managing land and water to meet human needs while conserving natural processes and biological resources.

· Finally, each biosphere reserve is a symbol of voluntary cooperation to conserve and use resources for the well being of people everywhere.

As on 31st march 1994 there were 421 wildlife sanctuaries, 75 national park, 14 biosphere reserves in India.

Importance of National Parks and Sanctuaries

Plants and animals are very important part of our environment. They maintain the balance of environment and also maintain the food chain and food web. They also provide raw material to many industries thus helping economical development of a country. It also has cultural and religious importance.

Since so many years human beings are constantly depleting the natural resources by cutting down forests, thus making species endangered and extinct. To protect them from extinction national parks and sanctuaries were made. Today in India we have – 75- national parks and -421- sanctuaries. They are important due to following reasons.

1. We can conserve the plants and animals who are on the verge of extinction
2. We can go for captive breeding for rare animals
3. Animals are given natural environment, food, water
4. We can stop poaching of any kind
5. We can increase the green cover by not cutting trees.
6. Forests are important in controlling pollution
7. Apart from supplying raw material to industries forests also provide material for research. Where people can study vegetation, animal behavior, growth development, prey predator relationship, habitat etc.,
8. Conservation of natural resources tries to bring back the balance of nature
9. Forests also reduce the spread of deserts
10. It provides aesthetic beauty, adventure in wilderness and scope for scientific research.
11. They provide a place to study environmental education also
12. They are places of national importance
13. Wild life gets protection

There are many national parks and sanctuaries

Sasan Gir, Ranthambore, Danchigam, Jim Corbett, Jaldapara, Madhumalai etc.,

Nalsorovar, Koeladev, Bharatpur, Rangantitoo are famous bird sanctuaries.

Difference Between National Parks and Sanctuaries: National Parks Sanctuaries

National Parks	Sanctuaries
• A National Park is a relatively large area of one or several ecosystems	• A wild life sanctuary is a relatively small area of one ecosystem
• In a National Park plant and animal species their site and habitats are preserved and protected	• A sanctuary is dedicated to protect the wild life and concerned species
• The wild life and plants species are preserved for special scientific education and recreation	• The threatened and endangered animal species are protected and efforts are made for their growth
• Hunting and grazing activities are absolutely prohibited	• Hunting without permission is prohibited and grazing and movement of cattle is regulated
• Human interference or any type of human activity which disturbs the biodiversity is completely prohibited	• Human activities with certain conditions are allowed without disturbing the ecosystems.

Water Conservation

Water is the elixir of life. One cannot imagine life without water. 90% of the body weight of the living organisms is made up of water. The increase in population has led to heavy demand on water in the urban set up. We have heard of riots on drinking water and its supply in many countries. We have hardly 3 % of potable drinking water. Water gets contaminated by sewage lines, leading to gastroenteritis and related diseases. Apart from sewage lines water is getting contaminated by solid waste, fertilizers, chemicals, heavy metals, mercury, cadmium, lead, fluorine etc., Apart from industries mining and quarrying activities, effluent waste from industries and sewage from the drainage system is also causing water pollution. (Water pollution has also been discussed in unit 4)

Conservation of Water

1. Water can be conserved by reducing the use of chemicals and fertilizers
2. Treating sewage and drainage water before being discharged in water bodies.
3. Waste water treatment plants have to be developed.
4. We need to harvest rainwater and recharge ground water.
5. Do not waste water, repair any leaking tap immediately.

Project on cleaning rivers

National River Conservation Directorate

The National River Conservation Directorate (NRCD) which functions under the ministry of Environment and Forests provides assistance to various State Governments for implementing the River Action Plans in 29 identified grossly polluted stretches of various rivers of the country under the National River Conservation Plan (NRCP). The objective of NRCP is to improve the water quality of these rivers. Which are the major fresh water sources in the country, through the implementation of pollution abatement schemes? The important works being taken up under the NRCP include:

Interception and diversion works to capture the raw sewage flowing into the river through open drains and divert them for treatment.

- Sewage Treatment Plants for treating the diverted sewage.
- Low cost sanitation works to prevent open defecation on riverbanks.
- Electric crematoria and improved wood Crematoria.
- River Front Development works such as improvement of bathing ghats etc.

Ganga Action Plan

The first River Action Plan to be taken up under the NRCD was the Ganga Action Plan. The objective of the GAP phase 1 was to improve the water quality of the river Ganga as per the following standards:

Bio chemical Oxygen Demand (BOD)——3mg/l maximum

Dissolved Oxygen ——5mg/l maximum
Total Coliform Count ———10,000MPN per 100ml
Faecal Coliform Count ———2,500 MPN per 100ml

Pollution abatement works under this plan have been taken up in 25 class I towns population above 1 lakh in 1985 of which six are in U.P., four in Bihar and 15 in West Bengal. The action Plan primarily addressed itself to the interception and diversion for treatment of 873 million liter per day (mld) of municipal sewage. To accomplish the task, 261 schemes of pollution abatement concerning municipal activities have been sanctioned under the GAP. These include 88 schemes of interception and diversion, 35 of sewage treatment plans, 43 of low cost toilets, 28 of electric crematoria, 35 of river front development and 32 of miscellaneous category. So far, 259 schemes have been completed. The remaining two schemes of STPs are in Bihar. Meanwhile, GAP phase I scheme has been closed w.e.f. 1-4-2000. A sewage treatment capacity of 865 mld has been created under the programme so far.

An amount of about 452 crore has been spent on the GAP phase I. The entire funding has been provided by the Central Government.

It was initially expected that programme would be completed in 6-7 years. However, it has been delayed considerably due to land acquisition problems, court litigation and lack of experience in implementing a programme of this nature and magnitude.

Problem Areas under Ganga Action Plan

With the completion of the Ganga Action Plan phase I, bottlenecks have appeared in respect of operation and maintenance (O&M) of the assets created under the programme. Expenditure towards operation and maintenance of facilities like sewage treatment met by the center up to September 1989 and thereafter was shared equally with the respective State Governments from October, 1989 onwards till March, 1997. As decided during the initial periods of GAP, the responsibility of O&M

of assets created during the initial periods of GAP, the responsibility of o and M of assets created under the GAP thereafter rested with the concerned State Governments. While O and M of assets is unsatisfactory in Bihar and to some extent in U.P., O&M of major assets in West Bengal is generally satisfactory.

U.P. and Bihar have not been able to provide uninterrupted electricity for running the facilities. Electric crematoria's are reported to be running satisfactorily in West Bengal only. But in Bihar and U.P., O&M of these assets is not satisfactory. A total of 128 bathing ghats have been constructed and most of them are not being maintained properly. Now the ministry approves only those projects where State Governments give firm commitment for operation and maintenance of assets created under the scheme. Emphasis on appropriate technologies aimed at reducing these pollutants is being increasingly given under the GAP –II

Impact on River Water Quality

Out of the total sewage generation of 1,340 mld from 25 class I towns (as of 1985), it was targeted to intercept, divert and treat 873 mld of sewage under GAP Phase I. As against this target capacity to treat 965 mld has been commissioned so far.

The water quality of river Ganga is being monitored at 27 locations from Rishikesh in Uttaranchal to Ulubcria in West Bengal by reputed academic institutions such as Bharat Heavy Electrical Limited (BHEL), Haridwar, CPCB zonal Office, Indian Institute of Technology, Kanpur, Patna University and Bidhan Chandra Krishi Vishwavidyalaya Kalyani. As a result of the schemes completed under GAP Phase-I, the water quality of river Ganga for the year 2002 shows improvement in respect of the Biochemical Oxygen Demand (BOD) which is a major indicator of pollution. Monitoring of rivers under GAP II namely Yamuna, Western Yamuna Canal, Gomti and Hindon is continuing. Rivers of NRCP are being included in the water quality monitoring programme as and when the core schemes for the towns on that commissioned and operational is an integral part of water quality Monitoring.

All the participating laboratories involved in water quality monitoring have been subjected to Analytical Quality Control (AQC) by the CPCB. The institutes/ universities carrying out water quality monitoring have been entrusted with the additional responsibility of evaluating the performance of the sewage treatment plants set up.

National River Conservation Plan (NRCP)

The Ganga Action Plan model with necessary corrections on the basis of the lessons learnt and experience gained from GAP Phase 1 has been applied to the polluted major rivers of the country under the National River Conservation Plan (NRCP). Since Ganga Action Plan Phase I did not cover the pollution load of Ganga fully the 2nd Phase of Ganga Action plan which covers tributaries Yamuna, Gomti, and Damodar beside river Ganga itself was launched and approved in stages between 1993 and 1996 for implementation. Simultaneously, the NRCP was also launched in 1995 to cover other major rivers in the country. After the launching of the NRCP in 1995, it was decided to merge the Ganga Action Plan Phase II with NRCP. A notification to this effect was issued on 5-12-1996. The present approved cost of NRCP as a whole stands at Rs. 3438.08 crore covering pollution abatement works in 155 towns along polluted stretches of 29 rivers spread over 17 States.

Soil Conservation

Human beings get food, shelter and support from earth. Earth is the only planet that supports life. Water and oil is also obtained from earth. We get many minerals from soil. Human efforts have led to contamination of soil due to high toxins in the form of pesticides and chemical fertilizers plus dumping of waste materials, hospital waste, garbage this leads to soil pollution.

Soil also gets eroded due to storm water, rivers, winds, reduced number of plants and productivity of soil.

Reasons for Soil Erosion

1. Quarrying and mining activities to obtain coals, petroleum, natural gas and minerals.

2. Denudation of forest cover, removing vegetation due to lack of vegetation there is soil erosion.
3. With the rise in population concrete jungles have taken place of actual jungles leading to soil erosion
4. Industrial and household waste dumped on soil is causing soil pollution.
5. Irrigation systems also lead to water logging and increase in the salt content of soil leading towards low productivity.
6. For construction of railways and roadways productive land becomes useless.
7. A number of natural causes lead to soil erosion, river, cyclone, storm water, earthquake, and volcano also damage soil.
8. Chemical fertilizer, salt water and spread of desert lead to pollution of soil

Ways to Conserve Soil Erosion

The topsoil of 6 inches is the most fertile layer it takes a longer time to form and gets washed and withered with minimum effort. So we need to conserve it.

1. Reduce the use of fertilizers and pesticides.
2. Grow more and more trees as the trees hold the soil
3. Afforestation drives should be increased.
4. Quarrying and mining activities should be reduced as earth has sufficient to fulfill peoples needs but not for greed
5. Solid waste and garbage management is needed the industries should have effluent treatment plants. Biological waste can be converted to fertilizers using vermiculture.
6. Water harvesting can be done to stop storm water from running away. We can also have mechanism for ground water recharging.
7. We need to have bunds, reels and terracing to reduce soil erosion.
8. Wind belts can be made using trees so that soil erosion can be controlled.

Many efforts were made by government to conserve the wildlife one such experiment is the tiger project.

Project Tiger

Tiger populations declined drastically from estimates of 40,000 at the turn of the century to 1800 by the 1970's. This led to 1973 in the initiation of project tiger with the objective of conserving and rescuing this species from annihilation. Twenty-three tiger reserves were set up along with the imposition of a total ban on hunting and trading in tiger products at the national and international levels and the implementation of habitat improvement and anti poaching measures. Between 1973 to 1989, the species showed a marked recovery resulting in an increase in number to more than 4000 by 1989.

Promoting networking and sharing of information is essential for an informed and inexpensive approach to biodiversity conservation.

Geographical Information systems (GIS) and remote sensing could help determine the rates causes and scale of biodiversity loss.

Number of parks and sanctuaries can be increased in India the protected area network is inadequate in protecting ecologically important and fragile ecosystems. Wetlands, mangroves etc. (detailed report in appendix)

Apart from government initiative people movement was also there i.e. the Chipko Movement.

Project Elephant

Project elephant was launched in 1991-92 to assist states having ranging populations of wild elephants to ensure long term survival of identified viable population of elephants in their natural habitats. States are being given financial as well as technical and scientific assistance in achieving the objectives of the project main activities of project elephants are as follows.

- Ecological restoration of existing natural habitats and migratory routes of elephants;

- Development of scientific and planned management for conservation of elephant habitats and viable population of wild Asiatic elephants in India.
- Promotion of measures for mitigation of man elephant conflict in crucial habitats and moderating pressures of human and domestic stock activities in crucial elephant habitats.
- Strengthening of measures for protection of wild elephants from poachers and unnatural causes of death.
- Research on project elephant management related issues
- Public education and awareness programmes
- Eco-development
- Veterinary care.

Objective of the project: Save the Asiatic elephant

The project covers the major elephant populations extending over 12 states and inhabiting an area over 60.000 sq. kms. The project is being implemented with the collaboration of the state governments with the aim to provide corridors of protected areas for the free movement of elephant herds.

This measure would help in the preservation of the gene pool and also minimize the man elephant conflict. The elephant population is not part of the elephant project, a nation wide conservation effort.

Threats for elephants

- The key problem is dwindling habitat and broken migratory corridors.
- Latest threat is an emerging market for elephant meat, particularly in tribal areas.
- The elephant population is vulnerable to unscrupulous poachers due to their precious ivory tusks.

Status of Elephants in India

Elephant habitats spread across 11 states in the regions, including Arunachal Pradesh, Meghalaya, Assam, Nagaland, Bihar, Madhya Pradesh, West Bengal, Uttar Pradesh, Orissa, Andhra Pradesh and Tamil Nadu.

Most of the forests have been destroyed. Moreover canals, roads, mines, dams, and urban complexes are tattering what few forests remain here. Confused hungry and angry elephants the used to live in peace with humans have increasingly taken to attacking humans. The problem is particularly severe in Assam, West Bengal and the Andhra Pradesh Tamil Nadu border. The solution being put forward is to capture elephants and put them to use. This is a euphemism for condemning them to a life of slavery, most often hauling timber or helping in the construction of roads which will further degrade their own homes.

Japan is one of the leading Ivory purchasers. African countries have been willingly feeding the demand of ivory. Keeping this in view, the future of elephants, including the Asian species, is at best bleak.

The situation in India was comparatively better, due to the veneration and respect that Indians had for the elephants. It was this reason, which allowed Indians to live in peace with elephants for thousands of years.

But something changed almost two decades ago. In India the large-scale poaching of elephants for ivory apparently started in right earnest in the late seventies.Some local people suggested then that because mature sandalwood trees were getting harder to find, traditional tree poachers began to turn to 'white gold'-ivory tusks.**ELEPHANT KILLING**: The best documented elephant killing had taken place in Mudumalai, where authentic records of nine adult elephants were made public, between October 1984 and September 1985; eight of these were tuskers. Poaching had been responsible for 80 per cent of the known tusker deaths in that one year. In addition, the Nilgiri Wildlife Association had sent in reports of a still more elephant deaths. It was a terrible shock for most people who had presumed that the solid amount of political support that Mrs. Indira Gandhi gave to wildlife, would result in things getting better, not worse. With each passing day, the situation worsened. In June 1985, two elephant carcasses (one partly burnt) were found at Masikoil, in the Segur Range, near a cattle station (called 'patti').In August two more tuskers were reported killed at Masipatti and angry allegations suggested that they had been burnt by the Forest Department mobile party in charge of elephant poaching control to prevent criticism for their own failure. Nevertheless, 11 forest staffers were temporarily suspended.In the first week of October 1985, another elephant was killed near Anaikatti. Then in December four adult tuskers were killed in the Coonoor Range, two near the Buddlguppa checkpost (near Thengamarada), one at Kallamvalaiya and one at Allimoyar (Varapallam). The press was full of criticism for the failure of the staff to protect an animal that was so publicly loved. This led to defensive reactions, including the certification of tuskers as females that died from, "natural causes".What is to be the fate of the elephant in India?Poachers know their migration routes even better than researchers and forest officers do. And with CITES in the clutches of wildlife traders, loopholes that allow them to continue to kill and profit seem here to stay for a while. What is worse is that the high stakes have led many people who should be protecting elephants to turn a blind eye, because they are in on the take.· Adding to the bleak future for elephants is the fact that they are intensely disliked by farmers, whose crops they raid and whose deaths they occasionally cause. And the retaliation is vicious. ·Live high tension wires from overhead electric lines are laid onto elephant paths.·Petrol soaked rags are lit and then thrown on their backs.·Barbed wire, laced with pesticides is hidden under the leaf litter on known trails to wound and thus kill the animals.PRESENT STATUS:For many years now conservationists have been asking the Central Ministry of Environment and Forests to enhance allocations for Project Elephant. But this highly politicized ministry has not responded positively. Instead, we see the elephant welfare being turned into a political game between the Centre and Tamil Nadu, with each party trying to demonstrate its love for elephants by "looking after" temple elephants.Meanwhile the rot that set in, in the eighties, continues to take its toll of wild elephant herds. And their migratory corridors continue to be snapped by industrial projects that the MoEF not only clears, but actually encourages in almost every elephant state in India, from Arunachal Pradesh, through Bihar, to Kerala.Project Elephant Project Elephant has played an important role in assisting elephant range States to ensure long term survival of identified viable populations of elephants in their natural habitat. Financial assistance to the extent of Rs.28.39 crores has been provided to the elephant range. States under this scheme during the IXth Plan. 25 elephant reserves have been identified by the Central Government during this period out of which, as on today, 3 elephant reserves, viz. Singhbhum (Jharkhand), Mayurbhanj (Orissa) and Garo Hills (Meghalaya), have been notified by the State Governments. Another important activity under the project is mitigation of human elephant conflict by providing adequate compensation.

Chipko Movement

This is the most famous and powerful people's movement in Garhwal region (Himalayan) of Uttar Pradesh. It originally started as the tribal women's protest against felling of trees by contractors but gained momentum under the leadership of Chandi Prasad Bhatt and Sunder Lal Bahuguna .

The term "Chipko" literally means "hugging". Dasholi Gram Swarajya Mandal (Dasholi Village Self Rule Forum) spearheaded the movement in Gopeswar, Chamoli district of U.P. The DGSM under the leadership of Bhat and Bahuguna started grass root level movement involving hill women to protect the hill ecosystem.

Reckless destruction of hill forests by timber contractors caused landslides and floods in the valley of Alaknanda and Bhagirathi and was destroying fragile ecosystem. The women had to suffer, as they had to walk 10-15 km everyday to collect fuel.

In the course of time the Chipko movement spread all along the hill region saving all hill forests and greenery and then moved to the south in Karnataka in 1983 when it was named "Appico" movement.

Environmentalists from France, Germany, Sweden, Switzerland etc., came to visit the Chipko camps and hailed the chipko movement. (detailed report in appendix). Environmental education is needed at every level in life. Teacher has to accordingly organize the teaching and learning accordingly.

Role of an Environmental Education Teacher

Planner: Any effective teacher undertakes a lot of planning. The teacher of environmental education is no exception. He/ she should prepare lesson plans and annual plans relating to environmental education.

Organizer: Any plan will meet with success only when it is implemented effectively. For this, the teacher of environmental education should tailor his teaching according to the learning abilities of the student and use the resources that are locally available, including the resource persons, to achieve his/ her objectives.

Guide: The role of a good teacher does not end with teaching alone. He / she should be a friend, philosopher and guide for the students. Should realize the needs aptitudes and interest of the students and motivate them.

Explorer: Environmental education is more an out door activity. Teacher should be inclined towards exploratory methods of learning. Teacher can assign some projects to the students.

Recorder; Environmental education is best imparted through experimental learning, by recording the changes in the environment.

The aim of conservation basically is to have sustainable development. Let us know about sustainable development.

Some Questions

1. Explain the need for conservation of Biodiversity in your own words with proper illustration.
2. Explain conservation of wild life and forest with suitable illustration.
3. Explain need and importance of soil conservation and ways of conserving it.
4. State the difference between
5. Write short note on (a) Project Tiger
   (b) Chipko Movement
   (c) Elephant project

7

Sustainable Development

Sustainable Development:

The World Commission on Environment and Development introduced the term Sustainable Development. (The Brundtland Commission) in its seminar report of 1987. "Our Common Future". It is defined as "meeting the needs of the present generation without compromising the needs of future generation."

It emphasizes upon using the earth resources judiciously and compensating for it in some sense. A balance has to be created between resource consumption and resource generation. In sustainable development two words are used let us understand. The meaning of these two words:

Sustainable: Sustainability is "that can be maintained" or "Keep goal continuously" in ecology it refers to "Conservation of ecological balance by avoiding depletion of natural resources". That means the resources that we have today should continue to exist tomorrow and ....for long times to come.

Development: The literal meaning of development is "the act or instance of growth, advancement" Here we are hinting the well being of human beings. The generation of comforts and luxuries brings environment under great stress. In the context of economical and technical development the world always had been better today than the world yesterday and will always be better tomorrow than today. But the condition of environment will be poorer.

We can't do much about past but certainly to give a good future to our children, we can use the resources judiciously in a prudent manner. We will have to work with environment ethics. That would mean, we control;

- Human population
- Loss of biodiversity
- Habitat destruction
- Ozone depletion
- Global climate change
- Pollution (air, water, noise etc.,)
- Food and energy supply

All these are concerns on the global scale.

Until environmental concern does not find space in our heart we would never be able to delicately handle our surroundings, when we are at home or in a public place we should recognize personal and collective responsibility to protect nature to create a sustainable environment.

Development model that we have adopted today, we are extracting natural resources like water, forests, fisheries, mineral, soil nutrients etc., at a pace faster than their capacity to regenerate. We are also pumping pollutants back into the natural ecosystem at rates far higher than they can absorb, or can be cleaned up. The result is unsustainable development.

According to Tata Energy Research Institute (TERI) the economic losses due to soil degradation, disease caused by pollution and forest degradation is between Rs. 100,000 crores to 450,000 crores. We cannot continue with this unsustainable form of development.

Sustainable development aims at improving the living standards and the quality of people's lives, both now and for the future generations. All countries strive to ensure that citizens both in urban and rural areas have clean air to breathe, safe drinking water and adequate supplies of clean and renewable energy.

Agriculture and industry are the important sectors in which natural resources, land, forests, rivers, oceans and mineral deposits upon which they rely have to be used efficiently and responsibly

Environmental problems are linked with economic issues like poverty and population growth puts pressure on natural resources as well as capacity to provide amenities like housing health care, education, safe drinking water and sanitation. The task before the government is to create development strategies that incorporates values of environment sustainability while increasing economic growth and providing adequate social services.

One way of looking at development would mean environmental data such as safe drinking water. In 1992 the government of the world at the UN conference on environment and development held at Rio-de-Janeiro signed a series of historic agreements and statements pledging their support for the move towards sustainable development. The development agenda for the 21st century called agenda 21 is an expression of collective aspirations and commitment of the signatories to push it forward from a statement of hope to a pragmatic blueprint for organizing a sustainable society out of the present economically and environment inequitable world.

The concept of sustainable development has its origin in the World Conservation Strategy (WCS) Report, published in 1980. It says, "Conservation is the management of human use of the biosphere so that it may yield the greatest sustainable benefits to present generation while maintaining its potential to meet the needs and aspirations of future generations."

Sustainable development should be a part and parcel of our National Plan. While noting population explosion and shrinking resource base, we should practice recycling and reusing materials.

The idea of sustainable development was strongly supported at the Earth Summit (1992) held at Rio de Janeiro, Brazil. The Earth Summit adopted a comprehensive plan for sustainable development.

The commission formulated following guidelines for achieving sustainable development

1. Sustainable reduction in population growth rates;
2. Housing, health care and education for the poor;
3. Education and empowerment of women, particularly in rural areas;
4. Afforestation (making up deforestation) in cities and rural areas.
5. Use of non conventional energy resources by industries and proper treatment of urban wastes and industrial effluents;
6. Conservation of land, soil, water, forest, wild life, fish and non renewable resources by application of modern tools of science and technology;
7. Efficient use of resources avoiding wasteful and excessive utilization;
8. A global and national strategy to eradicate poverty and
9. People's participation in conservation and improvement of environmental quality.

Sustainable use of environmental resources can be realized through

- Maintenance of the regenerative capacity of renewable resources and avoidance of excessive pollution which could threaten waste assimilation capacities and life support system of the biosphere and
- Utilization of the growing body of scientific and technological data to foster resource recovery and waste reduction.
- If extinction of natural resources is to be avoided, harvesting rates should not be greater than the rate of natural growth of the resources over prolonged periods of time. The rate of utilization of such resources should be defined by the level where the rate of "take" equals the rate of renewal, restoration or replenishment

The Rio summit through its agenda 21 gave priority to population control, poverty eradication and people's participation involvement in the management of natural resources. Sustainable development aims at creating chains of mutual social, economic and environment benefits for local, intermediate and global levels. Benefits of sustainable development at local level would mean provision of food, shelter and health.

The environmental problems that we face are serious. They are numerous and multifaceted: deforestation, soil erosion, degradation of marine resources, pesticide build up, domestic and industrial pollution, hazardous waste, etc., The damage caused to the environment is not as a result of mega industries rather it is due to lack of awareness and poverty of people.

Strategies for Sustainable Development

There are several mechanisms for sustainable development that have been found and applied to attain better resource management.

Economic and Environmental Consideration in Decision-Making

Economic and environmental concerns are not conflicting. Policies that conserve the land, forest, and agriculture and improve them in long term have to be applied. Efficiency in using resources and energy would reduce the cost and reduce wastage also. The traditional method of sectoral decision-making has caused the harm to various sectors. There is a need to look at intersectoral linkages in the process. Sectoral decisions lead to sectoral side effects, thus impact on forest is rarely considered by policy makers. This means that the process of development should be viewed from the multipurpose undertaking. Decisions will have to consider the impact on the environmental quality.

Proper Resource Pricing

The resources should be priced as per their availability and scarcity. So that there use can be authentic and systematic. They are not wasted. Ownership is another thing, which one must keep in mind. If you own something you are more careful about it.

Development of Integrated Protected Areas: There is a need to protect the wild life. The wild species have to be protected they have been the storehouse of our agricultural products, medicines and many other types of raw materials, directly or indirectly we get from the environment. Many of our necessities and luxuries are directly or indirectly coming from environment. Thus we need to spread awareness about the conservation and protection of the areas.

Residual Management

The growth in industrial production, energy conversion, and transport of goods and people is an important factor. These activities have reached levels at which the associated flows of materials and energy from concentrated states in nature to degraded and diluted states in the environment have begun to alter the physical and biological quality of the atmosphere. Many kinds of alien materials are being introduced into the environment. Residual management on the other hand, looks at the pollution problems with an overall framework of materials policy, which includes resource recovery, recycling, and by product design to save material and energy. Land treatment of wastewater uses the natural filtration of soils, the bacterial action of soil organisms and sometimes, the capability of plants to use the nutrients in wastewater directly. In the developing countries resource recovery is highly economical because materials and energy costs are high relative to labor costs. Paper, glass, metals, plastics, oils and other materials are recovered from waste streams and recycled by networks of workers.

Environmental Education

In general, the primary aim of environmental education is to enable citizens to understand and appreciate the complex nature of the environment, as well as the role played by a properly managed environment, in economic development. Only an informed, motivated and committed citizenry could provide the mass base necessary for the continued protection of the environment. On another level, environmental education can be instrumental in increasing environmental awareness among top policy makers in government. Decisions are ultimately a political responsibility, but the likelihood of the best choices being made is greatly enhanced when there is widespread knowledge and understanding of all the implications. So education, both formal and non formal, has an indispensable contribution to make. The task of education is to develop a rational for the study of the environment, and thus equip people to make up their own minds in an informed way.

Citizens Participation

Community based sustainable development programs work on the basic premise that people have the innate capability to improve their quality of life and the problems confronting them can be overcome through their own efforts with some assistance from government and non-governmental agencies.

In promoting the active participation of the citizenry for sustainable development, non-government organization can be the central vehicle in mobilizing people to participate, since they are the segment of population, which will work through community organizing, public information campaigns, research/ situation assessment environmental surveillance and monitoring.

Thus, sustainable development can be achieved with the help of proper policies their strict implementation. It would need the government as well as non-governmental intervention. The status of environment will increase when the citizens will be aware about the environment and its impact on human life than only they will participate actively in protecting their environment.

Characteristics of Education for Sustainability

Education for sustainability is

. **Contextual** – fully awake to and engaged in addressing the crises of modernity. **Logically** education that reproduces modernism uncritically cannot effectively be engaged in resolving the crises modernism has created. Where possible, education for sustainability should be applied and grounded in the local economic, social and ecological context and community, followed by regional, national, international and global contexts.

Innovative and Constructive – drawing inspiration from new paradigm postmodern thinking in a range of fields (including science ethics, politics, economics, design and psychology) offering insights and ways forward that promise a safe, humane and environmentally sustainable rather than threatened or chaotic future.

Focused and Infusive - primarily grounded in, but not limited to social development and human ecology equity and futures, at the center of a holistic approach which touches all other areas.

Holistic and human in scale- recognizing that all educational dimensions, such as curriculum, pedagogy, structures, organization and ethos are mutually affecting and need to be seen as a consistent whole; and that this works best at a scale that relates to the needs of learners and educators. It is also holistic

Integrative greater emphasis on interdisciplinary and transdisciplinary enquiry, reflecting that no subjects, factors or issues exist in isolation. Transdisciplinary means breaking free of disciplinary ways of working. Simply putting disciplines together, by contrast is often no more than sum of parts.

Process oriented and empowering rather than product oriented – Revisioning and revaluing education and learning as intrinsic to life. Education for sustainability is therefore engaged and participative rather than passive; the emphasis is on learning rather than teaching. In particular, action research with its emphasis on critical reflection, experiential learning cycles and democratic ownership of change is inherent in EFS.

Critical- ideologically aware and socially critical, Recognizing that no educational values are politically neutral, EFS should draw on the body of critical theory associated with deep green and red green orientation as these constitute the prime challenge to the modernist hegemony. At the same time, it must continuously appraise this theory and its own rationale critically.

Balancing- Seeking to rebalance correlated pairs that are disassociated and distorted in the dualistic dominant paradigm. These include personal aspects such as knowledge and values, cognitive and affective learning, rationality and intuition, object and subject, material and spiritual; collective aspects such as economy and ecology, present and future, local and global, individual and community.

Systemic and connective- Putting emphasis on relation and pattern (including dynamics and flows, distortions, feedbacks and causation); encouraging a participative systemic awareness and wisdom in relation to designing sustainable and multilevel physical, environmental, social and economic systems.

Ethical – Clarifying ethical issues, but also nurturing normative ethical sensibility that relates and renders seamless the deeply personal and collective, i.e., it extends the boundary of care and concern beyond the immediate and personal to a participative sense of solidarity with others, distant people, environments, species and future generations.

Purposive – exploring, testing, criticizing and nurturing sustainability values and alternatives, with an explicit intention to assist change.

Inclusive and lifelong – not selective, but for all persons in all areas of life, and extending throughout their lifetimes.

Environmental education has to be provided to all the sections of the society. The aim of environmental education has to be sustainable development. Growth and change are the order of today and tomorrow. Our way of life is in swift transition. Boys and girls of today will live as adults in a world whose features and potentialities are different almost beyond imagination from what we have previously known.

These changes will require new skills and understandings on the part of young children. The fact that our life is growing and changing makes it likely that secondary education itself will grow and change greatly during professional career.

How can we deal with the fact that all teenagers, far from being the same differ individually and come from differing social ethnic and economic backgrounds? The activities arranged in school should be so diverse that appeal to all types of students. The variety will help the students to select activity of their choice. It must also appeal to different senses.

Man, however, like any other species has to survive and cannot treat matters of survival as unimportant. It has lately become widely recognized that the ways of life fostered by our modern culture may sooner rather than later prove incompatible with human survival.

Even if the technical and professional basis exists, there remains the problem of achieving greater impetus in training deploying and making the best use of additional gifted environmental teachers.

One of the most outstanding changes of recent years has been the swift spread of public awareness about threats to the natural environment in which we live. There is little doubt that expansion of information services outside the schools, such as those provided by the media, the museums, the nature conservancy, the naturalists trusts, together with the increased provision of facilities in the form of National parks and other reserves have played a part in this increased awareness.

The teachers are also members of the public; this increased awareness has also made its impact on the schools which can be seen in the types of studies undertaken.

Environmental education will require field investigation undertaken on an individual basis, requiring several visits and a problem solving approach especially part of scientific investigations.

Organization of individual studies by pupils at school makes considerable demands upon the teacher. The emphasis is on the teacher as planner and organizer of studies undertaken by individuals or small groups than on the traditional role of a teacher of a class as a whole.

There can be different ways of organizing student's activities

1. Pupils work alone or in small groups, which accommodate individual differences among learners.
2. Pupils are encouraged to change their own topic of study and are involved in the decision-making concerning their work.
3. The individual pupil is free from constant supervision by the teacher in such a situation self discipline and self-evaluation is necessary. Carefully organized work to promote a positive and productive attitude.
4. Pupils can interact with each other when they need to which tends to reduce tension and anxiety.
5. It has been shown that when children work independently they conduct experiment, read books, watch films, talk to specialists, make models paint pictures collect material they learn better.

How do you become a good teacher? You know it takes more then just being a good scholar. You remember teachers who were fine scholars and poor teachers. You know it takes more than just being a technician. So you know now a teacher should know what he/ she is teaching, how to teach it. The teacher has to play a variety of roles as director of learning, as counselor, as liaison between school and community as a member of the profession, leader, facilitator, initiator, manager etc. Environmental education has to be provided to all and at every level to make this earth a beautiful place. What are the various laws and policies which help in maintaining the harmony and balance in environment?

Some Questions

1. Explain the concept of sustainable development.
2. What are the strategies to ensure sustainable development?
3. What are the characteristics of the education for sustainable development?
4. Explain the role of Earth Summit in bringing sustainable development?

5. As teachers and students what is our role in sustainable development? How can we contribute towards sustainable development?

8

Environment Policies and Laws

Since human society has progressed from hunting-gathering stage, man has started altering the natural environment in the pursuit of creating, an economic, social and cultural environment of his choice.

This has resulted in the depletion of natural resources, degradation of land and pollution of water and air. In order to protect ourselves, the animal and plant life and the environment from destruction, numerous laws have been enacted at the national and international levels.

Need for Legislation

The protection and improvement of human environment is a major issue which affects the well being of people and economic development, and it is the duty of all governments and people to exert common effort for the preservation and improvement of human environment.

The constitution of India has provisions to make environmental legislations. Consequently laws have been enacted on the following subjects.

1. The Factories Act , 1948
2. The Insecticides Act, 1968

3. The Wildlife Protection Act 1972
4. The Water (Prevention and control of pollution) Act 1974
5. The Air (Prevention and control of pollution) Act 1981
6. The Forest (conservation) Act 1980
7. The Environment Protection Act 1986.

Existing Legislation: Environmental laws deal with the problems of pollution by a set of rules under tort law as nuisance, negligence and liability i.e., if you are affected by poisonous fumes coming from neighboring industrial unit, or if constantly bothered by unbearable noise in the neighborhood you could go to a court of law and get your errant neighbor pay for his offensive conduct. Polluting of water of a public spring or a reservoir so as to render it unfit for human consumption is made criminal offence under section 277 of the IPC.

The Insecticide Act: Being aware of the prime responsibility of protecting the health of citizens and the environment, the government of India enacted the Insecticide Act in 1968.

This was enforced from 1971 to regulate import, manufacture, sale, transport, distribution and the use of insecticides with a view to preventing risk to human beings and animals.

The Wildlife Protection Act: The most serious threat to wildlife is posed by habitat destruction. Expanding agriculture, industry and urbanization etc., are the causes of this destruction.

Realizing the importance of wildlife resources, our country has set up an Indian Board of Wildlife (1952), creation of Wildlife Parks and Sanctuaries, enactment of an All India Wildlife Protection Act 1972. The Wildlife Protection Act governs wildlife conservation and protection of endangered species. The Act prohibits trade in rare and endangered species.

The Water (Prevention and Control of Pollution) Act: The water act defines water pollution, prescribes penalties and establishes an administrative machinery, called the Water Pollution Boards, at the Central and State level in order to control and prevent pollution of water. The Water Act prohibits the dumping of poisonous, noxious or polluting matter into streams and wells. The act subjects the discharge of sewage or trade effluents into streams and wells to the prior consent of Boards.

The Air (Prevention and Control of Pollution) Act: The Air act was passed in 1981 to mainly regulate and control emissions from automobiles and industrial plants.

After consultation with the State Boards the state government may declare any area as "air Pollution Control area", and prohibits the use of any fuel other than approved fuel in the area causing air pollution.

Further, no person shall, without the previous consent of the State Board, operate any industrial plant involving industries specified in the schedule in Air Pollution Control area.

Environment Protection Act (1986)

The Environment (Protection) Act was passed by the Parliament on 23rd May 1986. By virtue of this Act, the Union Government has armed itself with considerable powers necessary for the prevention, control and abatement of environmental pollution.

Environment Protection and its conservation has been a concern of India. And this act is a step towards improvement of environment. This issue emerged after the UN conference on human environment 1972 at Stockholm. This conference was followed by number of steps taken by many countries to save human beings and natural environment from the adverse effects of pollution. An attempt has been made to make an umbrella act, enacted after the Bhopal Gas disaster for the protection and improvement of human beings, other living creatures plants and property.

The coverage includes handling of hazardous substances, prevention of environmental accidents, research, inspection of polluting units, establishment of laboratories, dissemination of information etc.,

The power includes coordination of action by States Planning and execution of nationwide programs, laying down environmental quality standards, especially those goveming emission or discharge of environmental pollutants, placing restriction on the location of industries and so on.

The major provisions are:

- Planning and execution of a nation wide programme for the prevention control and abatement of environmental pollution
- Laying down standards for the quality of environment, for emission or discharge of environment pollutants from various sources what so ever.
- Laying down procedures and safeguards for the handling of hazardous substances and for the prevention of accidents, which may cause environmental pollution and remedial measures for such accidents, and preparation of manuals, codes or guides related to the prevention, control and abatement of environmental pollution.
- As per provisions made under the act no person carrying on any industry, operation or process shall discharge or emit or permit to be discharged or emitted any environmental pollutant in excess of such standard as may be prescribed. (Detail act is in appendix)

Drawbacks in Environmental Legislation: There are various drawbacks in the Acts enacted in relation to environment. Forest constitutes a vital resource of the nation. It is scientifically established fact that the forest covers should be at least one third of the land area for a healthy state of environment, but experts and the mass media have brought to the attention the fact that the forest cover of the country has been rapidly shrinking; it is not more than 12 per cent of the land area.

Laws aimed at protecting trees, animals and birds cannot in the process treat people as marginal.

Sometimes back, the Government came up with a well meaning draconian Forest bill- principally on two grounds. One that the Bill would make criminals of all tribal living in and off the forest, as it prohibited the taking of all the produce including leaves and fruits from the forests. Two, the proposed bill converted forest officers into judges and executioners at the same time. The bill failed to attract public support because it adopted an oppressive colonial model of law.

Water and air pollution Acts do not permit individuals and groups direct access to courts individuals have no locus standi under the said Acts.

Some like the Silent Valley, the Doon Valley, the Delhi gas leakage case etc., have attracted media and public attention. But they have also thrown up interactive issues of standing burden of proof, expert testimony and the very competence of the ordinary courts to handle environmental disputes.

An individual or even a committed group of individuals cannot be expected to submit authoritative proof of objectionable radiation level. The inequality of the resources available to the individual and their establishment make mockery of the rules of evidence in environmental disputes.

Difficulties in Enforcement of Environmental Legislation: Besides having legislative activity, the state of the environment in India continues to be gloomy. The rivers and lakes continue to be choked with sewage and industrial waste. Forest continues to disappear and the consequent loss of soil has led to the scourge of floods with sickening regularity.

Legislation is an expensive affair. Environmental legislation is more expensive than other type of disputes, since it involves expert testimony, technical evidence and so on.

The law must guide and help people to establish a trend of acceptance.

Sharing of costs of anti pollution measures taken by the industry seems to be a better strategy then state sponsored expenses and lengthy prosecutions. What is offered at school level and how can we deal with it is discussed in the next section?

Some Questions

1. What is the need for legislation in environmental issues?
2. What are the difficulties in implementing the environmental legislation?
3. Write short notes on the following:
   (a) Air pollution Act
   (b) Water pollution Act
   (c) Insecticide Act
   (d) Wildlife Act
   (e) Forest Act
   (f) Environment Protection Act 1986.

9

Curriculum for Environmental Education

What is Curriculum?

All purposeful activities

1. Planned inside or outside the class
2. Earlier it was considered as a single subject. But now it belongs to the curricula of all subjects.

Why it should be taught in school? What are the values that it fulfills?

Intellectual Value

Environmental Education allows us to think why the state of environment has reached its present state. It also makes one think about usage of some alternative strategies for its improvement. It has made us to think if few animals have become extinct today what will happen to the food chain and the food web. It makes us think how science and technology should be used in such a fashion that when we reap its benefits we do not destroy the planet where we live.

Utilitarian Value

The Nature has always been kind to human in giving its realms. Directly or indirectly we draw lot many things from nature and other life forms. We get fresh air to breathe, water to drink, sunlight, which directly gives us heat, and plants with help of sunlight prepare their own food. Clouds bring rain for us, we get many other things from nature like fruits, vegetable, milk, meat, leather, fertilizer's, pest control, medicines, fuel, chemicals, dyes, minerals, ores, coal, gasoline, petrol, metals, soil, tourism spots, forests, Lac, honey, precious stones, fishes and many other marine forms, etc. etc. We must learn how to conserve preserve and protect environment so that it could be used by our posterity also. We must use these assets of environment in a judicious manner.

Vocational Value: Environmental education has opened avenues for many professional one can do B.Sc. in environmental science, One can do environmental engineering, or environmental law, or become teacher to inculcate environmental values. Today many leading companies have environmental cell one could do environmental management cell and join such post. It can also act as a hobby wherein one can join the local club and local people's movement to solve environmental problems. Or one can work in one's own garden.

Cultural Value: Environment especially in India has been revered in the ancient period. Till date we do offer puja to plants, fire, sun, bathing in river is considered holy. Our culture is woven around the environment. Different religions have different ways of worshiping nature as the all giver.

Moral Value: Goodness, truth and beauty are the values, which have been revered for long. Environmental education is for goodness of every organism on the planet earth, it believes that the planet belongs to all organisms and must not be dominated by human beings. The lack of interdisciplinary researches has created many environmental problems. When one tries to look at truth from a micro specialization area the multidimensional truth is viewed as one-dimensional truth thus further complicating the environment. We thought that DDT would kill the mosquitoes but were unaware of its environmental truth. We thought of high rise buildings but only the devastating earthquake revealed the reality of their crash. We made indiscriminate use of fertilizers, detergents, and pesticides of course as a result of scientific discovery but were unaware of their fatal consequences. We set up huge power plants, nuclear reactors, heavy water plants, only the Chernobyl incident opened our eyes, and the Second World War was another eye-opener on how we share our boundaries. We realized the air, water, and other natural resources our commonly shared by the planet. It is our moral duty to look after this planet.

Aesthetic Value: A thing of beauty is joy forever. Nature is all enduring and bestows us with different gift from time to time. The green pastures, rivers, oceans, mountains, hills, forests, ravines, the beautiful snow clad mountains, meadows, grasslands, variety of animals, colorful birds their chirping, plants, flowers, fruits add to the aesthetic beauty of environment. Nature sings for us beautiful songs day in and day out. It is supreme work of art that is visible every where. The nature's clock is set beautiful it has flowers for different seasons.

Training in Scientific Method

The study of environmental education trains the students in attacking the problem according to a certain definite and distinct procedure, which we call as the scientific method. This training which he receives in studying environmental education can be applied to solve other problems arising in new situation. In brief, scientific method involves the following steps:

1. Making an accurate survey of the problem
2. Setting up the method of attacking the problem.
3. Collecting data regarding the problem
4. Drawing conclusions from the collected data.

It is due to this scientific method of attacking a problem that has achieved wonders in all the fields of human activity.

Development of Scientific Attitudes

This is the second value, which is transferable. The attitudes of an environmentalist would require keen observation, unbiased reporting of truth, open mindedness, free from superstition and false belief. The attitude once developed will be used in the later life of the child also.

Psychological Value

Principle of activity is the main basis of teaching. It satisfies the instinct of curiosity, creativeness, self- assertion, and self-expression etc. of the pupils. Learning by living and learning by doing are the two maxims of psychology, which can be fulfilled by environment as it is directly linked with the life of human beings. The problems related to environment are easily visible in the locality so action programs can also be targeted towards them.

Earlier it was considered as a single subject now if we see the textbooks till fourth standard there is separate textbook on environmental science but after fifth standard it get bifurcated into science and social studies also other subjects have some chapters on environment.

Curriculum Development includes following stages

- Operationalizing environmental education general goals into intermediate sub goals and objectives
- Delimiting curriculum scope (extent of coverage in terms of objective, cognitive, affective and psychomotor) and sequence (planning elements grade wise)
- Developing Environmental education curriculum blueprint following 3D model based on goals levels grade levels and across relevant disciplines
- Selection and defining contents
- Identifying teaching strategies and instructional activities.
- While breaking it up one must keep in mind the
- A. local regional and or national needs
- Logical and valid scope and sequence
- B. Three basic considerations i.e. socio – economic considerations, content considerations and the pedagogic consideration.
- It should be related to immediate environment of people. Content and methodology have to be developed to realize the set goals and objectives.
- The four goal levels are ecological foundation level, conceptual level, investigation and evaluation level environmental action skill level.

UNESCO in 1980 has given two models of curriculum development

- Inter disciplinary model and
- Multidisciplinary model

Characteristics of Environmental Education

- Environmental education should be integrated into the whole system of formal education at all level.
- It should be interdisciplinary in nature
- It should adopt a holistic perspective which will examine the ecological, social, cultural and other aspects of particular problems
- Environmental education curriculum should aim at building up a sense of values

Four strategies for curricular Patterns of Environmental education;

1. Single subject approach in which components are drawn from a single academic discipline
2. Interdisciplinary approach in which components are drawn from different discipline rolled into one subject and focus is on single topic
3. Multidisciplinary approach in which components are drawn from two or more academic disciplines and focused sequentially on a single topic
4. Holistic approach in which there is co-ordination of separate courses such that the diverse fragments of knowledge and understanding are woven together.

In the first approach the emphasis is on teaching environmental education as a single subject like the optional field of B. Ed where environmental education is a single subject.

In the second approach the emphasis is to make use of interdisciplinary where the content could be taken from all other discipline yet one discipline can emerge like we have B. Sc Environmental Science.

In the third approach the emphasis is to make use of multidisciplinary approach that is environmental education becomes an integral part of every subject matter, wherever there is any topic which has scope to integrate environment it is integrated.

Holistic approach emphasizes that when environment is taught it may need to be looked at from various angles and all this angles should be taught in a holistic manner.

William Stapp has given the phases of curriculum development for school's comprehensive environmental program.

Phase 1. Establish a committee to develop, implement and evaluate the environmental education programme and to facilitate communication;

Phase 2. Establish environmental education goals that the environmental education program will be designed to strive towards

Phase 3. Establish environmental education objectives that the program will be designed to achieve;

Phase 4. Review the literature regarding theories of learning instruction, and attitudes and behavioral change to serve as guiding principles in the formulation, implementation and evaluation of the environmental education program;

Phase 5 Establish Programme goals to help achieve stated environmental education goals and objectives

Phase 6. Establish the curriculum (instructional model) of the environmental education program

Part A: Philosophy and concept

Part B: Skill development

Part C: Value Clarification

Part D: The environment encounter

Part E: Emphasis of program at different age levels

Part F: Teaching and learning models

Part G: Guidelines for learners entering a community to work on local environmental problems

Part H: Handling controversial issues in the classroom

Part I: Program phasing sequence

Phase 7. Establish a comprehensive in-service teacher education program

Phase 8. Strategy to overcome program constraints; and

Phase 10. Develop instruments to evaluate the effectiveness of the environmental education program.

1. Making committee for environmental education. The Committee must have representatives from students, teachers, and non-teaching staff. The coordinator must co-ordinate the group. Principal should be the chairman and facilitator of the committee

Duties of environmental education committee are to:

- Assist in development of philosophy
- Identify changes needed to implement program
- Develop the strategy
- Implement the program
- Maintain communication both within the school and with community
- Evaluate the effectiveness of Programme in achieving stated goals and objectives
- The goals of the program must be in coherence with the goals of environmental education and the guiding principles given by the Tiblisi
- Obtain an understanding that people are an inseparable part of an environmental system and whatever they do alters their surroundings in both harmful and beneficial ways.
- Obtain an understanding of how environmental problems can be solved
- Develop analytical thinking and action skills for understanding preventing and helping to correct environmental abuses.
- Enunciate the goals of environmental education in such a way that they become manageable and achievable objectives.
- Review the recent literature formulation implementation and evaluation of the environmental Programme
- Behavior that are reinforced are most likely to recur Desired behaviors should be reinforced by home, school, community, religion and media

- The most effective effort is put forth when learners try tasks that fall in the range of challenge not too easy and not too hard – where success seems likely but not certain.
- Learners are most likely to throw themselves whole heartedly into any project if they themselves have a meaningful role in the selection and planning of the enterprise.
- Reaction of excessive direction of the teacher is likely to be apathetic conformity defiance or escape
- Instructions must be based on learners motivation
- Different methods must be used
- Learning is retained when followed by action
- Learning takes due to active behavior of the learner
- One exciting way of learning is self discovery
- Helping learner acquire only technical knowledge will not help learner
- Learners are more likely to become involved in environmental issues if they personally believe they can have some effect upon decision making
- Individual apathy can result when a person feels a lack of confidence in her/his ability to change or influence decision
- Program goals should be same as goals of environmental education as given by Tiblisi conference
- Concepts related to environment. Each concept must be looked at primary secondary and tertiary level 1. Ecosystem 2 Population, 3. Economics, 4. Technology 5. Environmental Ethics 6. Some important skills in identifying and helping solve environmental problems are the ability to

A. Recognize environmental problems
A. Define environmental problems
B. Listen with comprehension
C. Collect information
D. Analyze information
E. Generate alternative solutions
F. Develop a plan of action
G. Implement a plan of action
H. Evaluate the plan of action
I. Develop critical thinking

Value Clarification: In order to make environmental education effective we must address the root cause of the problem rather then treating the symptom. We must try to change the life style/ pattern of a person. A student picking up litter would treat the symptom. Developing the concern to change a person's behavioral pattern that causes him to drop the litter would focus on the root cause.

In the value clarification process a learner begins to develop one's own set of values when he/she starts to consider alternatives, the consequences of alternative before he/she acts.

Steps

1. Learners are presented with an issue
1. Learners suggest alternative solutions
2. Learners consider the consequences of each alternative
3. Learner express their feelings about each alternative and
4. Learner make a free choice

The value clarification approach helps learners become aware of personal beliefs, attitudes, values and behaviors, which they prize and are committed to both in and out of the classroom. The learner should be provided with opportunities to explore his immediate environment with all of his senses- sight, hearing, smell touch and taste. Experiences should be provided for different types of cnvironment to know their relative strength and weakness.

If a child learns to appreciate and respect environmental resources, he/she may want to learn more and be willing to protect what he/she appreciates.

Guidelines for learners for entering a community to work for local environmental problems: Learners entering a community to work toward the solution of local environmental problem should receive intrapersonal and interpersonal training. It is also important that consideration be given to the process of identifying, selecting, implementing and evaluating community action projects.

Handling controversial issues in the classroom

The issues should be discussed form various angels, divergent views can be presented one must respect the various views. One must consider social implication of the action.

Environmental Encounter

It is important that the learner had direct experience with the environment. Environmental encounter are designed to assist learner in integration of

1. Concepts
2. Problem solving
3. Values

Personal involvement through following steps

1. Define the problem
2. Become informal
3. Identify alternative solutions
4. Evaluate alternative solutions
5. Develop a plan of action
6. Implement
7. Evaluate

At primary level – appreciation of nature

- A visit of school site can be arranged
- For upper grades problem solving can be arranged
- Action phase is most important
- Making posters
- Setting aquarium
- Feeding fishes
- Picking up litter
- Writing slogans
- Letters.

Environmental education activities must focus on the affective (feeling), cognitive (knowing) and skill behavior domains (skills) In the early year emphasis should be on the affective domains and later on the affective behavior and later it should be on cognitive and skill.

Evaluation of Environment Education Curriculum

Evaluation of EE may be considered under three heads

1. Evaluation of learners
2. Evaluation of strategies and methodology
3. Evaluation of curriculum

Conventional methods and techniques adopted for evaluation may be inadequate because of multidisciplinary nature of the subject, problem centered approach, value oriented nature of the discipline and community oriented strategies.

Evaluation of Learners

Learners are to be evaluated according to the instructional objectives. It will include both cognitive and affective domain. Individuals or committees interested in evaluating environmental education programs should become familiar with the evaluative instruments reported by the following: Bennett, 1976;, Doran, 1977; Hekstra; 1977; Larson, 1972; Rentsch, 1973; Robinson, 1970, Roth, 1972, Stapp et al.,1972; Swan, 1969; and Webb, 1970.

A very well designed instrument for evaluating a comprehensive environmental education programme was developed by Dr. Dean Bennett (1976) for UNESCO. This instrument could be modified to meet the needs of many environmental education programs.

The ERIC system, (ERIC school of natural resources, The Ohio State University, Columbus, Ohio) has produced a series of research guides providing sample research instruments in the cognitive, affective and skill domains for evaluating instructional programs in environmental education. Individuals or school systems interested in considering instruments useful in evaluating environmental education program should consider acquiring these booklets.

It is important that the evaluative instruments be as objective and reliable and valid as possible. It is vital that environmental education programs be evaluated and reported in the literature.

Content of curriculum for Environmental education as suggested by UNESCO. Leticia Cortes

Content of the Frame work

Basic Ecological Concepts

1. Human is an important part of the ecosystem. He/ she must understand how the components of the ecosystem interact and depend on each other.
2. Nature has its own way of maintaining environmental equilibrium.
3. Human's culture including his technological activities create imbalance in the ecosystem.
4. To restore balance in nature, human has to reassess his attitude, behavioral patterns and ethical standards.
5. Some currently accepted values are in conflict with existing responsible environmental actions/campaigns
6. Individuals, government and non-government agencies, national and international must work for sustainable development to reduce depletion of resources and reduce environmental problems.

Energy

1. Energy flow in the biosphere
2. Energy is transferred from producers to primary consumers, then to secondary consumers in a food web.
3. The sun is the primary source of energy that supports life on earth.
4. Plants convert the solar energy to chemical energy.
5. The shorter the chain, less energy is wasted.
6. Toxic substances can be transported through the food chain and eventually reach man.
7. Safety measures in the use of pesticides, insecticides and herbicides, and the proper disposal of household and industrial waste and other toxic substances should be looked into.
8. Energy cannot be created nor destroyed but it can be transformed from one form to another.
9. Energy utilization
10. Energy shortage causes various socio-economic and political problems
11. Countries need energy for development and progress.

12. Energy must be wisely used (at home, in commerce, and in industry).
13. In the extraction and use of energy, pollution of the environment may occur.
14. More research should be done to reduce energy costs and to find alternative and indigenous sources of energy such as biogas, biomass, solar, wind, geothermal and energy from waves.
15. Pollution
16. pollution refers to adverse changes in the environment which affect biotic and abiotic components
17. Pollution is a problem associated with development activities, and may be the price paid for progress.
18. The main channels of global pollution are air and water.
19. Pollution results in damage to vegetation, animal lives, human lives and man's property.
20. Different pollutants come from a variety of sources.
21. Meteorological conditions as well as socio-economic factors affect the accumulation and dispersal of pollutants.
22. Indiscriminate use and mismanagement of water resources due to human's selfish motives have resulted in global water pollution.
23. Pollution control requires multi sectoral participation. The participation / action of each individual increase the probability of success of any pollution control program.
24. Population:
25. Population growth is self-regulating. Regulation is determined by the carrying capacity of an ecosystem
26. Human can raise the carrying capacity of the environment by applying science and technology principles only up to a certain level.
27. Technological activities have an impact on the population of human and non-human species.
28. Human has developed techniques to alter genetic composition.
29. Population of the world is increasing at an alarming rate.
30. Population growth is influenced by physical, biological and socio-cultural factors.

31. Population density is generally higher in developing and underdeveloped countries then in developed countries
32. Over population brings about environmental and socio-economic problems as it increases the demand on the resource base.
33. The present world population situation and the carrying capacity of the environment dictate the need for population control.
34. All living organisms are interdependent.
35. Current value systems need to be reassessed.
36. Population growth can be controlled naturally or by artificial means. Population control depends on well-defined policies and regulatory measures.
37. Cities represent a highly dense ecosystem.
38. The continuous migration of rural people to urban communities (urbanization) creates environmental problems. There is an urgent need to plan measures to improve the quality of life of rural people.
39. Urban communities have a greater demand for the basic human needs such as food, air, clothing, housing, health services and transportation.
40. Population problems can be reduced through a multi sectoral approach.

Basic Needs

1. To live we need air, water, and food.
2. We need to take in oxygen from the air.
3. Planting greenery helps to purify the air
4. Green plants need water and energy, among other factors, in order to manufacture food.
5. The natural sources of fresh water on earth are surface water and underground water.
6. Surface water such as in rivers and lakes originates from watershed forests.
7. Underground water is tapped by the construction of wells.
8. Dams are built to store water for use when needed.
9. Water needs to be purified before it is taken by the human body.

10. In addition to water, human obtains other sources of food through agricultural practices.
11. To increase the yield of food, human uses fertilizers and pesticides.
12. The misuse of fertilizers and pesticides affects human's health and degrades the environment.
13. Some kinds of food have to be processed and preserved before they are transported to the consumers.
14. The preservation of food through the use of chemical additives might be hazardous to health.
15. To live clean and healthy, human should preserve the quality of air, water and food.

Health and Environment

1. Health hazards caused by noise, air, water, solid and toxic waste pollution leads to.
   · Impairment of hearing
   · Formation of smoke and smog which cause respiratory problems
   · Food poisoning and diseases due to contaminated food crops.
   · Formation of acid rain, which affects cultivation of food, crops
   · Contamination of water supply due to dumping of industrial toxic wastes
2. Health hazards caused by overpopulation include:
   · Poor sanitation and ventilation due to bad housing conditions;
   · Poverty and malnutrition
3. Deforestation leads to a reduction in the supply of herbal medicines and thereby affects medical research.

Natural resources

1. Forest resources are useful in many ways. They:
   · Are sources of fuel, building materials, medicine.
   · Are habitats of wildlife.
   · Help regulate CO2/O2 in air.
   · Provide watersheds
   · Help maintain rainfall

2. The destruction of tropical forests to obtain fuel and building materials and to utilize the land for growing crops and other developments such as building industries, houses roads, dams, etc. would cause;
   - soil erosion.
   - Imbalance of CO_2/O_2 in the air
   - Reduction in rainfall
   - Flooding
   - Extinction of species (wildlife)
   - Displacement of inhabitants living in the surrounding affected areas.
3. The clearing of mangrove forests for fuel, building materials and commercial fresh water farming will cause the destruction of the ecosystem, the inundation of the shoreline/ inland area and the reduction of food supply.
1. Planting of trees can help
   - Prevent soil erosion
   - Regulate CO_2/O_2 in the air
   - Cool the surrounding area.
2. **J.Water Resources**
   - lakes
   - rivers
   - ponds
   - reservoirs
3. Water is essential to sustain life.
4. Water is used in:
   - Agriculture
   - Industries
   - Generating hydroelectric power
   - Domestic and recreational activities
4. The demand for usable water is increasing due to the rapid growth of population and industrial development.
5. The quality and quantity of water resources are affected by the way human use water.
6. Water resources must be managed intelligently through
   - Reducing water use
   - Maintaining and preserving watershed
   - Controlling water pollution
   - Recycling water.

Marine Resources

1. Marine resources constitute one of the world's principal renewable resources,
2. They are the only natural resource based on the productivity of the ecosystem.
3. They Include marine fishes and other organisms in the seas and oceans, and the estuarine or coastal fishes and organisms.

Marine fishery

4. There is a direct and an indirect utilization of the marine ecosystem.
   - The direct use is the harvesting of fish, marine mammals and other organisms(fishery)
   - The indirect use is the ocean role in determining climate, producing O2 and diluting wastes (ocean)
5. There are conflicts between fishery use and ocean use of the marine ecosystem.
   - They exist mainly in the areas of:
   - Transportation via ships, boats, tankers and supertankers
   - Mining and dredging of the seas
   - Waste disposal and pollution
   - Oil exploration and production
   - Overexploitation of marine fishes and mammals leads to depletion of (food) resources. Economic losses occur and fishermen (and consumers face food demand-supply problems).
   - Industrial pollution causes hazards. Examples like Minamata and Itai-Itai in Japan and red tides almost everywhere are causes for concern. Diseases and sometimes death do occur.
   - Nations impose 200-mile limits to conserve their own marine resources. This has led to disagreements or dispute among nations over national boundaries.

Estuarine resources

6. Where the salty seawater meets the fresh water abundant plant and animal organisms thrive- estuarine resources.
7. Rivers supply rapid replenishment of plant nutrients to the estuarine ecosystem

8. Estuarine resources may be divided into mangrove forests and aquatic inhabitants.
9. Mangrove forests
10. Aquatic organisms
   - Common aquatic organisms in an estuarine ecosystem are fish, crustaceans and mollusks.
   - These are part of the food chains of the estuarine ecosystem
   - Nutrients come from the estuarine waters themselves
11. Problems in estuarine areas include the following:
   - Depletion of mangrove trees/forests
   - Overexploitation of estuarine resources
   - Pollution from up-river or pollution from the sea is washed up during high tides;
   - Use of estuarine areas for drainage and development due to pressures from an expanding population nearby.

D. Wildlife Resources

- Wildlife is important for maintaining the balance of ecosystems and the preservation of our cultural heritage and as a source of valuable information for scientific studies
- Conservation of wildlife species can be conserved through proper management of their habitats and adequate control mechanisms.
- Endangered wildlife species can be conserved through proper management of their habitats and adequate control mechanisms.
- Wildlife sanctuaries are often destroyed by indiscriminate destruction of forests through logging, burning and poor agricultural practices.

E. Soil Resources

- Soil is usually taken for granted as a natural resource, the most important function of which is to support plant life.
- The ability of the soil to support the growth and development of plants depends on soil condition, the quality of the plants and climatic conditions.
- Aside from food taken from plants grown in soil, plants provide life sustaining oxygen forest products like wood, natural fibers and native fuels.

- Soil is made up of inorganic substances from parent rocks which have undergone several physical and chemical changes, together with organic substances from decomposed plant and animals remains.
- Fertile soil lost through thoughtlessness of people and through erosion resulting from clearing of forests and mining activities could take centuries to be retrieved.

Corrective measures

1. All types of pollution may be reduced through
   - Proper enforcement's of laws
   - Increase public awareness of environmental issues through information campaigns and mass media
   - Public participation in environmental management activities,
2. Over population can be controlled
   - Proper family planning
   - Proper housing and town planning
3. Deforestation can be controlled by
   - Proper enforcement of forestry and laws
   - Recycling of wood products
   - Optimizing land use by integrated farming method.

Environmental Education Curriculum in India

Environmental studies provide the cohesive center of interest which gives meaning to the unrelated aspects of the curriculum. And in doing so, they furnish "interest factor" which increases motivation. The early period of elementary education uses the social living aspect of environmental studies. This subject provides a variety of experiences so that the childs learning can be all round and well balanced. Different facets of man's experiences that are provided through this subject could give a comprehensive idea of human society to children.

It encompasses the wide frontiers so that the vital element are fused in a way which can give the children a phenomenal amount of information the social, physical and cultural world around him and at the same time deepen his understanding and interest in man and his environment.

Thus, Environmental studies occupies very important place at elementary level. Not only it enables the children to understand and appreciate their social cultural and physical surrounding from the beginning can be very useful for the harmonious and peaceful existence at the later stage; that is when they will be adult members of the society but this subject can also replace both science and social science at elementary stage as at this level many concepts of these two subjects overlap and these concepts are related to our bio physical, cultural and social environment. Thus by introducing environmental studies in an integrated manner at elementary level, in the multidisciplinary manner one subject can be reduced.

Looking at the school curriculum scene, we would find that various elements of ecology and conservation education had already been included in the school curricula and textbooks from class VI to XI prepared through the study group during the period 1968-72. In primary (Classes I-V) curricula, the science concept had been carefully interwoven with the immediate environment and day to day experience of the child.

Subsequent generations of school curricula and textbooks developed at the national level since the 1970s also adequately represented the environmental education dimensions.

The current curricula and textbooks were developed in response to the National Policy on Education 1986; the Environmental Education dimensions have been reinforced at all levels. The NPE 1986 prescribes environmental protection as a core element of the national curricula. Basic elements of environmental education have been covered concentrically and spirally in different levels of school education including plus two levels. Various concepts have been integrated into Science, Geography, Chemistry, Biology, Physics, Social studies and other subjects.

NCERT in 1995 undertook a Programme of massive curricular revision of textbook for school stage making the curricular material environment based. The project activities envisaged under the schemes are adoption of monuments, nature study, study of ecological problems of a village, adoption of municipal ward or locality to study its social and ecological environment, history and culture and their dissemination, review of curriculum to make it local specific through curriculum workshops, preparation of textbooks/ instructional material, slides audio and video tapes, films of environmental conservation, plantation of trees, visit to zoos/ wild life sanctuaries, tracking, nature walks, measurement of environmental erosion etc. Ministry of Human Resource Development (MHRD, 1988). The scheme is being implemented in collaboration with state government departments like Department of Forest and Environment, Pollution Control Board and Non Governmental Organizations in the state with 100 percent financial assistance from Government of India. The Government of India has also taken up programs for imparting environmental education through Center for Environmental Education (CEE), Central Board for workers Education (CBWE), Indian Institute of Ecology and Management (IIEM) etc. But these few institutes cannot meet the requirement. Many voluntary and non-governmental organizations have been dealing with the local and regional problems. Several women organizations have also been coming forward to take up environmental awareness campaign. The National Curriculum Framework and CBSE 2005 have introduced environmental education as a special and separate subject at school level. For the above mentioned curriculum and its transaction we would need various methods to achieve aforesaid objectives.

Some Question

1. What are the values that environmental education fulfills?
2. What are the characteristics of environmental education?
3. Explain the stage involved in the development of curriculum?
4. Explain the comprehensive model of curriculum development for school program.
5. As a school teacher and as a citizen of India what according to you should be included in the curriculum of environmental education?

10

Methods of Teaching Environmental Education

For teaching environmental education a teacher can make use of various methods conventional as well as modern some of the methods for teaching environmental education have been discussed here.

Exhibition:

All of you are aware about exhibition; you might have seen many exhibitions and trade fairs. There are stalls with entrance tickets, where number of exhibits are exhibited and sold. The items are grouped according to the similarities and dissimilarities.

In Environmental Education fair the exhibits are related to environment. They are in the form of models, charts, specimen, poster, new projects from industries to control pollution, projects from other schools, modified instruments, techniques, along with awareness camps related to health and misbeliefs.

In addition to the exhibition there are bookstalls, refreshment stalls and entertainment in the form of cultural program, plays based on environmental issues, debate, seminar symposium with poster (awareness) competition.

Every year such exhibitions must be arranged. For organization of the fair, students should actively participate.

Why there should be an Exhibition?

- Exhibition provides an opportunity to the pupils to show their hidden talents.
- General public becomes familiar about many concepts and phenomena related to environment. In short it helps to make people aware about current environment.
- It generates awareness among people
- Children learn from their peer's projects and models.
- It develops team spirit, sharing, creativity gets a channel
- School contact increase.

For organization of any Exhibition

Teacher has to plan the work, distribute the work, and design the display of the exhibition hall or ground.

Planning

- Permission
- Declaration and Invitation to various institutes
- Finance
- Resources
- Date/Time
- Venue
- Publicity

The planning would begin with the permission from the head of the institution.(i.e. the Principal). The next step would be to declare the exhibition and invitation for various organizations. For this purpose one needs to make a circular, in the circular one must mention the date, the venue, the themes, for how many days, the timing, the last date for submission of entries, the name and address of contact person plus their phone numbers. If there is any participation fees than that should be mentioned. Once the entries start coming they can be classified on various themes. Depending upon the number of entries and the various projects one can design the venue and number of stalls. The venue is selected keeping in mind the available finance and other resources in the school. The entire exhibition must be publicized properly so that maximum number of people can take advantage of it.

Distribution of Work

The distribution of work must be done based on the talent of the student. We will need some volunteers, some student leaders to manage groups and other problems. We need children with good hand writing, good writers and good speakers. We need children to demonstrate their work etc.

A number of committees must be made like the advisory committee, Executive committee, reception committee, General management committee, sectional seating and publicity committees plus sub committees all the committees must be guided by the teacher in charge.

The work should be assigned according to the age, ability, and interest in the field.

How to arrange the display?

There should be enough space between two models or charts or posters. They should be self-explanatory. The experiment, which needs electricity, should be arranged accordingly. The write up with the experiments and models should be clear and bold enough to be read from a distance, properly labeled and carrying name of the students and the school. The demonstrators should be properly trained and demonstrations must be properly rehearsed.

The stalls should be scientifically decorated and not artificially. Proper lighting should be there.

Execution

As per the planning, organization, distribution of work and way to display, the work should be executed. When the exhibition is ready it must be inaugurated. After inauguration there should be judgment and evaluation of the projects presented by students.

Judging

Different committee of judges for different items of exhibition should judge the exhibits. This judgement should be before opening to common public and other school students.

There should be some criteria:

1. Scientific approach 30%
2. Originality 20%
3. Technical Skill 20%
4. Thoroughness 10%
5. Dramatic Value 10%
6. Personal Interview 10%

After the exhibition is over the teacher and students should review and evaluate the entire process from planning to exhibition and find out whether the objectives were achieved or not. If there was any problem it can be improved next time.

Exhibition for environmental education is very important method because through such exhibition the new environment friendly habits and technology can be introduced to the students in particular and community in general.

Role Playing

Since childhood we have seen children use this technique to emulate the people in their environment. They try to act like their mother or father or friends or actor, actresses of their favorite serial and films. By enacting and pretending to be like postman, or fireman, they learn what makes up the job of a postman or a fireman. When the role-play helps in understanding social phenomena it is known as sociodrama, but when it tries to understand a personal emotional relationship than it is known as psycho drama. Therapists and psychologists use psychodrama. Only specialists should use psychodrama.

Role-playing is basically unprepared unrehearsed dramatization. For e.g. if we take the topic of say cruelty against animals, here we can depict two characters one a happy animal and other ill-treated animal both can share their feelings and children can be sensitized towards animals and their care. After the portrayal entire class discusses what was the cause of (A) animal's happiness? And what was the cause of (B) animal's sadness? How should they be treated and why?

Role-play can be used to

- Clarify attitudes and concepts;
- Demonstrate attitudes and concepts;
- Deepen understanding of social situations
- Prepare for a real situation
- Plan and tryout strategies for attacking problems
- Test hypothetical solutions of problems
- Practice leadership and other social skills.

How role-playing is different from drama?

Role-playing differs from the usual type of dramatic work in that no script is needed, no memorizing on parts, no rehearsal. It requires spontaneity of presentation. The action comes directly from the individuals' creative use of there own experience.

Pre Requisites for role playing;

1. The class should have a cooperative group feeling and common interest.
2. The participants should have the issue clear in mind.
3. The experience should be regarded as a means of learning and not entertainment.

Steps involved

Selecting the situation

Say Garbage disposal in a locality is causing problem to the residents of the area. And the people come together raise their voices to the municipal corporation members. The situation should be a simple one from their day to day life. If the situation is complex than the role will fail, as the students would not have experienced such situation in the real life. For role-play take a local level problem. Once the students comprehend the situation, take some time to discuss the roles with the players. The rest of the class becomes the audience.

Selecting the Cast

Here the students can be asked to volunteer for different roles. Chance should be given to various students in order to avoid stereotype thinking. The teacher is usually tempted to give chance to particular student repeatedly depending on his / her enacting and communication skill. Some students may not be very skilled but may definitely have different thinking and experiences to share.

Playing roles

As it is a spontaneous activity some students may become very nervous the teacher must help them. First few lines could be rehearsed in order to boost the confidence of the students. One must avoid rehearsing as it curtails spontaneity. Only to boost confidence few lines can be rehearsed. The roles must be properly explained to the role players.

Follow up

Any role-play must be followed by discussion. In order to make role play more effective and interactive, a part of role-play can be shown and than stopped to know what will happen next. The students must analyze and discuss the action and interpret its significance. This discussion must end in some generalization.

Limitations of a role-play

1. Pupils do not always take role-play seriously. They often think of it as entertainment.
2. Unless pupils are well prepared, the role playing may become superficial and result in stereotype thinking
3. The role players must know the characters and their situations.
4. It is time consuming activity
5. It is dependent on atmosphere
6. Supporting free discussion and inquiry.
7. Try to have pupils play a number of different types of roles in order to avoid stereotype roles and stereotype thinking.

Quiz

In order to conduct quiz competition one needs to have many questions. A teacher can prepare a large question bank pertaining to environment. A date can be announced for competition. A circular can be sent to various schools regarding, date, time, venue, last date for entries, age group valid for competition and address and phone number of contact person.

Once the entries start pouring teams and rounds can be decided. If there are many entries than a written test can be conducted to find the team members. We can take the top scoring members say we get the top sixteen students, out of the sixteen students we can mix and make eight teams. While making the team one care should be taken the two students representing the team are in tune with each other. I.e. thc group dynamics must be taken care of, it should not happen that we place together two such students who do not talk with each other. Now we can prepare our students to participate for quarterfinal in pool A we can have 1,3,5 7 and in pool B we can have 2,4,6,8. From the quarter final there will be quiz round between team 1-3, 1-5, 7-3, 1-7, 3-5, and 5-7 we will get two winning teams in each pool. Say for e.g. we get 1-5 and 3-7 as quarter final winners similarly from pool B we will get quarter final winners. Say we get 2-6 and 4-8, after each has got chance to play with the other the losers drop out of the game and the team winning maximum time wins eventually.

Preparation of items for quiz

In order to conduct a quiz there is need to prepare a question bank. The question bank can have, pictures of various, plants, birds, animal, geographical locations, voices of birds and animals. Apart from audio and video there can be question on various concepts related to environment, causes, problems, effects on health, national parks, sanctuaries, gadgets used to measure environmental problems, units, environmental adaptation in plants and animals, medicinal plants, completion of some puzzle related to environment, name of NGO's associated with environment, renewable, non renewable resources, environmental tragedies, environmental conferences, some environmental acronyms, Some laws related to environment, some questions related to mythology, some magazines, some books etc. etc.

Some rules must be made for quiz

Like will the question pass from one team to another, or will it go to the audience. Different people involved in conducting quiz. Rules for tie: both will be declared winners or a tiobreaker will be played. Marks can be assigned to different rounds

1. Quiz Master: The role of quizmaster is clear, he/she is the one who conducts the show and asks various questions. His/her verdict must be considered final to avoid any confusion. Quizmaster can have number of rounds; audio, visual, audio-visual, a question, specimen, model or a puzzle can be set for students to solve and speed round.

2. Scorer: The score keeper keeps the score. The rules decided for scoring can be given to the scorer. After every round the score keeper announces the score.

3. Time keeper: In the speed round time is of great importance here the students have to finish an activity in a stipulated time. The time has to be kept by the time keeper.

4. For visual aids a technician may be required: We may have to show a slide, or a film or even a tape recorded voice. For all such activities a technician is required.

Debate

Debate can be other activity in environmental education. If we see the content of environmental education there are many issues which have inherent contradiction. For e.g when we talk of science and technology and environment. Should we stop development if the environment is at stake? Will global warming phenomena lead to nuclear winter or melting of snow will lead to submergence of low-lying area? How far the war is an answer to establish peace? Are dams friendly or not? Should we have Zoo's? Should we have bonsai's? And many more questions are worthy of debating from environmental perspective. The students can be given these topics well in advance. They can select whether they are going to vouch for it or against it. A date can be given and competition can be arranged. There can be a panel of judges to decide upon the winner. All the judges can be given a checklist and a rating scale to rate the speaker. On the date and time decided for debate the participants participate in the activity and the rest of students become the audience. After every presentation some audience must be given an opportunity to question the speaker, for some doubt or clarification. Debate will help in giving both the sides of the problem so the students will be able to know every problem has many sides. When a decision is taken it has to be taken in the larger interest and not as a part of selfish interest.

Field Trips

- Are purposeful visits to places of scientific interests and provide valuable experience in the process of learning environment and science.
- Provide students a first hand knowledge of science and stimulate their interests & motivate them to learn.
- Field trip term can be applied to any activity outside the classroom in which the pupils participate.
- A field trip may vary in duration and organization from one to a few hours to an extensively organized lasting a day or more.
- For full benefit, a field trip must be carefully and properly planned.
- It should be considered as a holiday trips though it is a sort of enjoyment but be considered as a serious undertaking.

Purpose of Field Trips

- For collecting various types of seeds leaves, fruits, flowers, rocks etc.
- Studying the habits of migratory birds
- Learning about the habit and habitat of animals in natural habitat like forests and artificial habitats like Zoos, Sanctuaries etc.
- Studying animal behavior
- Learning about cultural practices like Fish Culture, Prawn, Pearl, Lobster etc.
- Knowing how silk is processed from silk worms in Factories
- Honey & Lac production
- Visit to Family Planning centers and Population control centers
- Visit to Veterinary Centers to learn about how animal care is provided

- Dairy visits to get information about how milk is processed find learn about cryopreservations.
- Understanding hybridization through visits to Genetic Engineering Centers
- Learning about wild species and cultivated species through visits to forests & forms respectively.
- Visits to pharma industries to understand role of biotechnology in field of medicine.
- Trips to science exhibitions, symposium, and seminars.

How to Make Field Trips a Rich Educational Experience?

Planning

- The visit or excursion should be planned well in advance with the active co-operation of Teacher and pupils in the light of its purpose.
- Here the teacher incharge is expected to seek permission from the place where the visit has been arranged. Prior to taking permission from the place where we are going we need to take permission of principal (management) and parents. It has to be organized in such a way that minimum disturbance is made in the regular timetable. After we get the permission we have to decide route to be traveled, the time schedules. Next, one would need to arrange for the transport and lodging facilities and the expenditure to be borne by the pupils, the luggage and other necessary articles to be taken along etc.
- The most important aspect of planning is to arrange for finance.

Finance Arrangement

- After listing out the probable field trips during an academic year, it is very essential to make a rough estimate about the total expenditure.
- After accounting for the total expenditure, it is estimated as to how much expenditure should be borne by the school as well as by the individuals.
- Prior sanction of the accounts department is to be sought.
- It is also to be seen whether any concession is possible for the student's in railway, bus fares etc.

- The expenditure should be in terms of the financial status of school and aids reserved for such trips.
- Teacher in charge should submit a detailed list of the number of student, place of visit, the duration of stay, the mode of travel, lodging facilities, the necessary articles to be taken along etc.
- Teacher should be resourceful enough to collect grants for the trips.
- The fee structure should be such that a part of it is to be devoted to the expenditures procured due to field trips.

Preparation

- After planning, students and teachers should prepare for the trip
- Should know the purpose of visit, the things that they should look for? What things are to be collected? What type of information is to be recorded?
- Directions of activities.
- How to record?

Execution

- Teacher acts as a guide and supervisor
- Reaching the place, teacher must direct the students. Also see to it that all students follow the instruction.
- Draw student's attention to the important things and make certain that all the pupils participate and get the desired information.

Places of field trips

- Zoo
- Museum
- Bird sanctuary
- Dairies
- Hospitals
- Aquaculture farms
- Tea Gardens
- Botanical Gardens
- Green Fields

- Forests
- Ponds, lakes, stream
- Fish farms
- Research laboratories
- Poultry farms
- Veterinary Centers
- Sea shores
- Visit to Polluted Sites
- Tissue Culture Centers
- Vermiculture Centers
- Nature Parks
- National Parks & Sanctuaries
- Science Exhibition & Science Fairs
- Population Growth Centers

Advantages of Field Trip

- Every thing cannot be learnt in the classroom, hence excursions provide opportunities for direct experiences & thus learning becomes more accurate & meaningful.
- Provide first hand information to supplement and enrich classroom Instructions.
- Co-relate the school life with the outside world and community.
- Create situations, which develop a spirit of scientific inquiry.
- Application of learnt knowledge.
- Provide basis for a number of projects and study materials.
- Pupils learn planning, co-operation, etc.
- Learn to discharge responsibilities.
- Arouses interest of students, and vitalizes instruction
- Students' get opportunities to collect things and preserve them.
- Provide recreational dimension to study
- Students see the relation between science and society

Disadvantages of Field Trip

School program is disrupted. Field trips usually require at least a complete day or minimum 5 to 6 hours. This means that on such days no-classes will be held so the school timetable is disturbed. Also frequent field trips may cause lack of time for completion of the school syllabus.

waste as fuel. A sharp rise has occurred in the price of wood and coal in the last decade. Development of alternative sources like solar, nuclear, wind and tidal and biogas holds promise for solving energy crisis.

Ecological Disruption

The subtle and fragile relationships in an ecosystem can be disrupted due to external factors like human intervention. Any change in an ecosystem that is imposed from outside often triggers off a chain of reaction that dismay sometimes be irreversible. All the environmental problems described above are cause as well as manifestation of an ecological crisis in environment. Extinction of 'Dodo' and the threat from hydro electric power projects are two classic examples that amply illustrate the ecological imbalance due to human intervention. Dodo, the flight less bird of Mauritius became extinct due to hunting by colonial rulers and the dogs that they brought with them. Calvaria majora, a species of plant whose fruit was eaten by Dodo and the hard seeds passing through its digestive tract became softened facilitating germination after excretion by the bird became nearly extinct after disappearance of the bird. Recently few seeds have been germinated after being forcibly fed to turkeys.

Largely hydroelectric projects, once considered a blessing and architectural wonder are being looked with skepticism from environment point of view. President Hosseni Mubarak once said that the challenge before Egypt is to cope with Aswan dam. Such projects are ecological disasters as they submerge vast tracts of forestland, uproot people mostly tribal from their home and hearth, cause water logging and salination due to canal network, change microclimate of the area, create breeding ground for disease vectors like mosquitoes and snails etc., Dams also have potential for causing earth quake due to reservoir induced seismicity.

Despite protests by the activist groups Government of India has given green signal to such hydroelectric projects like Sardar Sarovar, Narmada Sagar and one at Tehri. Fasts undertaken by Mr. Sunderlal Bahuguna, Baba Amte have produced no effect. However, Kerala Shastra Sahitya Parishad's struggle forced government to shelve the 'Silent Valley Project'.

Observation – Demonstration

Dictionary meaning of Demonstration "A public showing emphasizing the salient merits, utility, efficiency, etc of an article or product"

In teaching demonstration means showing how something is to be done or not to be done. It involves the art of depicting the skills associated with an action, idea, attitudes, processes and other intangibles.

Major Characteristics of Demonstration

It is a good method for displaying skills in operation.

Demonstration is facilitated by audio-visual materials, like a chalkboard, a filmstrip, a film, a recording, a diagram, a chart.

Things to keep in Mind

1. Establishing Rapport: Maintain a friendly relationship with students show enthusiasm, arouse curiosity.
2. Ensure that the key points are communicated emphasize the key points. (repeat)

Steps

1. Preparation for classroom demonstration:
2. To plan demonstration that will create interest among students
3. Plan every step carefully
4. Plan for all requirements and arrange them as per need.
5. Rehearse your demonstration
6. Outline the steps on chalkboard
7. Make sure that everyone can see and hear
8. Prepare written material.

Performing the Classroom Demonstration

Key Points

(a) Arouse curiosity, generate interest.
(b) Keep demonstration simple
(c) Not digressing from main idea
(d) Checking continuously that demonstration is understood

(e) Not hurrying through the process
(f) Not dragging the demonstration
(g) Clear visibility
(h) Summarize the demonstration
(i) Distribute handouts at the end.

Evaluating the Demonstration

It can be done with the help of discussion or a test. Demonstrator can also do self evaluation.

Merits

- It is economical compared to laboratory method
- Lesser finance and infrastructure is needed
- It makes teaching learning more concrete
- Visual memory helps in retention
- It takes lesser time
- It has advantage of both lecture and demonstration

Demerits

- It gives no scope for hand on experience
- It is dominated by teacher
- It does not cater to individual differences
- No skills are developed
- In discussion also few students participate

Project Method

Project means a bit of real life, which isn't theoretical or bookish. According to Kilpatrick, "A project is a unit of whole hearted purposeful activity carried on preferably in its natural setting". Project is a problematic situation, which comes to completion with the required solution from school. Project method lays stress on the role of project to develop social skills. According to Stevenson "A project is a problematic act carried to its completion in its natural setting".

According to Ballard, "A project is a bit of real life that has been incorporated into the school.

Learning takes place in the natural setting. Students interact with nature.

Importance of Project Method

It is based on the psychological principle of learning by doing. The learning gets consolidated faster. The concept can be learnt at depth involving various discipline students learn creativity. They learn to solve problems. It emphasizes experiential learning.

Steps involved in Project Method.

1. **Providing a Problematic Situation.**

   The problem should not be imposed on students.

   Teacher should provide interesting situations.

   (a) The teacher may organize field visits the students can be involved in collection of flora and fauna.

   (b) Different types of projects can be mentioned and students can opt for the project of their choice.

   (c) Teacher can demonstrate experiments to show importance of sunlight, chlorophyll etc.

   In the discussion students can be motivated to take up various experiments.

   (e) Silent demonstration can be placed in the laboratory or in the classroom for e.g. an aquarium can be placed in the class or a potted plant. The new element in the class can raise questions in the mind of students.

   (f) Certain wild life documentary, films can be shown to arouse interest.

   (g) Discussion of content can be done which can arouse interest in students.

   (h) Teacher may ask students to view a few Internet websites to generate interest in them.

   Thus, in the given ways one can generate a problematic situation in front of students.

2. Selection of a Project

Student is able to sense the problems and depending upon interest, time and available resources plus the aptitude required for carrying it out.

The students after discussing common interest in a group – select a project. It is a group activity and a co-operative venture.

3.Planning: - Planning in project is a group activity where the task at hand is thoroughly discussed. Students should be asked to read in the area of project. Students should consult people in the community and experts in the area. The project should be specified and further divided in the group so that people are given task according to their abilities and choices.

4.Execution: - Meaningful implementation of planning is execution. The students' carryout the task after consulting with their teacher. The teacher guides the students whenever they have some difficulty. A teacher must see that every member is working independently and few members do not dominate the group.

5.Evaluation: - Evaluation of the project should be two sided that the teacher evaluates the project plus the participants also evaluate their project in the light of given objectives. Evaluation of individuals' task is difficult, as it is a group effort.

6.Recording/Report: - Project Report is the end product and the compilation of the team effort. It must have following things.

1. Introduction.
2. Problem.
3. Hypothesis.
4. Methods and Material.
5. Experiment.
6. Results and discussion.
7. Summary.
8. References.

If it is visit to some site than pictures, specimen submission, herbarium preparation etc., is to be submitted with the report.

A good project must keep in mind the age, ability, interest, aptitude, and availability of time, resources, and maturity, individual differences that naturally exist among students.

Merits: -

1. It is based on the principle of learning by doing and learning by living.

2. Understanding of the content is better.
3. Students develop a lot of social skills.
4. They learn to solve problems.
5. They learn co-operative thinking and decision-making.
6. Students learn self study habits.
7. Students can develop scientific attitude and scientific temper.

Demerits: -

1. It is very time consuming.
2. Expectations from teacher are very high.
3. Good library is required to use this method.
4. A good laboratory is also required to teach through this method.

Role of Teacher

The teacher in the project method plays many roles facilitator, motivator, guide, manager, helper and supervisor.

The teacher first has to provide different situations to the students. Next the teacher must check the plan before execution to see that the leader of the group properly distributes the work after looking at the potentials of the members. The teacher also has to give deadline for the completion of the project. Finally, the teacher is supposed to evaluate the project report submitted by the students.

Projects for Students

- **Collecting leaves:** A collection of different types of leaves may be made which can be used as teaching aid to explain the structure; function (modification, adaptation) of leaves and the trees to which they belong could be identified.
- **Collecting feathers:** A collection of fallen feathers of birds can be made. This could be used to discuss the plumage of birds, adaptation and the identification of the birds of which the feather belong.
- **Making Herbarium:** Making a herbarium collection of local plants to understand the flora of the region.
- **Greening the School:** A collective, sustained activity by students through which the school campus can be made environmentally sound and aesthetically pleasing.

- **Studying the Tree life around:** Observing and studying all activities of living organisms around a tree to understand life supporting system.
- **Recycling material:** Reusing discarded tins, cartons, envelops etc. to create forms to emphasize the value of recycling materials.
- **Testing water pollution:** Take water samples from various sources and compare them with clean water to understand the levels of water pollution in such water bodies.
- **Insects in School Campus:** Observe and study the different species of insects in the school campus to understand their variety diversity and adaptation
- **Trees in School Campus:** Identifying and distinguishing the characteristics of trees in the school campus.

Poster Presentation: Posters are the two-dimensional sheets of paper which communicate some message to its viewers either through a picture alone or a picture plus a slogan or only slogans. The posters are helpful in catching the attention of the viewer. Long and lengthy messages given through print or any other media may not be read at length but the posters if they are properly done leave an impact on the mind of its viewer. They are a good source of informal education. The people passing by day in and day out watch these posters and learn about the concept. We can make use of poster presentation to teach environmental education. We can select a theme and on a particular theme we may prepare posters and show them along with commentary

Criteria to be kept in mind

- A single poster must have one clear idea
- It should be large enough for a class to see
- Colors can be harmonious in a poster
- Letter size should be large enough to be visible to the whole class.
- It must contain picture, message or slogan for environmental education on a relevant theme.
- It should be properly paced and nicely explained.
- After presentation there should be discussion on the theme. The discussion should tell what the students learned. It should not be considered as an entertainment program.

- **Games:**
- **Various games that can be played.**
- **Web of Life:** Materials requires 100 meter of string

Cards with names of various objects in nature written on it.

Method

Distribute one card to each card to each student. Ask them to pin it on. Make the whole group sit in a circle. The ball of string represents energy. Take the ball of string and give it to the "sun". It is suggested that the game start from the sun, as all life on earth depends on it. The Sun winds the string on his finger and passes the ball to the grass as it need the sun's energy for photosynthesis. The grass may then give it to the deer, as it feeds on it. Each one winds the string around a finger and passes it on. Repeat these up and down food chains till all the students are involved and a tight web is formed. The web is stretched tight.

Now ask them, what happens if one member of the web is taken away e.g., if all the tigers are killed. To demonstrate this effect the tiger pulls on the string. As a result the number of deer will increase; the demand on the grassland system will increase. This exercise is repeated till the web is destroyed.

This game can be modified for senior students by asking them to select organisms according to different ecosystems such as forest, grassland, etc.

This also demonstrates how each system has a large number of linked species that are not found in other ecosystems.

2. Equitable Distribution of Resources

Method

Seat children in two circles on inside and the other outside. Place some sweets in the center of the circles.

Ask each child to pick a sweet, not more than one at a time. Gradually add sweets to the center of the ring.

Children in the inner ring will be able to take more sweets than those in the outer circle. Since children will pick up sweets more quickly than they are added, some will get very few sweets than those in the outer circle. At this point ask those who have fewer sweets to grab sweets from others who have more than their share.

The inequitable use of resources is thus shown to lead to conflict.

Examples from real life.

Nations : Northern developed Vs southern developing
Urban Housing : Apartments Vs slums
Agriculture : Irrigated farms Vs Rain fed Farms

3.Traditional and Modern Pattern of Resource Use

Method

Select two groups of children. One has tall students the other has short children. Place sweets within reach of tall children, but out of reach of short children. In the first round of the game, select only two tall children. Ask them to get sweets. Most of sweets (resources) will be taken by the two tall children. Then ask the tall children to keep half of the sweets with them and distribute the rest of the sweets. (This is the traditional pattern of resource distribution.) In the next round of game an equal number of tall and short children. Repeat the exercise. Very few sweets are left for distributing to the short children. (This is the current pattern of resource use.) The tall students signify the developed nations and short children signifies the developing nations. It also gives the message go by the need and not the greed.

4. Water Conservation Game

This activity shows that in most situations people are careless about how they use resources, and have no value for its conservation till it is totally depleted.

Method

The students are asked to form a row. They are shown a bucket of water, which represents all the water in the earth's hydrosphere. A mug of water is taken out of it. This represents the world's fresh water. A spoonful of water is taken out of the mug and handed to the first student. They are than asked to quickly pass it to the end of the line.

All the water from the spoon is usually spilled and wasted. The last few students thus get no water.

The activity demonstrates the need to conserve water by its careful use. The game can then be repeated with the new awareness at least some of the water is likely to remain in the spoon at the end of the line.

They are then told that the spoonful of water is the small quantum of water that the hydrosphere makes available for all our requirements. If it is misused none would be available for our future generation.

5. Conservation

This game can be used to create awareness of the need for conservation of resources.

1. Divide students into three groups. The first group contains 7 or 8 students, the second group of 4-5 students and the third group of 1or 2 students.
2. Give the first group a sheet of paper and a box of crayons. Allowing unlimited time, ask them to draw whatever they want.
3. After they have finished drawing, give the same paper to the second group and ask them to draw anything they want on it, but give them only those colours which were not used by the previous group. Give them time limit of three minutes.
4. Pass the same paper to the third group and ask them to draw anything they want on it, but give them only those crayons that were not used by the other two groups. If the other two groups have used up all the crayons then the third

group uses none. This group has only one minute to draw or work on the picture in whatever way they can. (they cannot use their personal pens or pencils to draw).

5. Ask them to think of the paper on which they were asked to draw, as representing the earth or land and the crayons as the resources available. The first group used up a major part of the land and resources without thinking about its conservation for future use. As a result the second group, which represents the next generation did not have enough while the third group was left with nothing at all. This is how the resources of our earth have been utilized at present, without a thought for tomorrow, or the needs of the future generations. This demonstrates the importance of conservation.

6. Who am I?

This game could be used to clarify concepts on classification of animals. One student from the class is selected and shown a card with the name of an animal or bird written on it. The other students from the class have to guess, the name of the animal or the bird. The questions should usually follow the given sequence to which the student who has the card only as a yes or a no.

Are you a living? If yes
Are you an animal? If yes
Do you have four legs? If yes
Are you found in the forest? If yes
Are you carnivorous? If yes
Are you Brown in color? If yes
Usually 8 questions are permitted.

7. Antakshari

Method

Students can be divided in two groups and they can be asked to sing songs related to environment. Turn by turn and the score can be maintained. They will be able to see the incorporation of environment in song. Is it in the same pristine environment as depicted in the song? What can be done to bring that beauty back?

8. **Cross Word Puzzle:** A crossword puzzle can be prepared on environment and its issues. (individual)

9. **Monopoly:** It is a game of business, which can be modified to environment, where punishment and bonus can be in terms of environment. (Game for four)

10. The game of **snakes and ladders** can also be modified into aquatic or terrestrial ecosystem and its biotic and abiotic components. (Minimum two, maximum four)

· **Puppets:** Environmental messages can very well be communicated with the help of puppets. They are simple to make and use.

Materials required for **glove puppet;**

Glove Puppet

- Plastic ball, old socks, stickers, paper, wool for hair/ black cloth one plain cloth half a meter and one printed cloth and a card board.
- With the help of hot knife dig out a small hole in the ball so that the first finger can pass through it easily. Insert a rolled chart paper or cardboard, which is rolled in a form of hollow cylinder, through which the first finger can pass. Remove the hollow cylinder take the plastic ball stick some paper ball for nose; now push the ball into the old sock. Decorate the face with eyes, mouth, you may use colors and do some make up as per the need of the script. Stick the wool in place of hair/ or fix black cloth.
- For the body of puppet, prepare the glove in such a way first finger goes into the head through the neck (cylinder) and three fingers go on one side and the thumb goes on the other side to make two hands of the puppet. In the hand region stick cardboard in the shape of a palm.
- You may first draw the palm on paper and than cut the cloth by folding it. Stitch it in such a way that a glove is made.

Now one can make different dresses for different gloves. Dresses can depend on the theme, background of the script.

- **Stick puppet:** Compared to glove puppet they are easy to make. On a Firm and slightly thicker stick a picture can be cut out and stuck on the stick.
- A curtain can be used to tell about the setting or the background. On the curtain pictures can be fixed.
- Puppets make a good learning resource.

We have seen many games and resource that can be used and prepared for teaching environmental education. You may have a question in mind when and how can we do so many activities school timetable is often very tight and we can only do curricular and co-curricular activities. Some of the co-curricular activities can be related with environment. There is one place where number of activities round the year can go on for a better environment. This place is the Nature club. Now let us see how nature club can be beneficial for environment.

Nature Club

The nature club is a group of young people, which can spread conservation in the society. Since a club represents the collective will of its members, it can generate conservation awareness in a most effective manner. But such activities must be organized in an imaginative manner to be effective.

Nature Club Activities

- The following activities are included in Nature Club movement:
- Organizing seminars, competitions, debates, discussions, poster presentation, quiz's etc. on various occasions
- Nature trails, Nature study Projects
- Tree planting compost preparation, paper recycling and Vermi compost.
- Articles and contributions for nature news, school and other magazines
- Water pollution monitoring and conservation demonstration projects for local community.

How to form a Nature Club? As given in the National Green Corps document 2001.

We all know that we are part of the environment we live in. And the solution of many environmental problems lies in our attitude towards environment. Be it awareness to keep our surroundings clean or the realization to conserve natural resources by re using and recycling wherever possible, they all are attitudinal. On the surface it looks simple. But changing the attitudes of 100 crores people is not going to happen overnight. The best way to attempt to bring about a change in the attitudes in the society is through the children. They have no vested interest. They are impressionable. They are our future. They are the single most important influence in any family. With this realization the Ministry of Environment and Forests, Government of India has decided to launch the National Green Corps program NGC in all districts of our vast country.

Objectives

1. To provide possible solutions for existing problems
2. To make children understand opportunities for school children
3. To provide environmental education opportunities for school children
4. To utilize the unique position of school children as conduits for awareness of the society at large.
5. To facilitate children's participation in decision making in areas related to environment and development
6. To bring children into direct contact with the environmental problems facing the society they live in and make them think of solutions
7. To involve children in action based programs related to environment in their surroundings
8. To develop a sense of scientific inquiry into environmental problems

Coverage

The NGC program will be implemented in all the States and Union Territories.

Membership

About 100 schools in every district in the country

In addition all the Kendriya Vidyalayas and all other schools under CBSE and ICSE

Methodology

The scheme will be operated through Eco- clubs to be formed in the member schools. Each such club will have 30-50 children, who show interest in environment related issues each such club will be supervised by a teacher in-charge, who is selected from among the teachers of the member school on the basis of his / her interest in environment related issues.

Each eco-club will be provided with a kit of resource material in the language of their preference, apart from a token monetary grant of Rs. 1000/- per annum for organizing different activities. There will be district implementation and monitoring committee to supervise, organize training for in-charge teachers, and monitor periodically the implementation of scheme at the district level.

There will be state steering committee to oversee the implementation of the scheme. The State Nodal Agency will coordinate the implementation of the scheme in the state and organize related activities like training to master trainers. The National Steering committee will give overall direction to the program and ensure linkages at all levels.

Criteria for Selection of Schools

All Kendriya Vidyalayas, Navodaya Vidyalayas and all other schools under CBSE and ICSE

About 100 schools in each district under the respective state / UT boards. The schools must be preferably of secondary and senior secondary level schools, upper primary schools can be selected

Those schools who have prior experience in running Eco-clubs or other environment related program would be given preference.

Selection of Master Trainers

From each district, the District implementation and Monitoring committee would select one or two Master Trainers. They can be from among the In- charge teachers of selected schools. They would be first trained at the state capital. They in turn would train In-charge teachers.

Finance

Financial Implications

1. Each school with an Eco-club would be given an annual financial assistance of 1000/-. The student members of the Eco-club and In-charge teacher would decide on using the sum for their activities in consultation with the Principal/ head Master.
2. The state nodal agency would be given 5 per cent of total annual expenditure on the scheme in that state towards administrative expenses.
3. For selection, printing and distribution of locally relevant resource material, the Nodal Agency would be given a Financial assistance at the rate of 50 per Eco club
4. For organizing the training of in- charge teachers, the Nodal Agency would be given a financial assistance at the rate of Rs. 990/- per master trainer. (It would be calculated at the rate of 1.6 Master trainer per district)
5. For organizing the training of in-charge teachers, the Nodal agency would be given a financial assistance at the rate of 335 /- per In charge teacher.
6. The state resource agency would be given 3% of total annual expenditure on the scheme in the state as their honorarium. The sum includes travel expenses and other administrative expenditure. No other financial assistance would be given to the resource agency for their assistance in the implementation of the scheme.

Fund Flow Mechanism

1. Except for the funds meant for Resource Agency where the money would be directly released, all other funds would be routed through the State Nodal Agency.

2. First installment of financial assistance released to the State Nodal Agency would consist of :

a. 100% funds meant for selection, printing and distribution of locally relevant resource material.

ii. 100% funds meant for training of Master Trainers.

iii. 100% funds meant of training of In-charge teachers.

iv. 50% of funds meant for financial assistance to Eco-clubs.

Second installment would be released after the training for in-charge teachers is completed and resource material is distributed to Eco-clubs would be released. Final installment would be released subsequently.

The funds meant for State Resource Agency would be released directly to the agency.

Activities

Organize seminars, debates, lectures and popular talks on environmental issues in the school. Field visits to environmentally important sites including polluted and degraded sited, wildlife parks etc. Organize rallies, marches, human chains and street theater at public places with a view to spread environmental awareness. Action based activities like tree plantation, cleanliness drives both within and out side the school campus. Grow kitchen gardens, maintain vermi – composting pits, constructed water harvesting structures in school, practice paper recycling etc., Prepare inventories of polluting sources and forward it to enforcement agencies. Organize awareness program against defecation in public places, pasting posters in public places and to propagate personal hygiene habits like washing hands before meals etc. Maintenance of public places like parks gardens both within and outside the school campus. Mobilize action against environmentally unsound practices like garbage disposal in unauthorized places, unsafe disposal of hospital waste etc.

Role of Implementers

Role of State Nodal Agency

- To nominate a Nodal Officer

- To ensure identification of member schools by the district committees and organize training for them with the help of Resource Agency.
- To select locally relevant resource material in consultation with the Resource Agency and get it printed.
- To ensure identification of Master Trainers by District Committees and organize training for them with the help of Resource Agency.
- To ensure training program for in-charge Teachers in Districts.
- To ensure distribution of grants and resource material to Eco-clubs
- To receive quarterly reports from District Committees and compile them in the form of reports and send them to Central Nodal Officer in the given format.
- To organize State level activities and co-ordinate them.
- To organize publicity for the program to encourage more schools and students to join Eco-clubs.

Role of Resource Agency

- Each State/UT is being provided with the services of one Resource agency for the better implementation of the scheme. The main role of the Resource Agency is that of a consultant and a facilitator. The Agency is expected to perform the following functions;
- Assist the State Nodal Agency/District Committees in the identification of schools in each district
- Help the Nodal Agency in selecting locally relevant resource material.
- Help the Nodal Agency in organizing training program for Master Trainers by providing technical inputs to resource persons.
- Assist District Committees in drawing up action plans and in organizing District level training programs for in-charge Teachers by providing resource persons as well as in drawing up training schedule.
- To advise the State Nodal Agency in all the aspects of implementation of the scheme.

Composition and Role of State Steering Committee

Composition

- Principal Secretary, Environment and Forests
  Chairman
- Or officer of equal rank
- Secretaries or their representatives from state departments of education, health and other concerned departments
  Members
- Representative of Resource Agency
  Member
- Head of the Nodal Agency
  Member
- Two eminent NGOs working on environmental issues
  Member
- State Nodal Officer Member
  Secretary
- State government can nominate other officers and individual relevant to this committee.

Role

- To coordinate implementation of the scheme.
- To encourage different activities to be taken up at District level
- To select the best district, best Eco-club and give publicity to their activities so that other districts and Eco-clubs can adopt them.

Composition and Role of District implementation and monitoring committee

Composition

District collector / DM — Chairman
Conservator of Forest/ DFO — Member
District level officials of Department of Environment/ State pollution Control Board and Department of Health — Member
Two eminent NGOs working

on environmental issues — Members
Heads of five schools from
among the selected schools — Member
Representative of the Resource Agency — Member

District Education Officer/ District Scientific Officer Member Secretary

The State government can nominate any individual who is relevant to the committee

Role

- To identify the Member schools in consultation with State Nodal Agency and Resource Agency
- To motivate Heads of schools to initiate participation in the scheme.
- To select Master Trainers and send them for training organized by the State Nodal Agency
- To identify In-charge Teachers in consultation with
- School principals and organize training for in-charge Teachers
- To distribute Resource material to in charge teachers at the time of training
- To identify the activities to be taken up at the District level and organize them. Co-ordinate supervises and monitors the implementation of the activities by all the Eco- clubs in the district.
- To keep the State Nodal agency informed of the activities undertaken by the individual members as supervisors for a group of 10-15 schools and review their reports.
- To send the monitoring report to the State Nodal Agency as per the schedule.

Role of Teacher In-Charge of Eco club

- The Teacher In charge of Eco club plays a key role in the implementation of the scheme. He/ she should encourage more and more students to join the club. He/she should take up imaginative steps to implement the activities suggested in the scheme, which are relevant to that region. Main functions of in- charge Teacher are

- To assemble the Eco-club members every week for one hour at least and take up some activity
- To encourage the students to suggest activities for the following weeks and make a list of it. Make necessary preparations for their execution in consultation with the Head master Principal.
- Send monthly activity report to the District Committee
- Coordinate with the District committee for taking up district level common programs.

Monitoring

Performa for Schools National Green Corps

Monitoring Performa –A For schools

To be submitted every month to the district implementation and monitoring committee)

Report for the Month of _______year.

1. About the School
2. Name of the School
3. Total Students Strength
4. Boys Girls/ Co education:
5. Do you have Nursery? Primary/ secondary sections:
6. Medium of Instruction
7. E-mail Address If any
8. II About the Scheme
9. Have you appointed Teacher in-charge; (If yes give name)
10. Has he/she attended the orientation programme:
11. How many students are taking part in the scheme break up of girls and Boys for co- education schools :
12. Break up of primary / secondary students:
13. Have you received Resource Material:
14. Have you received Grant Have you received Caps etc:.

Activity	No. of students participated	Date/Duration
1. Seminar/ Talk/ Debate		
2. Camp /Field Visit		
3. plantation/cleanliness drive		

4. Awareness by rallies etc
5. others (specify)

Date

Signature of Head Master
with Principals stamp

Performa for District Implementation and
State Monitoring Committee
National Green Corps
Monitoring Performa B-1 (District level)
Activity Report
(To be submitted to the State Nodal Agency for each quarter ending in September / December/March/June by the 15th of following month)
Name of the district number of participating schools
Number of participating students;
I. Activities by individual schools:

Activity conducted	*No. of schools which participated*	*No. of students participated*
1. Seminar/ Talk/ Debate		
2. Camp /Field Visit		
3. Plantation/cleanliness drive		
4. Awareness by rallies etc		
5. others (specify)		

II . Activities conducted by District Committee:

Activity	No. of schools which participated	No. of students who participated

III. Monitoring Status

1. Has the Monitoring Committee met during this quarter Yes/ No
2. Have the Committee members inspected the working of Eco-clubs in schools: yes /No
3. If yes No. of Schools visited:
4. Remarks:

Date: Signature of DEO /
Member Secretary with Seal

C. Performa for State Nodal Agency

National Green Corps
Monitoring Performa C-1
Activity Report

(To be submitted to Central Nodal Officer half yearly in the first week of May and November)

1. Name of the state:
2. Number of districts covered under the scheme:
3. Number of participating Schools:
4. Number of participating Students:

1 Activities by Individual Schools

Activity	No. of schools which conducted	No. of students participated
1. Seminar/ Talk/ Debate		
2.Camp /Field Visit		
3.Plantation/Cleanliness drive		
4. Awareness by Rallies etc		
5. others (specify)		

II . Activities conducted by District Committee:

Activity	No. of district	No. of schools which participated	No. of students who participated

Monitoring Status

1. Has the monitoring committee met during this Quarter: yes / no
2. Have the committee members inspected the working of Eco-clubs in Districts/ Schools : yes/no
3. If yes, Number of Districts/ schools Visited

   Remarks:

Date: Signature of
Nodal Officer with Seal.

National Green Corps is a good scheme to target the problem of environment through schools. They can form eco club, it has been implemented in many schools. Schools are clear they know what to do and how to go about, they have appointed in charge teachers for eco club. The students meet twice a week and do some activities like planting trees, cleaning up school campus, and carrying out marches, rallies for public awareness. Teacher also calls expert for talk on environmental problems, they have also surveyed nearby area and given complaints to the municipal corporation. Teacher in charge has also started with the help of student's vermicompost preparation for school garden. Whereas there are some school they have received the grant but they have not yet started activities, even the in charge teacher has not been appointed. The schools where eco club activities are going on they are in search of more activities and more resources so that they can take up more activities, projects and take charge of one kilometer range area of their school and maintain its cleanliness and greenery.

For teaching environmental education there are numerous methods that can be easily applied. Schools where environmental education is separate and compulsory subject many activities can be directly carried out to inculcate environmental values. The schools where environmental education is not yet compulsory, they can integrate it with subject teaching. Along with teaching of languages, social sciences, commerce, drawing, science etc. environmental education and its inputs can be provided. The teacher will have to use ecological approach for dealing with such issues. It can be done in two ways.

Classroom approach: After organizing field trips and asking questions to students why such a problem has come up? Who is responsible? Who is the beneficiary? Who will sensitize the public to take more responsibility? For example teacher can ask questions about global warming. Why the temperature variations are occurring in the globe?

Second approach is more suitable for higher secondary students as it is the field activity. The students are given the problem to study vegetation in different regions, like garden, near residence, on hill side, in desert, near traffic signal, near the industry, on the bank of river. Find out the reason for the change in foliage. Similarly different topics and chapters in different subjects can provide for either ecological discussions in the classroom or they can also go for project based learning. Apart from various methods of teaching we will not need the support of media for transacting the curriculum of environmental education.

Some Questions

1. Design and implement a project to teach environmental education write its steps and procedure.
2. Organize a field trip to near by polluted areas. What preparation will you do? How will you evaluate it?
3. What care will you take in demonstrating a topic related to environmental education?
4. As a teacher you want children to bring about community awareness. What steps will you follow to organize such a program?
5. Suggest five environmental games. With respect to; things required to play the game, rules if any the objectives they will achieve. (Benefits)

11

Role of Media

Media has touched our life in every way since morning to evening we are so used to these technological gadgets like radio, television, taperecorder (music system, c.d.'s, DVD's, mobiles, computers ICT is soon reaching the masses plus print media. Apart from the popular media that come to us there are some other which can be used to bring awareness among the people like rallies with tableaus depicting environment and the needed improvement, street plays, use of folk theatre, drama, role-play etc. Let us discuss them one by one.

Radio: Today FM radio is catching up it has really become very popular among the youngsters. This media can be tapped properly to send the environmental messages. We can make attractive jingles and advertisement having the environmental value as the theme. We can also invite guest speakers to talk on issues pertaining to environment. If we have some local exhibitions we can publicize on radio. Radio drama can be broadcast based on the environmental theme.

Television: Television is another powerful medium where celebrities could join hands to bring awareness about environmental problems. They can also advertise Eco- friendly products. Films, documentaries can be shown on conservation and preservation of environment. Television as a media can reach every age group. Cartoons can be used to send messages regarding environment. For older children documentaries, national geography chronicles and films can be used. For city dwellers there can be program on greening the open to sky space and its maintenance. For farmers Eco- friendly farming could be showcased. For the television soap addict's serials should have environment as its theme. In the above-mentioned ways Television can provide environmental education to different age groups.

Music systems: music system is another popular media used by general population. All the songs that are made half of them describe the beauty of nature. The picture perfect beauty of nature is deteriorating day by day by human interference. So a slogan or a rhyme could be added to these music audio video's on imagine how it would look if........... Happens (polythene bags, rotten eggs were lying all around) planet is our house and its cleaning our responsibility.) Such small two minutes rhyme containing messages can be sent to various individuals through audio cassettes and CDs. Apart from advertisement, rhymes music videos could be shot with environment and its problems as theme. No one may buy a CD that's totally based on environmental messages unless it is musically composed in the most popular manner. But environmental messages can easily be sent with the popular music CDs and Video's.

Mobiles: Today the network of mobile is also spreading very fast. We see many people are using mobile. SMS (short messaging service) is the fascination today. SMS could be sent on environmental themes. Small rhymes, advertisements could be made to sensitize the mobile user on saving electricity, using dustbin, conserving water etc. it will help in inculcating environmental friendly and healthy habits for healthy living.

Computer: The use of computers is increasing at enormous rate in every trade. Nature provides wonderful screensavers. Screen savers along with slogan on environmental theme could be made. Apart from slogan some computer aided Instruction (CAI) could be made based on various environmental problems with ameliorative strategies. CAI could be developed on environment and health related issues. Advertisements could be floated on Internet. Virtual seminars, symposium could be conducted based on environmental themes.

Newspaper: It is the most popular media available in any country It can help in bringing awareness regarding environmental issues. Studies related to environment and their finding could be circulated to the masses, public interest advertisement, publicity about various environmental programs, activities done by and for community could be widely publicized by the newspapers. Newspaper can present data pertaining to environmental pollution in the region and the state. The activities conducted by the school can also be presented to the community through the newspaper the students can contribute posters paintings and articles in the children's column of the local newspaper. Special program leaflets can be circulated in the locality with the newspapers. Thus, newspaper can help in increasing the cause of environment. These promos, and slogans related to environment should be really attractive otherwise they will go unnoticed.

Magazines: They are as important as the newspaper but their circulation is less than the newspaper. The articles related to environment could be published for wider awareness. The articles could present the data available regarding environmental degradation and development in the area, it can have columns on pollution watch, story , jokes, cartoons, advertisements related to Eco-friendly products, interviews of environmentalists, award winning work, projects, review on books. Policies and law related to environment, report of programs conducted in a particular area can also be published in the magazine. A picture story on one of the sanctuary and bio-diversity therein could be one of the regular features. Any particular and special change in the environment or its policy should become the cover story. The magazine could be a hard magazine or a soft magazine on the Internet.

Folk Theatre: The folk theatre is another popular media in Gujarat Bhavai is famous in Rajasthan the puppet and in north nautanki is famous. All these media can be used to further the cause of environment. The stories and the background for the puppet show, bhavai and nautanki could have the environmental theme. Folk media has the traditional image and a wide reach in the rural, remote and tribal areas. Even the areas not connected by the technology network can have environmental programs through the popular folk theatre, which runs shows in different parts of the area.

Selection of various media

Which media should be used to teach which type of topics is a common question which emerges? Environmental education definitely requires a multi pronged approach to attack various problems that we see in our vicinity. For selection of proper media we can follow the cone of experience given by Edgar Dale.

The Cone of Experience

The cone describes various stages from direct experiences to pure abstraction. The section at the base of the cone represents concrete aspect of living and learning: the most immediate, direct purposeful experiences. As you proceed up the cone, section by section, the experiences become progressively more abstract and less direct. At the apex of the cone, most abstract, is the section including verbal symbols. Dale emphasizes that we should not view the bands of the cone as rigid, inflexible divisions. Nor does he wish us to see the various bands as being arranged in order of difficulty or importance. They do, however, help us to see experiences of living and learning in an order of increasing abstractness as one move away from direct, immediate reality. All these levels of experience, with the material that accompany them can play a significant role in effective teaching and learning.

Direct, Purposeful Experience is the real stuff of life. In it, we participate directly, with responsibility for outcomes. Dale calls it the bedrock of all education.

At the first level of abstraction, contrived experiences are replicas or simulations of reality. Often it is too difficult to study reality directly. Perhaps the reality in question is too large, or too small, or too dangerous to approach easily and directly in the classroom. Training programs in military and commercial aviation utilize contrived experiences on an extensive scale.

Dramatized Experiences are, in a sense, a kind of contrived experience. Participation in a dramatized experience can help us capture some of the feeling of a reality. It is possible for us to role-play human problems and human relationships. In dramatized participation, as in other contrived experiences and in direct reality the learner is primarily a doer. He is a participant, an actor rather than an observer.

Demonstrations are visual presentations of things, processes, facts, or ideas to be learned. They are traditionally a vital part of science teaching, although they are typically used in other subjects as well.

Field trips put one in the position of a spectator, looking at things or observing processes and people at work. It is not we who are responsible for what happens, but the "they whom we are observing who have the "real" stake in the activity or situation. On the other hand, when our field trip involves interviewing, seeking out, questioning people, finding facts, ascertaining data, we become participants as well as observers. Field trips provide both abstract and direct experience that cannot be gotten in the classroom.

Exhibits are almost necessarily less direct and more abstract than field trips in the quality of experience they provide. Primarily the exhibit is something one sees as a spectator. The exhibit is the representation of reality, often simplified to emphasize particular characteristics, processes or relationships. Color, design, lighting and symbols all help determine how much impact the exhibit will have. In viewing readymade exhibits prepared by a manufacturer, museum or some other source, we are pure spectators. Some exhibits that we prepare using variety of materials there we are spectators as well as makers.

Television and Motion Picture bring us sensory concreteness, a feeling of realism, and a unique clarity. They possess an almost hypnotic power to command our attention. Motion pictures can abstract reality so that it becomes clearer and more comprehensible for us. They can compress time and space, so that in a thirty minute film about population explosion, or industrialization and its impact, can cover a wide range of area which cannot be physically covered by travelling in as much time. We are spectators of the event, away from seeing, hearing, touching, smelling and tasting. Television can also do all these functions. Television provides directness of communication, whose values and impact we are just beginning to absorb.

Still Pictures, Radio and Recordings are all less direct and more abstract than the experiences and materials we have mentioned so far. As Dale points out these are "one sense" materials. The still picture, whether it is viewed directly or projected on a screen, remains a still picture, it lacks motion and sound. Similarly a radio broadcast or recording depends primarily on one sense for its impact. These materials, either give us representations of reality or a portion of reality itself, can be powerful aids to learning. In them, however certain elements or dimensions are abstracted.

Visual symbols, including flat maps, diagram, charts, and other materials and devices, involve us in a different kind of communication from those we have discussed. We use dollar sign to symbolize money, a line on a graph to show change in time, bars to show portions, symbols on map to show direction. etc.,

Verbal symbols are at the apex of the cone of experience, because of all our experiences these are most abstract. What is a word or a number? A verbal or quantitative symbol whether word or letter, or number, is a designation for an idea or a thing.

What the cone of experience emphasizes is that learning situations and materials differ in their level of abstraction. No single kind of experience and material will prove equally effective with all students. Each level has unique functional value. It is the teachers challenge to help the learner by providing materials and an environment in which, as needed, he may use symbols, use vicarious experience, and use direct purposeful reality to master his learning tasks.

Radio Script

The script can be written for radio, television or even stage drama. Role-play does not require any script. For all other types script is needed. The script is basically thematic write-up of the drama. Based on this thematic write-up the dialogue and screenplay are written. For radio script we do not need screenplay but for Television, films and also drama, we need screen play.

Radio Script on Environmental Education

Based on the theme, the characters required for the play are decided. Usually minimum of two characters is taken. One character is environment friendly and other is not so environment friendly. The theme is set in a background of a market, school, or village or space, or university or playground, or animal court. The theme is written keeping in view the audience age, socio-economic background interest level and their daily life style. Same theme can be treated differently at different levels. Depending on their requirements for e.g. the theme is disadvantage of using plastic bags age group is secondary school children. Here the theme could be set in between two friends, as the secondary stage belongs to adolescence stage and they like to be with friends.

Other factors to be kept in mind;

- The script must focus environmental value.
- It should be for 20-25 minutes (the time can be flexible depending on the concept.)
- It should focus on problem
- It should focus on the causes of problem.
- It should focus on consequences of overuse.
- It should focus on available alternatives and ameliorative measures.
- It must sensitize the listeners.

Presentation and Recording

For presenting radio drama we do not need many things. We may need speaker system, recorder, some musical instruments and of course some speakers depending on the number of characters in a script. The speakers should be very skilled because voice is the only media that is reaching to the audience. We don't have any properties or screen play to explain the circumstances.

Presentation

The dialogues are written keeping in mind the common lingo used by the students of a particular group. Their vocabulary and their level must be kept in mind. Basically it must psychologically appeal to the listeners.

The introducer introduces the theme and the background of character. The characters read their lines with emotion and much needed zeal. The presenters must read the lines in a live manner. Whenever required the musical instruments must be used to create the special effects like tapping of shoes (someone is coming) laughter track for group laughter, knock on the door, clapping for a positive value. Etc. Voices and music must be recorded as and when needed.

Requirements for recording

Apart from the recorder it would need a silent area, where no other noise interferes with the drama (for e.g. horn, other vehicles, a fan making noise, children playing etc). Allow the students to write their own lines and allow them to rehearse. Train them in phonetics for proper voice modulation and intonation; make them aware about punctuation's in a drama. Give them direction about relevant emotion and expression in a line.

Record the presentation

Record the presentation on the audiotape and play it in the class. The good tapes can also be broadcast on local radio station. Through such broadcast we can make people aware about environmental issues.

Limitations

- It should not be considered as an entertainment program.
- It lacks a screenplay
- Students may not be skilled in writing dialogues and presenting them. It is time consuming activity
- In the times of advanced technology radio has relegated into the background as a thing of past.

Drama Script

Script has to be on environmental theme. Again the theme has to be set in some background. The background can vary depending on the environmental theme and the target audience. The target audience will have an impact for life, so they are important components.It will have following stages:

Planning: Any activity that is carried out requires planning. Drama requires lot of planning. The steps begin with permission from the principal. Then bring out a circular. The circular will give the details regarding, date and venue plus the theme and name of drama. Participants could be asked to volunteer their names to the in charge teacher. The circular could be placed on the bulletin board and its copies could be circulated in the secondary classes. Once we get the entries next stage is to do selection.

Writing of script: Depending on the theme characters is selected and a background is selected around this background a story is developed and dialogues are written which include the problem, its causes, consequences and action needed. The script should be written in interesting manner keeping in view the age ability and interests of the students. Language should be simple and local.

Selection of characters: Here we screen the students for the drama depending on the characterization of the characters in the drama and the requirement of the theme. The students are asked to read their lines of the characters in front of the panel of judges. From these the best are selected.

Rehearsal: Next stage is rehearsal where the selected students practice their parts with each other. The director of the drama trains the students in expression.

Direction, screenplay, dialogue writing should be done by the students as far as possible under the guidance of the teacher in charge. For screenplay the students and the group will need the curtains to show background. Apart from curtains they would need furniture and other properties to give it real life like look. Big papers could be used for curtains or even projection from a LCD can help to create the visual effect for background. Some students can also make use of mask or special dresses to add to the decoration of stage.

Presentation: Screenplay helps in communicating the idea without using too many words for e.g. a 'poor boy' the description of poor boy in his house would require too many words but a picture can tell about the reality most effectively.

Properties: Properties are the objects used in a drama to depict the reality. (E.g. of properties trees, benches, brooms, polythene bags, etc.)

Costumes: Selection of costumes is another important feature in drama. The costumes must be as per the requirement of the drama and lighting. General rehearsal and dress rehearsal is required for a drama. One must rehearse every move in a drama, as there is no provision of retake or editing. On one side when rehearsal is going on other students must be involved in the publicity of drama.

Speaker system: The mikes could be hanged as per the placement of the characters on the stage and their to and fro movement.

Placement: Placement of actors could be marked with chalk on stage so that the lightman can focus the light on actors. The lightman must be given the dialogue sheets so that they know where the light must move.

Publicity: Publicity is important, one drama can send message across to a large group. Some leaflets can be stuck in various places in the community also. If there is a large drama competition than its leaflets could be printed and circulated along with the local newspaper.

Fees: Some nominal fees can be kept, this fee could be collected and deposited in the ecoclub fund, properties, costumes and other facilities could be arranged for the drama. Fees will also solve the management problem to some extent.

Setting the stage: Stage setting is important as the stage speaks much about the background of drama. In order to give special effects sound and light may be used. Sound could be recorded on a tape recorder and played as and when required.

Recording: If there is a facility of video camera in a school than such drama can be recorded on a video camera, which can later be converted into a CD and good CDs can be beamed on a local cable network for general awareness of people.

Discussion: After the drama is over the teacher can take students to respective class and a discussion should be held on the message of the drama. If the drama is in evening than the discussion could on the subsequent day. Through discussion teacher would know whether students have got the necessary values and attitude.

In this chapter various media and their role in imparting environmental education have been discussed. While teaching various topics we may come across issues which are dilemmatic and need proper analysis to take proper decisions. For this Value Analysis Model will come to our rescue.

Some Questions

1. According to you what should be the role of print media in disseminating environmental education.
2. Explain with suitable illustration the use of drama/ radio/ computer and internet in teaching environmental education.

3. Explain the “cone of experience” given by Edgar dale.
4. How will you as a teacher select appropriate media/ activity to teach environmental education?
5. According to you, is the role of media effective in providing environmental education? Justify your answers with proper illustrations.

12

Value Analysis Model (VAM)

Conflicting values lead to Dilemma, which further leads to value conflicts one is not clear what one can do in a given situation. Here one needs to analyze the problem at hand through many angles in order to reach to an amicable solution to a problem. How does this model function?

In this model there are eight steps;

Syntax

1. Presenting the Dilemma

The dilemma can be presented orally with the help of over head projector or a film. Develop the environmental problem.

2. Asking for facts

Why has this dilemma occurred what is the actual problem? Ask the students to share their experiences, views and observations.

3. Identifying and Clarifying Facts

Filtering and selecting directly responsible variables and than clarifying.

4. Ask for conceivable alternatives

Dividing the class into small groups and allowing them to discuss and find alternative solutions to come out of the current dilemma

1. Every group has a chairman and a recorder. They come up with 2-4 alternatives

5. Asking for possible consequences of each alternative.

Facts alternatives Consequences Consequences long range

Self others self Others

6. Asking for evidences to support the likelihood of desirable consequences occuring

Possible evidence or actual evidence of something that has happened elsewhere.

7. Asking for the Evaluation of likely consequences occuring.

Alternatives open to central character	Consequences	Their desirability from various points of views				Algebraic score of consequences	Ranking
		moral	legal	economical	aesthetic		

The highest ranking alternative is the most feasible alternative.

8. Asking for judgement as to which alternative seems to be best and why (discuss)

The ranking of individual student may vary and therefore at the end discussion is important to clarify the alternative chosen and its justification.

Should there be dams

Cleaning of rivers

Connection of river should it be there.

Reduction of vehicle on road

Is the ban on more than 8year old vehicles in Bombay a better decision?

Environment protection can become a reality only if we bring change in our value system. The nature we enjoy today is not our property. We are only the caretaker, we have to hand over property to our posterity safe and sound. Any thing that is not good for nature is also not good for human beings and other organisms on earth. Mere consumerism and materialism will only increase piles and piles of garbage and pollutants on planet earth, rendering dangerous impact for survival or living organisms. The judicious use of natural resources, without greed if we take what ever is required for us to live, can save us from the jeopardy. There is ample amount of substance on mother earth.

Our values will tell us what is useful and good for us and nature at large. These values are deeply integrated in the Indian culture. Right from childhood, we try to teach children that trees and animals get hurt, we must not disturb them, we must keep our body clean, we must keep our house clean, we must use dustbin. One must not spit here and there. Poor environment is as a result of poverty, which is as a result of consumerism and materialism, few people's materialistic approach leads to excess utilization of resources by one group living little for other on the periphery. Spirituality can help in reducing the race for materialism and consumerism. The next chapter deals with Management of environmental education.

Question

Q. Take any dilemmatic situation related to environmental education and apply value analysis model for its resolution.

13

Management of Environmental Education

Environment education is education through environment, about environment it is both a style and subject matter, if education as style is concerned, it means using environment as a teaching learning aid and as an approach to education. In so far as the subject matter Is concerned, it means teaching about the components and constituents of environment. In so far as the teaching for environment is concerned it means controlling the environment, establishing proper ecological equilibrium which entails proper use and conservation of resources and also involves control of environmental pollution. It also includes proper environmental planning so that environment is not only functionally useful but is also aesthetically enjoyable this aspect would include horticultural planning and urban planning. If we look at the urban development and the national news we find there are number of problems reported by the residents of many areas, regarding the approach road, concretization, taking away common plot area, cutting down of hillock, mining etc. These problems are continuously denuding the beauty of the environment. The scenario is not just in the urban sector even in the rural sector we find number of problems reducing number of trees, the water bodies drying up faster; people have to travel a lot of distance to get fodder and water. Even some villages are suffering from social problems like people do not give their daughter for marriage in certain villages due to the shortage of water. Number of trees is reducing in urban as well as rural sector. If we have to tackle these problems we will have to see the principles of environmental education.

Principles

The educational principles that buttress support to the inclusion of environmental education in school are:-

1. Environmental education help in programming experience from simple to complex.
2. Environmental education helps children to proceed from indefinite ideas to definite ideas.
3. Environmental education helps children to proceed from the concrete to the abstract.
4. Environmental education helps the ordering of learning experiences from the empirical to the rational.
5. A corollary of the foreign principle which is so clear to the hearts of educationists is that education should help the children in process of self development.
6. Besides forgoing principles, one other which is so obvious and visible in programmes of environmental education is one of the enunciated time and time again that same sequence as existed in the education of the child must follow the same sequence as existed in the education of mankind considered historically.
7. The next important educational principle which is germane to the programmes of environmental education is the pleasurable excitement which these program create in pupils.
8. The last but not the least important principle of environmental education is its relevance to man's interaction with his physical and social environment, its relevance to changing human attitudes which cause man to hate man and beget hatred that participates war the hatred that we detect and yet it exists and explodes in the world.

Environmental education is based on sound psychological principles and helps in inculcating positive attitude towards environment.

Now let us see some recommendations concerning environmental education.

Recommendation concerning Environmental Education

1. Environmental education programmes in most countries has yet to become fully established and therefore, government should be urged to emphasize environmental issues in the educational scheme.
2. The deeper understanding of the environment prevailed in the Vedic period and Mahatma Gandhi had included this concept in the basic scheme. Awareness in the past could get a straight into the approaches necessary in the future.
3. Environmental action needs a pre-requisite commitment at the individual and national level. A clear national policy on environment is thus essential and without this, curriculum development for environmental education would lack direction and purpose.
4. The main hurdle at present appears to be teacher training in environmental education. Appropriate teacher training programmes and materials for their use must be stated without delay in order to implement environmental education programs in schools.
5. To be meaningful, environmental education must relate to real world situations and should be linked to current development plans.
6. The multi- disciplinary nature of environmental studies must be recognized and accepted.
7. Further, in view of the influence if the culture, beliefs and literacy of the people on their attitude to the local environment, environmental instruction must integrate cultural, social and developmental needs and appropriate technologies for development.
8. All sections of human society must be exposed to some form and measure of environmental education for arousing their awareness, sensitivity and perception of environmental problems and thereby motivate them to get involved in worthwhile environmental action programs.
9. Fundamental issues in the process of studying the environment as systems could be related one or other hand,

location specific and comprehensive programmes stimulate enlightened decision making and community action.

10. Environmental education is a long term process beginning at the infant stage and continuing through formal preschool, school, and college and university stages and thereafter through non formal means throughout adult life.
11. Value orientation in environmental education has to be world wide movement.
12. Environmental education has to be useful and meaningful to him/her.
13. Environmental education policy must confirm to other related policies on population regulation, human settlement, land and water conservation and development.
14. Special attention should be given to environmental education focussed on non school going children, adolescent and women.
15. Environmental education is and has to be integral part of all educational programmes and also should become part of social, cultural and economic development education.
16. It might be useful to modernize inbuilt religious concepts relevant to environment and conservation such as those inherent in Vedas and smritis, Puranas classical works like Bible, Quran, and Torah and the messages of Buddha, Ashoka, Kautilya, Manu, Mahatma Gandhi and so on and incorporate these in the early education of infants, using the technique of story telling in the grandma's laps.
17. Every Country and community should develop and implement a master plan for environmental education. The plan should lead to the evolution of an ecological ethos that is a change of the present callous attitude of man towards nature and society.
18. Environmental education should enable people to perceive the environment in its totality that is the quality of physical biological, socio economic and cultural complex.
19. Clean environment must be made a fundamental right of all citizens.
20. Environmental education must aim at enlisting the cooperation and involvement of the people in environmental action.

21. Environmental Impact Assessment and its usefulness in anticipatory prevention of environmental abuse should be communicated to everyone.

Recommendations on Formal Education Needs

There is an urgent need for textbooks and teaching aids for environmental education programmes at all levels. Authoritative books on environmental protection as well as materials such as case studies, photographs, charts, maps, slides, films and other audio visual aids on environmental problems are necessary. Encouragement and financial assistance to scientists may be given for preparing such materials.

22. Environmental education at school and undergraduate levels should aim at creating environmental awareness. At higher levels the objectives should be to develop basic knowledge and skills for tackling and solving environmental problems.
23. Environmental concepts should be integrated in existing courses in physical, natural and social sciences.
24. Students should be exposed to the concept of nature education and the experience of participating in nature conservation programs, similar to the social forestry program in Gujarat.
25. Various educational bodies should reorient early education curricula to include environmental issues.
26. Co- curricular environmental programs for school children are a powerful tool for imparting environmental education to children and should be increasingly encouraged. Such program should incorporate four elements, namely, adventure, learning, grassroots action and links with both environmental offenders and beneficiaries.
27. Several techniques for providing co – curricular environmental education to school children are available. These includes sending out by mails or distributing in the class children entertaining magazines on environment, organization of nature and science clubs, visit to exhibitions, participation in community environmental action programmes and using songs, plays, folk tales, puppet shows and environmental games and puzzles.

28. At the higher school level, it would be more purposeful to involve youth in seeking and finding solutions to environmental problems and thus inculcate a positive environmental attitude.
29. Environmental magazines for the use of and by teachers should be brought out.
30. Periodical workshops and seminars on environmental topics should be arranged for teachers by organizations like the Indian Environmental Society.
31. Besides textbooks, other kinds of teaching aids for environmental education such as guides, handbooks, slides shows, film, models etc. should be developed.
32. Parent Teacher Association should discuss environmental education strategies critically and evolve appropriate school home integration for infusing the right attitude to environment in the children.
33. Programme suited for non school going children should also be developed.

University level

University should provide training for graduates, who can assimilate a comprehensive view of the environment and its problems.

34. All graduate courses should allocate a minimal period for classroom instruction, discussion or other suitable presentation of environmental topics.
35. At the university level also, it is best to integrate environmental topics into various subjects' streams such as physical, biological, social and economic sciences and in humanities.
36. University Grants Commission or other equivalent body should draw up the syllabi for various disciplines and induce their adoption.
37. Malaysian experience of post graduate diploma courses has shown that environmental awareness could be developed through discussion of real world environmental problems, that skills to identify, analyze and present environmental problems and solutions could be imparted and that

development of packages on environmental topics is feasible.

38. Carefully drawn syllabi for environmental training of teacher at the diploma, degree, and post graduate levels are urgently needed. These should include ecology, environmental economics, cultural perspectives causes of pollution and their control, resource management.
39. Environmental law should be taught in all law colleges and facilities for speculation in environmental law should be provided.
40. Graduate and post graduate programs in environmental management should be started at several centres.

Mass Media

1. Mass communication media was recognized as a powerful and effective tool for spreading information about the environment.
1. Media personnel should be trained to become proficient in spreading environmental consciousness.
2. Mass media, press, Radio and TV, should develop and employ environmental education professionals.
3. Mass communication techniques appropriate to the conditions of the target audience should be developed.
4. Traditional techniques of information dissemination like folk plays, puppet shows, balladeers, etc, should be used for environmental education.
5. Painting and essay competitions on environmental situations should be produced and exhibited widely.
6. Posters depicting environmental situations should be organized nationally.
7. Travelling environmental exhibition mounted on a bullock carts, camel carts or vans should constantly and periodically tour through rural areas.
8. Short, illustrated pamphlets, booklets, brochures on environment should be prepared by professionals and widely distributed.
9. Long distance rail passengers may be provided on entering the compartment, a booklet describing the ecosystem

components and impact caused on them by human and animal, pressure along the route.

10. An attractive environmental information folder may be given to every tourist arriving in the country.
11. A Gandhian style mass movement or satyagraha for environmental protection may be started.
12. Stories, cartoons and plays on environmental issues should be produced.
13. Feature films dealing with environmental protection may be supported by the films Finance Corporation.
14. Documentaries dealing with environmental questions of local, regional, national importance should be produced in all the official languages in India.
15. All popular environmental materials. (Books, periodicals, handouts, exhibits films, posters etc) must be simultaneously produced in all the official languages in India.
16. Representatives of the people should be fed with suitable environmental literature.

Role of NGOs

1. Directory of Government and Non Governmental Organizations in the field of environment should be prepared.
2. All NGOs should catalyze public involvement in environmental programs.
3. NGOs should include environmental education in their package of activities.
4. NGOs have a vital role to play in creating environmental awareness
5. NGOs should begin a decade of consumer and environmental education and involve youth organizations in their work.
6. NGOs can and should undertake environment based adult education.
7. The Department of Environment should provide a nodal point for NGO activities and act as a clearing house for information on NGO work in environmental education, action and programs.
8. NGOs should harmonize their activities with government bodies.

9. A newsletter of NGO efforts in the environmental field should be published.

Strategies at National, Regional and International Levels

1. Training programmes in environmental management should be set up at the regional level by regional organizations and national governments.
2. Environmental considerations should be integrated into economic development plans at the national regional and international levels.
3. Regional and international cooperation in and information exchange on environmental education UNESCO, UNDP and regional organizations.
4. Transfer of technology in environmental education management and action between developing countries could be freely promoted.

Action Plans

1. A wide range of environmental education materials for different sections of society must be produced urgently. The Department of Environment should support this endeavor.
2. Research in appropriate technology for environmental education should be promoted.
3. Problem solving and action oriented case studies on environmental issues of logical significance should be taken up and instructional materials based on these are prepared.
4. Surveys of present attitude of people towards the environment should be carried out to serve as baseline index to gauge the impact of environment education.
5. Pedagogic methodology for environmental education suitable for different levels must be evolved in a scientific manner.
6. Curricula in environmental education suitable for different levels from preschool to university have to be developed simultaneously with production of required textbooks, additional reading materials and audio visual aids.
7. Mass Media should produce professional material on environment for wide dissemination among the public.

8. NGOs should chalk out a national campaign for creating environmental awareness for target groups with built in periodical review and evaluation.
9. An information exchange network on environmental education should be setup at the national level.
10. A newsletter or news magazine exclusively for environment should be brought out.
11. Every news daily and magazine exclusively for environment should regularly carry articles of environmental interest written by professional and trained journalist.
12. Social Welfare departments must integrate environmental concerns in their programs
13. Health authorities should give priority to environmental health. They should prepare plans and schemes for preventive measures against environmental maladies and implement them conscientiously. They should also undertake environmental health education.
14. Persons with well developed environmental conscientiousness should be preferred in recruitment at all levels.
15. A National Committee or Board on Environmental education should be set up by the Department of Environment to promote Environmental Education programs, to review progress and evolve required policy at the national level, giving due consideration to the recommendations of this conference.
16. The Department of Environment in conjunction with the Ministry of Education, should convene a meeting with the Ministry of Education, in the states along with Secretaries of the Education Department and Directors of Education for adoption of a programme of environmental education in the schools.
17. NGOs should bend together in implementing a coordinated environmental perception programmes in a mutually reinforcing manner, using all media from TV to folk plays.
18. Mass media should mobilize itself for a comprehensive environmental perception program in a mutually reinforcing manner, using all media from TV to folk plays.

19. Information packs on environmental themes should be brought in different languages by NGOs with help from Department of Environment.
20. A nationwide reorientation programme in environment for educators, teachers and other professional should be started.
21. Appropriate training programmes in environmental management for largest groups should be started by Department of Environment in association training institutions, universities, school systems, staff training centers, management institutes. etc.
22. Teacher training in environment should be stepped up by all teacher training centers.
23. Environmental awareness programmes for women should be started urgently.
24. Regional and international co-operative activities in environmental education, including speedy information transfer, should be given top priority by UN and multilateral agencies.
25. The report and recommendations of the international Conference of Environmental Education should be published without delay and widely distributed to governments and concerned government departments.

Environment that we see around is changing constantly these changes are in forms of biotic and abiotic components. We have a stock around us of all the living and non living things necessary for survival. The stock must go on and on for generations together, if at all we wish to see life on Planet Earth. The stocks that we have are in the forms of birds, animals, forests, rivers, oceans; on the abiotic side we have minerals, sunlight, temperature, humidity, rainfall, gases, soil and climate. The abiotic make it possible for vegetation to grow and animals to survive. If the stocks are not managed properly there may be a major problem on the planet. The newer technologies can deplete the resources that we have. Therefore Environment management is necessary and very vital issue, as the physical resources that we have are non renewable and may not last forever.

Management of Environmental Education

Effective Management of Environmental Education is pivotal into child and man in their need for conserving, enriching environment. It helps sensitive individuals, families, schools, neighborhoods, communities and governments at various levels to solve environmental problems. It also helps develop knowledge, skills and attitudes required for solving these problems so that man stops causing havoc by spoiling wild forests and undertaking unplanned and unrestrained industrial activity in pursuit of ever increasing demand for consumer goods and fanciful gadgetry. Man, as we all, know, has been felling millions of trees for centuries to create pastures for his cattle and farms for agriculture, without realizing that by doing so he has been allowing rain and wind to erode soil. He, therefore without caring for the unintended consequences of his actions, has been opening the gate for floods to sweep, vast tracts of land cause dereliction. He has also been, especially since industrial revolution polluting air by allowing factories emit smoke which has increased carbon and sulphur content of the troposphere. He has got to be restrained throwing effluents in them. He has been dirtying rivers too by throwing effluents in them. He has got to be restrained from doing all this and from pushing the world further towards destruction, which will be possible only when he is exposed to a well planned and efficiently managed environmental education programme.

Now, management of environmental education programmes and activities is not easy task for it is beset with the problems of coverage and dimensions. It transcends the classroom and the school and covers the neighborhood, the community, the country and the whole world. It also cuts across and crosses several disciplines such as science of life, earth and physical phenomena, social studies, vocational subjects, arts and crafts, etc, It has therefore multi disciplinary character. To amplify this point, it may be added that owing to its multidisciplinary character the management of the curriculum of environmental education will not be amendable to the same pedagogical treatment as the curriculum of other disciplines, such as mathematics or history etc. The former will have two or three or more disciplines running into each other and may involve a lot many field visits, whereas the later will generally have little co-ordination with other areas of knowledge and may be restricted normally to the classroom. This unique feature of the management of the curriculum of environmental education is also a salient characteristic of the management of environment which is one of the applied sides of Environmental Education. The Bhopal gas tragedy is a glaring example of this characteristic. The tragedy makes it very clear that a chemical industry, if not managed properly, may usher in calamity not only for those manning it but also for those living nearby. It may be a catalysm or a holocaust for the entire city involving death, blindness and a great many diseases for thousands of people. Furthermore it may destroy animal life too, such as the pond and Lake Ecosystem, the birds and mammals and other vertebrates and invertebrates, etc.

In addition to these problems which complicate the management of environmental education, it involves a lot of running around, mustering of men, gathering of physical resources and doing work at one's own initiative without waiting for orders from above.

For illustration, if a group of individuals decides to grow some trees on the fringe of their village to check the winds that erode the humus of their farms and fields they have to go to someone knowledgeable about trees, to know which species they should select which will serve their purpose and which will grow in their climate and in the shortest possible time. Then they have to go to some other person say a shopkeeper from whom they may buy spades to dig holes for planting trees, to a nursery to get plants and to a manure shop, etc. In short they have to contact several people till they have planted the trees. After that too they have to care for the infant trees and save them from destruction by cattle and men. All this is possible if the concerned people are willing and dedicated workers, if they are imbued with fervor for conserving and improving their environment and if they possess a sound sense of values and work culture.

One other reason which complicates the management of environmental education and makes it more difficult is that man has been conditioned through the ages to using his environment recklessly. For instance seeing a flame of forest tree, known as Butea frondosa in Botany and as Dhak or Palash in Hindi, he may rush instinctively towards it to pluck its leaves for wrapping betel leaves or for packing other tit bits. He really runs berserk and ravages this tree when it blossoms in the month of March and April and when its branches, on after the other are adorned with flaming saffron flowers, which look like the rising sun in the lilac darkness of the twilight. He hopes off one whole branch every day, takes it home to decorate his drawing room till the entire tree is bereft of all branches and is reduced to a mere trunk. Similarly, he damages other trees by cutting their branches for using them as fuel. He has to be reconditioned and his attitude towards his environment has got to be improved. Now improving attitudes and teaching values is a task meant not only for teachers but also it is a challenge for managers who are responsible for achievement of all the objectives and for whom M.B.O., an acronym for management by objectives is very clear. Meeting this challenge is obviously difficult because it is a Herculean task to recondition a human being and to change his conventionalized behavior, caused by man created custom, attitudes and beliefs, behavior that has become a routine. Management in no other area or branch of learning is confronted with such a formidable challenge compounded by the intangibility of results.

Interpretation of Objectives

In order to meet this challenge and to accomplish all the objectives of environmental education cognitive, affective and psychomotor the first thing for the managers will be to understand their task very clearly, which will mean interpretation of the objectives of environmental education in operational terms, which lead to the achievement of objectives at various stages, say primary, secondary, senior secondary and non formal. For illustration the objectives at the primary level may be divided into operation such as a visit to a nearby pond with a view to understand its ecosystem, to a nursery to learn about plants and how to grow them, to an orbiculturist or horticulturist to learn how to care for trees, to neighborhood to survey the sources causing pollution of air and water in the community and to write down steps to be taken to keep the environment clean etc.

Planning

After the objectives have been delineated in operational terms, the next step will be planning of programmes and setting time limits for various targets and goals. Beginning from local primary school, it will encompass the community, block, district, state and go up to the country level. This sequence envisages communication from the top to bottom and from bottom to top and provides for interaction among the people working at the same level. It also assumes that planning would bring together school, families, communities and blocks etc. In the light of these assumptions, let us now begin with the planning at the primary school level, and for that matter, let us take the item 'planning planting of trees in the school compound'. The first step in this direction will be to divide students into groups and elect leaders so that a committee of students is formed at the school level to co-ordinate the project. Some teachers would decide, on the basis of suggestions received from different classes, which type of trees each class would plant so that the school grows the various types of trees required to meet its demands, namely of flowering trees, shade trees and fuel trees and of trees along the boundary wall. Obviously, the headmaster and other concerned administrators would also be consulted at each stage so that they too may make their contribution, give proper guidance and provide funds and other resources for obtaining sapling to be planted, keeping the requirement of the school in view, requirements in terms of fuel trees which may be used for holding camp fire, requirements in terms of a shady groove for conducting morning assembly and other functions which are normally held in an auditorium which the school cannot afford, requirements for conducting games and sports during schools hours in the season when the sun is scorching hot, requirements in the terms of fruits for children to be served to them as part of midday meals requirements in terms of the beautification of the school compound, etc.

When all the requirements of different kinds of shade, fruit fuel, ornamental and other trees have been laid down, the students will decide which species of each kind should they select out of those that can grow in their compound. Thus, for selecting flowering trees they will have to make a choice out of say Gulmohar (Poinciana regia), Jacaranda (Jacaranda minosaefolia), Amaltas (Cassia fistula), Colville's Glory etc. which can grow in that area. Such a decision has to be made keeping the surroundings in view so that the colors of flowers are neither subdued nor are they incongruous with the background. For example, planning Gulmohars amidst Colville's Glories may not look good as planting them near Jacarandas. Similarly a decision is to be taken about shade trees such as Neem (Azadiracta indica), Pakar (Ficus infectoria), Mango (Mangifera indica) Kadam (Anthocephalus cadamba), Pipal (Ficas religiosa), Cassia, Siam, etc. etc. and also about trees along the boundary wall, such as Ashoka (Palyathia longifolia), Silver Oak (Gaurillea robusta), etc.

The next decision that has to be taken is to select the sites for pits. They should be selected 3-4 month before planting saplings. One caution that must be exercised at this stage is that saplings should be planted at a distance of 15 to 20 feet from each other so that when they grow into full trees, the crown of one does not obstruct the growth of the other. A second caution must be that each pit should be dug to a depth and diameter of 4-5 feet, preferably in the month of March. It should then be left exposed to sun and rain. A month or two after that the sapling should be planted when it has started raining which means in any month from July to September. However, for planting deciduous trees, January and February are the best month, because during these month the trees are in a dormant state and therefore, the saplings can be taken out from one place and planted in another without suffering any damage during the process of transplantation. While doing that care should be, however be taken that balls of earth around the roots should not be removed or broken. A third caution should be that only the roots of the saplings should stand erect above the ground. Finally the plant should be drenched thoroughly. Similarly, all other precautionary measures should be planned to ensure proper growth of the trees to its full stature.

Similar steps can be delineated along with the cautions to be taken for planning other activities and programmes of environmental education such as identifying the source of pollution in the environment, launching cleanliness drives to spruce up the community, organizing educational tours to forests and other ecosystem to study the habits and habitats of vertebrates, etc. In so far as the planning of the theory lesson is concerned, it is advisable that the teachers prepare their plans keeping the multi disciplinary nature of the subject in view. For that matter they may consult encyclopaedias, books of knowledge and other literature. They may also consult leading magazines and newspapers carrying articles on environmental topics. In brief, these plans should include interesting and readable materials besides what is contained in the textbook so that they are related to the immediate environment and arouse student's curiosity to know more about it and its problems. It may be added here that the UNESCO, some international organizations, various governments, publishers and World wild life Fund have been bringing out useful information on environmental topics and on the animal and plant species that are facing extinction, which may be of interest to teachers at the time of planning their lessons. Many leading ornithologists and botanists too have several valuable contributions to their credit, which could also enrich teaching plans.

To summarize, each lesson plan should begin with a clear statement of objectives defined in behavioral terms and contain the material that would be used in the classroom by the teacher and the students for achieving these objectives. It should also contain the graphic materials; motivate students to learn the lesson etc. Furthermore, the plan should contain the evaluation procedures that the teacher would follow to assess whether or not the students have understood the lesson and achieved the prescribed objective. Finally, the plan should contain home assignments which may reinforce the learning outcomes of the lesson.

Teacher's lesson plans and the plans of activities and programmes to be undertaken by the students in their school and surrounding community will constitute the planning to be done at the school level. Next to it will be planning at the block level where the plans received from various school within the block can be scanned and their financial implications will be worked out, which should not be much, in any case because most of the work envisaged in the plans will be undertaken with the help of local community and inter departmental support. For example, spades and axes may be borrowed from the community development departments, or the students may bring them from their houses. Similarly sapling may be raised in each locality or village with the help of their concerned government departments or people. In essence, the whole effort should be directed at mobilizing local human and physical resources so that the plans at the school and block levels do not become prohibitively expensive. With this consideration in mind a consolidated plan may be prepared for the block figuring out the plans would form the basis for preparing district plan which in turn would lead to state plans. The state plans to the national plan which would be prepared keeping all the parameters of development in view so that regional imbalances are reduced and environmental education adds to the socio economic development of the country.

Organizing

Next to planning comes organizing for which once the plans have been prepared an organizational structure should be created for executing the plans. Really speaking the organizational machinery already exists. It is manned by almost adequate staffs that have merely to be informed of the mayhem caused by the indiscriminate exploitation of the environment and oriented about the needs and methods of environmental education. May be some adjustments or adaptations in the existing structure may appear inescapable in some cases but they will be minor. The existing manpower, or at the most a couple of personnel added to it, will fill the bill. What is needed is that they should accord priority to environmental education and volunteer to work on the committees constituted for the planning and management of environmental education. One such committee will have to be set up in the Ministry of Education at the national level that are concerned with the conservation and enrichment of environment, and also with the ministers and departments, such as of technology and industry etc. whose negligence may result in catastrophes and cataclysms for mankind. Vertical cooperation will include linkages with international organizations such as UNESCO, International Union for Conservation of Natural Resources (IUCN), World Wild Life Fund (WWF), etc. Similar committees will have to be set up at the state, district, block and school levels which will assist in the planning and implementation of all environmental education activities and programmes.

All these committees will also coordinate the orientation and in-service education courses and management training will be the quintessence of the scheme of environmental education. For conducting these courses and training programmes some additional staff may be required at the national and state levels. For that matter, perhaps a small cell may have to be added to the National Institute of Educational Planning and Administration. The cell at the national level would conduct orientation courses for top level administrators and those at state level for middle level administrators, school principals and teachers. Staff requirements for each cell, may be worked out keeping in view the number of persons to be trained. The minimum staff required for the cell at the national level will consist of a high level management man having experience in environmental education, an expert in the social aspects of environmental education, and expert in conservation, three office assistants who know shorthand and typewriting, a librarian and a staff car driver. Staff requirements for the cells in the State Institutes of Education can be worked out by states keeping their need of training in view.

The syllabus to be covered in the training course for top levels management may cover the following topics.

1. Environmental map of the country which will take into account the aspects of land and land form patterns of the country, environmental problems in various areas, prevalence of disease, etc.
2. Rural and urban problems relating to water supply, health, disease and sanitation.

3. Population and demographic problems and their control.
4. Safety requirements and standards to be followed in chemical industries, thermal power projects and atomic energy installations.
5. Endangered valleys, such as silent valley, Nubra Valley, forests that force extinction for example, if resin tapping continues in its present form in Jammu and Kashmir, about half of the pine trees would try up within twenty years the present ' French Cup and Lip, method has got to be substituted by the 'rill method' which increases the yield and at the same time ensures the health of the rest.
6. Social forestry
7. Solar energy
8. Biogas
9. Rare animal species, wild life, food chains, ecosystems
10. Marine and Fresh Water Biomes, etc.

The aforesaid outline is merely illustrative and not exhaustive list of topics to be covered in the management course on environmental education, it will also involve showing of films on the havoc already caused by indiscriminate deforestation, mushroom growth of industrial estates in metropolis and big urban conglomerations and on the loss of life caused by water pollution. The purpose of these films would be to develop in the participants an awareness of the environment a concern for conservation and enrichment. The films along with other course material will also aim at informing the participants of the latest methods and techniques of influencing educated people and changing their work culture. Changing work culture is important because the main reason for low performance in developing countries in all spheres of life, and especially in education, is lack of motivation and willingness to work. It is common experience that teachers at all levels show such an apathy towards their work that even the best scheme of education, handled by them falls on rocks and falls miserably. Environmental education is not an exception to it and will meet the same fate unless the management at the top level shows concern for changing the teacher's principal's and education officers attitudes towards their work, so that they may be able to overcome their sloth and resistance to adoption of innovations. In order to be able to do this, the top level managers will have to be kept abreast of the theories and models of management followed in various parts of the world for managing service organization in which results are intangible and the tools of measurement imprecise. They have to be appraised of the hierarchy of human needs, of the difference between the 'X', 'Y' and 'Z' theories of management will function in a country unless it has its tools in the culture of that country. In the background of this knowledge, they will have to work out a management model of environmental education for their country.

Staffing

When the model of management has been worked out and the administrative organization compatible to it outlined, the next step would be to select and recruit new staff or to train the existing manpower so that sufficient number of skilled personnel are available to run the scheme of environmental education. Doing this would involve forming of recruitment rules and setting up of a training wing or an institute where existing teachers of science and social studies who would be given the job of teaching environmental education, would be trained or those newly recruited would be oriented so that they become conversant with the philosophy, contents, programmes and activities of environmental education, and also with the methods and models for teaching it. Methods and models would, of course, include the following;

1. Those applicable to classroom instruction;
2. Those germane to conducting educational excursions, environmental surveys and field trips;
3. Those pertaining to doing practical work in the school and the community towards conserving renewing and enriching the environment; and
4. Those relevant to preventing people from causing any damage and deterioration to environment such as Chipko Movement for stopping people from destroying forests felling trees and looting away their boughs and branches.

Directing

When the staff personnel have been recruited and trained the next task is to take from them, which would entail a lot of decision making, communicating and exercising of controls.

Decision-making in environmental education will have to be somewhat a departure from the traditional or conventional method, as it is about activities and programs to be undertaken by them, mostly on their own or after receiving very little or no direction from their teacher. For instance, say, if students of IIEE undertake the activity "Survey of the sources of pollution of the Ganga in Patna", they have to traverse along its bank from west to east identifying all pollutants they come across and noting them down. Their teacher can obviously be of little help to them in this, because it may not be possible for him to accompany all the students who would be busy in various places. In sequel, students would be left to themselves to make their own decision. Moreover, imposing decisions on them or telling them what to do will not involve them fully in the activity. A better method would perhaps be sitting together and discussing with them the alternatives. A drawback in this method is that it sometimes generates more heat than light, as some students tend to stick to their guns for emotional reasons, which they perceive as most rational ones. To obviate this difficulty, it is better if each student can sit together and exchange their notes and make decisions. In this process, the emphasis would shift from seeking a quick solution to understanding the problem in its actual setting and getting involved in it. In other words, what is needed is that the students should not only be rationally but also emotionally integrate with his environment so that whatever decisions he might make, he should be able to carry them out.

Closely related to decision making is the pattern of communication in the organization. Top to bottom communication will not work in managing environmental education, because people involved will not work fully, receive a message and act upon it, unless they are emotionally prepared to accept and implement it which means that the receiver's perception and willingness are more important, than the clarity of the sender's words and expression, although the latter too are important. It follows from this that the receiver's mental and emotional state is very important in the communication pattern used in the management of environmental education. It may be further added that the message communicated should also be in the vocabulary and language of the people who are involved, the words to be used for communicating with them should be within their range of perception and should also be collateral to their aspirations, values and purposes so that they are received well. It may be remembered at this stage that effective communication is a very powerful method of converting people and changing their personality, values, beliefs and aspirations which is one of the significant purposes of environmental education.

Along with decision making and communicating, exercising control mechanisms is also a vital link in the managerial process. However, it is easier said than done because the results of environmental education are intangible to a great extent and therefore, tend to elude the controls. For example, it is not possible to measure reliably environmental renewal and enrichment. This intangibility factor is further complicated by the fact that the observer by his mere presence changes the event under observation. For some activity, his very presence affects the performance of the student. Even so, it is very necessary to measure their results, so that feedback is available on every programme and activity and it may be possible to take follow up action and remedial measures in time. And results pertaining to knowledge, comprehension, application, analysis, synthesis, evaluation of ideas and the entire cognitive domain can be measured by a battery of tests supplemented by an essay type of examination. However, the objectives in the affective domain, those pertaining to changes in attitudes, values, beliefs and aspirations cannot be measured as the 'uncertainty principle; applies more rigorously to them. In spite of this limitation, efforts must be made to exercise controls in this domain too.

Coordination

The next element to management is coordination. Coordination for the management of environmental education will be both inter and intra departmental. Inter departmental coordination would mean, first of all coordination among students within a class or its section, if any, so that practical work and activities are performed in a systematic manner and students may not squabble with each other about who should use the space and who the hammer and thus create a pandemonium. Intra-departmental coordination would also mean coordination among various classes in the school so that equipment and material required for various classes in the various activities are used sagaciously and prudently allowing the optimum use of scarce physical and human resources. A third level in the intra departmental coordination will be a horizontal link with the national government. Thus intra departmental coordination will aim at establishing connection between students teachers, principal and officers of the education department so that they can join to generate such scintillating wit and action as it electrifies the entire department and energies it to undertake and complete environmental renewal activities with grit and gusto.

Intra departmental coordination would mean coordination between the school and other departments such as the forest department, the department of urban and country planning, the horticulture department, the local industries that tend to pollute or actually pollute air and water, the experts on environmental education who live in the community, with all these departments would provide the school a perspective for understanding the problems of enriching the curriculum for it would enable students to visit these departments in a planned and guided way and to acquire practical knowledge as to how food water and air are polluted and how pollution could be stopped. In other words, it would provide for the students a very big laboratory where they will learn by seeing and doing. Thus, by effective intra-departmental coordination at its own level the school can accelerate and enrich student's learning outcomes. Similarly, by intra departmental coordination at district, state and national levels, education departments can secure a great support for environmental education programmes and activities.

Reporting

In order to ensure effective coordination, it would be very necessary to keep a proper record of correspondence to write proper minutes of all meeting, and to send reports to the departmental authorities and other concerned people at different levels so that they may take appropriate action and make environmental education a really applied subject.

Budgeting

Finally, keeping all the requirements in view, budget has got to be prepared in time so that the programmes do not suffer for want of funds.

In the end it may be repeated that management of environmental education is a far more difficult task than management of a factory or a firm, for it involves higher managerial skills and a dedication. It requires the fond attention without which the child will not have that glow and smile on its face which exudes health. It requires the tender care of a gardener for his plant, the care without which it will not grow and blossom and will remain stunted and dwarfed. It requires the skill of a leader who by using his wit and words mobilizes resources for social development and by using grit and gusto can achieve a formidable task. It requires in brief personal attention, dedication, determination, mental agility, social skills, a physically active body and an architect's and country planner's perspective, and above all, an indomitable will to succeed. Success would be a mistress of one who possesses these qualities. And environment around would be a beautiful heaven for humans.

Some Question

1. Why do you think environmental education should be managed?
2. Why environmental education needs a multi pronged approach of training from grass root level to top brass?
3. What are the stages of the management of environmental education?

Appendix

1. Glossary

Atmosphere: The gaseous envelope around the earth, the air. It has many gases but nitrogen, oxygen and carbon dioxide and water vapour are most important. It exerts a pressure of 14-7 pounds per sq. inch or in terms of column of mercury equivalent to 760 mm.

Autotrophs: Produce their own food, such as the green plants.

Biological Magnification: Successive increase of some chemicals through different food level organisms such as DDT from water to algae to herbivore fish to carnivore fish eating birds and to man.

Biosphere: All parts of earth where organisms live.

Carnivore: organisms feeding on other living organisms or flesh.

Carrying capacity: The holding capacity of the ecosystem is known as its carrying capacity.

Conservation: Keeping or not wasting; conservation of energy more efficient preventing loss of heat from buildings. Conservation of soil or soil conservation = preserving soil from being eroded or over cultivated. Maintenance of environmental quality or resources by use of ecological knowledge and principles.

Nature conservation =preserving nature as it is at present and taking steps to make sure that it is not polluted or disturbed. Conservation implies sound biosphere management within given social and economical constraints producing goods and services for human without depleting natural ecosystem and acknowledging the naturally dynamic character of biological systems.

dB: Decibel, a unit of sound intensity on a logarithmic scale.

Density: Number of individual per unit area.

Diversity: The process of different species growing together.

Desertification: The process of desert formation, permanent loss of plant life in a region, loss of capacity to sustain good plant growth.

Ecad: or Ecophene: Is a form variation within a species associated with some environmental condition but the character is not genetically fixed.

Ecological boomerang or backlash: The unforeseen canceling of projected gain or unforeseen adverse or catastrophic reaction from a natural system in response to human interference, management or developmental activities.

Ecological pyramid: Diagrammatic representation of numbers, biomass, energy or productivity of different trophic level organism with autotrophs at the base superimposed by those of herbivores, carnivores of the first order, second order and so on.

Ecosystem: The structural and functional entity of biotic communities and their environment. It may be of any size.

Ecotone: The transition zone between two communities showing characteristic edge effect.

Effluent: Liquid discharges or flowing out materials that usually pollute the environment.

Emission standards: The maximum permissible or safe limit of discharge of pollutants.

Environment: The totality of all kinds of influencing forces that surround an organism, both non- living and living.

Erosion: The physical removal of topsoil by wind or water; wearing under the forces of wind, rain beating, water current, trampling scrapings etc.

Eutrophic: Lakes rich in nutrients and productivity i.e choked with rich growth of vegetation.

Fall out : The descending radioactive fission products from atmosphere to earth's surface.

Fault: Deep cracks in earth's surface, fractures in rock layers etc. due to geographical events.

Feed back: The reverse direction flow (of information or any other thing) from the products back to the reactants.

Fission: Splitting of atom into lighter fragments and release of energy and neutrons.

Flow meter: The instrument used to measure the quantity of water or effluents flowing out of a system over unit time.

Fly ash: The dust and other small fragments of burnt up material dispersed by gas mixtures usually emitted through chimneys.

Food chain: The sequence of different trophic level organisms starting from primary producers to top carnivores.

Food web: The network of food chains in an ecosystem.

Fossil fuel: The fuel produced out of fossil plants and animals such as coal, petroleum gas.

Fresh water: Drinking water; less than 0.2 % salt content.

Fusion: Combining of nuclear or other things combination of atoms such as hydrogen forming helium and associated with release of energy (as in sun).

Green House effect: The heating effect through re radiation. In glass house the sunlight enters, but on re radiation the heat is trapped inside the glass house thus increasing the inside temperature. Similar effect is caused by atmosphere, dust, water vapour, ozone, carbon dioxide, etc. which allow the sun light to reach ground surface but trap the re radiating heat waves.

Gross Production: The total increase in organic matter, energy fixation due to photosynthesis over a unit area (or volume) and time. If the loss due to respiration is deducted it is net production.

Half life: The time taken by a radio active isotopes(or by pesticides) to come down to its half strength or decay to its half life level from the initial.

Holistic: Taking all the aspects and components of ecosystem into consideration.

Homeostasis: The capacity of ecosystem to resist changes due to disturbances or to return to balanced state.

Humic acid: The different kinds of acids formed due to partial decay of litter in the soil. These are decay resistant dark colored acid.

Humus: Dark colored fine powder of organic matter formed after the decomposition of litter.

Hydrology: The study of water storage's, distribution and movement on earth's surface.

Hygrograph: Instrument to measure relative humidity.

Incineration: Complete combustion of materials in a controlled condition.

Infiltration rate: The maximum rate of water entering the soil system through soil pores when it is abundantly available at its surface.

Infra red radiation: Wavelengths just larger than the red wave between 0.7 to 1um. It has a heating effect.

Ionosphere: The upper most layer of atmosphere above the stratosphere, where ionization takes place. In daytime its lower limit is 56km and in night 96 km above the earth's surface. It reflects radio signals.

Isotope: Forms of an element with same number of protons but different number of neutrons. They differ in radioactive behavior and atomic weights but have the same atomic number and chemical properties.

Microcosm: A miniature ecosystem often controlled to study the cause effect relationship of environmental factors on test organism or populations. Often used in aquatic ecology.

Migration: Movement of plant diaspores or of animals such as birds to distant places along some set routes.

Mist: Fine droplets larger than fog(i.e from 40um to 500um) of liquids in the air.

Monsoon: Monsoon the rain laden seasonal winds originating in Indian Ocean and Bay of Bengal.

Necrosis: Death of plant parts and its consequent discoloration.

Niche: The location and function of an organism in the context of ecosystem.

Nitrogen fixation: Conversion of free atmospheric nitrogen into combined form.

Oligotrophic: Nutrient wise poor lake with clear water.

Overburden: The deposits of surface soil or other material overlying usefully mined material like coal or other ores by open cast mining.

PAN: Peroxy acetyle nitrate, a secondary pollutant in smog formed by the action of light on hydrocarbons and nitrogen oxides of air.

Pedology: Study of soils.

Permafrost: Permanently frozen zone of the ground.

Pesticides: Chemicals used to kill pests such as herbicides for killing weeds, fungicides for fungi, insecticides for insects, rodenticides for killing mice, rats, etc. Permanent pesticides continue their killing property even after one year of its spray.

Photoperiodism: Control of phenological events by the day length time, such as leaf fall, flowering, migration of birds etc.

Pollution: Undesirable effects of foreign material on the natural environment.

Potable water: Clean water suitable for drinking and cooking.

Ppb and Ppm: Parts per billion or 1ug /1 and part per million or 1mg /l .

Primary production: Gain in biomass or energy by photosynthetic activity.

Preservation: Maintaining the natural conditions as it is. Like national parks and sanctuaries.

Remote sensing: Obtaining information about any aspect of ecosystems from far away recording device such as by aerial photography, lasers, ultraviolet and infrared detectors, radars, etc.

Resource: Materials useful to man and to other organisms

Secchi disc: A painted disc to measure turbidity of water.

Sewerage: The system of sewer collection, treatment and disposal.

Soil Profile: A section of soil column from surface to lower horizons.

Surfactant: The chemicals producing lather in detergents; these are phosphate rich and cause eutrophication.

Synergistic effect: Enhanced effects of two combining substances than the total effect of both in isolation.

Trophic: Related to food and feeding habit.

Troposphere: The zone of atmosphere containing clouds and moisture.

Watershed: The area drained by a stream or river.

Water table: The upper layer of ground water.

ZPG: Zero population Growth, i.e., each couple producing only two children so as to stabilize the population at the existing level.

2. **Some Important days and their Celebration**:

5th June: World environment day
22nd April: Earth day
21st March: World forest day
1st week of October: Wild life week

1st July: Vanmahotsav
28th February: Science day
1st May: Solar day
Nov. 19 to Dec. 18th: Environment month
7th April: World health Day
18th April: World heritage day
3rd May: International energy day
31st May: No Tobacco day
16th September: International Ozone Day
4th October : World animals' day
5th October : World Habitat Day
1st November : Forest day
3rd December : World conservation day
14th December : World Biodiversity day

Source : Gir Foundation Srushti.

3. Wild life Sanctuaries of India

Andaman and Nicobar islands: Arial,Bomboo, Barren, Battimalv, Belle, Bennett, Isamdn, Blister island, Bluff Island, Bondoville, Brush, Buchanan, Chanel, Cinque Islands, Cycle, Cone, Curlew (B.P.) Curlew, Cuthbert Bay, Defence, Dot. DottellDuncan, East, East of Inglis, Egg, Elat entrance, Gander, Girgan, Glathea Bay, Goose, Hump, Interview, James, Jungle, Kwangtung, kyd, Landfall, Latauche, Lhabarrack (saltwater crocodile) Mangrove, Mask, Mayo, Megapode, Montogemery, Narcondam, North Brother, North, North Reef, Oliver Orchid, Ox, Oyster Island-1 oyster island II, Pager, Parkinson, Passage Patric, Peacock, Pitman, Point, Potanma Islands Ranger, Reef, Roper, Ross, Row, Sandy Sea Serpent Shark Shearme, Sir Hogh Rose, Sisters, Snake Island1 Snake Island ii , South Brother, South Reef, South Sentinel, Spike Island I, Spike Island ii, Stoat, Surat, Swamp, Table(Delgarno) Table (Excelsior), Talabaicha, Temple, Tillongchang, Tree Tribly, Tuft, Turtle Islands, West, Wharf, White cliff.

Andhra Pradesh: Coringa. Eturnagram, Gundla Brahmeswaram, Kaundinya, Kawal, Kinnerasani, Kolleru, Krishna, Lanja, Maduugu, Sivaram, Manjira, Nagarjuna Sagar Srisailam, Nellapattu, Pakhal, Papikonda, Pocharam, Pranahits, Pulicat lake,

Rollapadu, Sri Lanka Malleshwaram, Sri Penusila Narasimha, Sri Venkateshwara.

Arunachal Pradesh: D'Ering Memorial (Lali), Dibang, Eagle Nest, Itanagatm Kamlang, Kane, Mehao, Pakhul, Sessa Orchid, Talc Valley.

Assam: Bardoibum-Beelmukh, Barnodi, Burachapori, Chakrashila, Diparbeel, Garampani, Gibbon, Laokhowa, Pabitora, Padumani-Bherjan-orajan, Panidihing, Sonai Rupai.

Bihar: Barela S. A. Z. S., Bhinbandh, Gautam Budhha, Kanwarjheel, Kaimur, Nagi dam, Nakti Dam, Rajgir, Udaypur, Valmiki, Vikramshhila Gangetic Dolphin

Chandigarh: Sukhna lake

Chattisgarh: Achanakmar, Badalkhol, Barnawapara, Bhairamgarh, Gomardha, Pamed, Semarsot, Sitanadi, Tamorpingla, Udanti.

Daman and Diu Fudam

Delhi Indira Priyadarshini (Asola)

Goa: Bondla, Chorao island (Dr. Salim Ali), Cotigaon, Madei, Mollem, Netravali.

Gujarat: Balaram Ambaji, Barda,Gaga Great Indain Bustard, Gir, Hingolgadh, Nature Reserve, Jessore, Jambogadha, Lala Great, Indian Bustard, Kachchh Desert khajiyaar, marine (Gulf of Kachchh) Nal Sarovar, Narayan Sarovar, Paniya, Porbander, Lake, Purna, Rampurs Vidi, Ratanmahal, Shoolpaneshwar (Dhumkhal) Thol Lake, Wild ass.

Haryana: Abubshehar, Bhindawas, Bir Bara Ban, Bir Shikargarh, Chhilchila, Kalesar, Khaparwas, Naharm Saraswati Plantation.

Himachal Pradesh: Bandi, Chall, Churdhar, Daranghati, Darlaghat, Dhauladhar, Gamgul Saibehi, Govind Sagar, Kais, Kalatop, Khajjiar, kanawar, Shoshan, Kibber, Kugti, Lippa Asrang, Majathal, Manalim Naina Devi, Nargu, Pong Dam Lake, Renula, Rupi Bhaha, Sianj, Sangla, Raksham Chitkul), Sechu Tuan Nala, Shikari Dev, Shilli, Shimmla Water Catchment, Simbalbara, Talra, Tirthan, Tundah.

Jammu & Kashmir: Baltal-Thajwas, Changthang, Gulmar, Hirapora, Hokersar, Jasrota, Karakoram, Lachipora, Limber, Nandini, Overa, Overa-aru, Ramnagar Rakha, Surinsar, mansar, Trikuta.

Jharkhand: Dalma, Hazaribaugh, Koderma., Lawlong, Mahaauaduar, palamau, Palkot, Parasnath, Topchanchi, Udhwa Lake.

Karnataka: Adichunchunagiri, Arabithittu, Bhadra, Billigiri Rangaswamy Te,mple, Brahmagiri, Cauvery, Dandeli, Doraji Bear, Ghataprabha, Gudavi, Melkote Temple, Mookambika, Nugu, Pushpagiri, Ranebennur, Ranganthitu, Sharavathi Valley, Shettihalli, Someshwara, Talakaveir.

Kerala: Aralam, Chimmony, Chinnar, Idukki, Neyyar, Parambikulam, Peechhivazhaani, Peppara periyar, Shendurney, Thattekadu, Wayanad.

Madhya Pradesh: Bagdara, Bori, Gandhi Sagar, Ghatigaon, karera, Ken Gharial, Kheoni, National Chambal, narsinggarh, Nauradehi, Orcha Panchmarhi. Palpurno, Panna (gangau), Panpatha, Pennch, Phen, Ralamandal Ratapani, Silana, Sanjay Dubri, Sardarpur, Singhori, Son, Gharial, Veerangna Durgawati.

Maharashtra: Amba barwa, Andhari, Aner Dam, Bhamragarh, Bhimahanke, Bor, Chandoli, Chaprala, Deolgaon-Rekhuri, Dhyanaganga, Gautala, Great Indain bustard, Jaikwadi, Kalsubai, Karnala, Katepurra, Koyana, Lonar, Marine (Malvan), Mayureswar, Supe, Melghat, Nagzira, Naigaon Mayur, Nandur

Madhameshwar, Narnala, Painganga, Phansad, Radhanagri, Sagareshwar, Tanse, Tipeshwar, Yawal, Yadsi Ramlinghat, Wan

Manipur: Yangoupkpi-Lokchao

Meghalaya: Baghmara Pitcher plant, Nongkhyllem, Siju

Mizoram: Dampa, Khawnglung, Lengteng, Ngengpui

Nagaland: Fakim, Puliebadze, Rangapahar

Orrisa: Badrama, Baisipalli, balukhand, Konark, Bhitarkanika, Chandaka, Dampara, Chilka (nalaban), Debrigarh, Khalasuni, Kotagerh, Kuldiha, Lakkhari Valley, Nandankanan, Satkosia Gorge, Simlipal, Sunabeda.

Punjab: Abohar, Bir Aishvan, Bir Bhadson, Bir Mehaswala, Bir Motigagh, Harike lake, Takhni- Rehampur

Rajasthan Bandh, Darrah, Jaisamand, Jamwa Ramgarh, Jawahar Sagar, kela Devi, Kesrbagh, Kumbhalgarh, Mount Abu, Nahargarh, National Chambal, Phulwari Li nal, Ramgarh Vishdhari, Ramsagat, Sajjangarh, Sariska, Sawai Man Singh. Sher Garh, Sitamatam Tal Chapper, Tadgarh, Raoli, Van Vihar.

Sikkim Barsey Rhododendron, Fambong Lho, Kyongnosola, Alpine, Maenam, shingba (Rhododendron)

Tamil Nadu: Chitangudi, Indira Gandhi (Annamalai), Kalakad, Kanjirankulam, Karaivetti, karikilli, Kilaselvanur-Melaselvanur, Kuthnkulam-Kadankulum, Mududmalali, Mundanthurai, Point Calimere, Pulicat Lake, Srivilliputhru (Giant Squirrel). Udayamarthapuram Lake, Vaduvoor, Vedanthangal, Vellanadu, Vellode, Vattangudi.

Tripura: Gumti, Rowa, Sepahijala, Trishna

Uttar Pradesh, Bakhhira, Chandraprbha, Hastinapur Kalmut, Katernaighat, Kishanpur, Lake Bahosi, Mahavir Swami,

National Chambal, Nawabganj, Okhala, Parvati Arnga, Patna, Ranipur, Saman, Samaspur, Sandi, Sohagibarwa, Sohelwa, Sur Sarovar, Surha Tal, Turtle, Vijai Sagar

West Bengal Ballavpur, Bethuadahari, Bibhutibhusan, Buxa, Chapramari, Haliday Island, Jaldapara, Jorepokhri, Slamander, Lothian Island, Mahananda, Narendrapur, Raiguanj, Ramnahagan, Sajnekhali, Senchal.

4. Project Tiger

Initially, the Project started with nine tiger reserves, covering an area of 16,339 sq km. with a population of 268 tigers. And at present there are 27 tiger reserves covering an area of 37,761 sq km. with a population of 1498 tigers. This amounts to almost 1.14% of the total geographical area of the country. Details of various Tiger Reserves along with their location and area are given in Table-4. The selection of reserves was guided by representation of eco-typical wilderness areas across the bio-geographic range of tiger distribution in the country. Project Tiger is undisputedly a custodian of major gene pool in the country. It is also a repository of some of the most valuable ecosystem and habitats for wildlife.

The Tiger Reserves are constituted on a 'core-buffer strategy'. The core area is kept free of biotic disturbances and forestry operations, where collection of minor forest produce, grazing, human disturbances are not allowed within. However, the buffer zone is managed as a 'multiple use area' with twin objectives of providing habitat supplement to the spill over population of wild animals from the core conservation unit, and to provide site specific eco-development inputs to surrounding villages for relieving the impact on the core. No relocation is visualized in the buffer area, and forestry operations, Non-Timber Forest Produce (NTFP) collection and other rights and concessions to the indigenous communities are permitted in a regulated manner to complement the initiatives in the core unit.

Project Tiger has put the tiger on an assured course of recovery from the brink of extinction, and has resurrected the floral and faunal genetic diversity in some of our unique and endangered wilderness ecosystem. The population of tigers in the country has increased significantly to about 4000 from less than 2000 at the time of launch of the project.

The effective protection and concerted conservation measures inside the reserves have brought about considerable intangible achievements also, viz. arresting erosion, enrichment of water regime and thereby improving the water table and overall habitat resurrection. Labour Intensive activities in tiger reserves have helped in poverty alleviation of the most backward sections and their dependence on forests has also reduced. The project has been instrumental in mustering local support for conservation programme in general.

Approach

- Elimination of all forms of human exploitation and disturbance from the core and rationalization of such activities in the buffer.
- Limitation of the habitat management to repair damage done by man.
- Researching facts about habitat and wild animals and carefully monitoring changes in flora and fauna.

The effective protection and concerted conservation measures inside the reserves have brought about considerable intangible achievements also viz. arresting erosion, enrichment of water regime and thereby improving the water table and overall habitat resurrection. Labour intensive activities in tiger reserves have helped in poverty alleviation of the most backward sections and their dependence on forests has also reduced. The project has been instrumental in mustering local support for conservation programme in general.

Most of the negative consequences of Project Tiger stem from increased human-wildlife conflict in the reserve areas. Some particular types are:

Predation/attacks by tigers on humans - earlier in this century, it was thought that man-eating tigers were those that had been

Indian Tiger Reserves showing year of creation / state / area

No	*Year of creation*	*Name of Tiger Reserve*	*State*	*Area (in sq kms)*
1.	1973-74	Bandipur	Karnataka	866
	1999-2000	Nagarhole (extension)		643
2	1973-74	Corbett	Uttar Pradesh	1316
3	1973-74	Kanha	Madhya Pradesh	1945
4	1973-74	Manas	Assam	2840
5	1973-74	Melghat	Maharashtra	1677
6	1973-74	Palamau	Bihar	1026
7	1973-74	Ranthambhore	Rajasthan	1334
8	1973-74	Similipal	Orissa	2750
9	1973-74	Sunderbans	West Bengal	2585
10	1978-79	Periyar	Kerala	777
11	1978-79	Sariska	Rajasthan	866
12	1982-83	Buxa	West Bengal	759
13	1982-83	Indravati	Madhya Pradesh	2799
14	1982-83	Nagarjunsagar	Andhra Pradesh	3568
15	1982-83	Namdapha	Arunachal Pradesh	1985
16	1987-88	Dudhwa	Uttar Pradesh	811
	1999-2000	Katerniaghat (extension)		551
17	1988-89	Kalakad (Mundanthurai)	Tamil Nadu	800
18	1989-90	Valmiki	Bihar	840
19	1992-93	Pench	Madhya Pradesh	758
20	1993-94	Tadoba-Andheri	Maharashtra	620
21	1993-94	Bandhavgarh	Madhya Pradesh	1162
22	1994-95	Panna	Madhya Pradesh	542
23	1994-95	Dampha	Mizoram	500
24	1998-99	Bhadra	Karnataka	492
25	1998-99	Pench	Maharashtra	257
26	1999-2000	Pakhui- Nameri	Arunachal Pradesh-Assam	1206
27	1999-2000	Bori,Satpura, Panchmari	Madhya Pradesh	1486
				37,761

Extracted from the MoEF Annual Report 2003

injured or otherwise handicapped in hunting their usual prey, or those that had accidentally acquired a taste for human flesh. These explanations seemed to be borne out by observations of game hunter-turned-conservationist Jim Corbett, who was responsible for hunting down several man eating predators.

The tiger population increase over the first decade of Project Tiger resulted in a spate of human deaths from apparently healthy tigers. These 'outbreaks' occurred mainly in the Sunderbans mangrove swamps of the Gangetic delta in India and inland swamps on the Nepal-India border. The Sunquists who studied tiger ecology in the Chitwan Reserve of Nepal, attribute this phenomenon to the crowding of tiger territories within a limited area, that results in the competitive displacement of some individual tigers. These tigers then resort to prowling on the fringes of the reserve, where encounters with humans are more likely. The problem is aggravated by the open nature of the vegetation at the forest border, that makes it attractive to other tiger prey as well. In similar habitat in Dudhwa, North India, sugarcane cultivators had taken to planting their crops well within the parks buffer zone. Sugarcane fields make ideal nursery grounds for tigresses, that attack humans when they come to harvest their crop. In areas like Dudhwa, villagers have retaliated by attempting to destroy tigers whenever possible. In 1986 and 1987 alone, twenty-five tigers had been found dead.

Encroachment into reserves - Humans have historically been venturing into India's forests in search of firewood, minor forest produce (fruits, leaves etc.) and fodder for their livestock. Project Tiger severely limited this access, denying people entry into the core areas, and restricting access in the buffer zones. Burgeoning human and livestock populations have exacerbated the situation. Habitat destruction and cattle grazing are the main offenses recorded, constituting 69 % and 20 %, respectively, of the tiger reserves and other protected areas.

In some areas, entire villages were relocated following re-designation of the forests as tiger reserves. For example, twelve villages in the Ranthambore Park of Rajasthan were disbanded by 1979, six years after it was declared a tiger reserve. While monetary compensation was offered, it was rarely considered adequate by the locals, who had often lived in the area for generations, to leave. As of 1986, there were upto 15,000 people and about 40,000 head of livestock around Ranthambore. Laws prohibiting encroachment into the villages are constantly violated, resulting in often disastrous consequences. Inadequate rains in 1984 caused acute fodder shortage around Ranthambore - graziers and grass-cutters swarmed the 400 sq. km reserve, causing much damage to wildlife habitat. A forester attempting to intervene was stoned to death by the graziers, and several others were injured.In

1987, a local administrative official yielded to pressure from villagers and granted them permission to graze their cattle in the park. This decision was quickly reversed by the Central Government, but the damage had been done and several thousand cattle had browsed the park cover.

Intensive grazing has also depleted natural corridors connecting tracts of forest in many tiger reserves, increasing the potential for contact with tigers that move between what are now fragments of forest.

Villagers protesting against wildlife and forest legislation set fires to major areas of the Kanha and Nagarhole tiger reserves, causing both habitat destruction and physical threat to a park ranger.

Other hurdles to tiger conservation

Besides increased conflicts between humans living around the park and the poisoning of tigers to protect livestock, the 1980s have seen a sudden increase in poaching in response to international demand . The biggest market for the fur trade - Japan - priced tiger skin at nearly US $95,000 in 1981. Tiger bones and whiskers are highly valued for apparent medicinal and spiritual reasons in China and other countries of South-East Asia. A single brewery in Taiwan is said to import 2000 kg of tiger bones a year from which it brews wine. Notwithstanding CITES and national-level legislation against wildlife trade, the market for tiger parts is flourishing. A tiger-breeding program has been set up in Beijing with Siberian stock from North American zoos, which might alleviate atleast some of the pressures on wild populations.

Suggested management strategies

Since much of the pressure on tiger reserves (and more generally, national parks and wildwife sanctuaries) comes from human and livestock populations, tackling these should be the priority for further management efforts. These require coordination between many governmental programs such as agro- and social forestry, animal husbandry, tourism, family planning and wildlife management that are administratively distinct. Some suggestions are given below: a detailed management plan has recently been prepared by a non-governmental agency in India.

(i) Reduce fuel/ fodder demands on protected areas: This may be done by encouraging plantation forestry in the common lands outside of the parks. A very small fraction of parks and sanctuaries currently have such schemes in place so there is much scope for this. A discussion of common property rights and legal reform is beyond the scope of the present discussion. Briefly, villagers have traditional access rights to some of the government-owned lands surrounding the settlements - if such land falls within protected areas, alternate sites must be made available. Relocation of villages is an option that has been partially successful, incentives to move must be strengthened.

(ii) Compensation for livestock damage by wildlife: Tigers are the major cause of livestock loss. Adequate compensation for this loss is currently in place only in a few areas. Amounts vary in orders of magnitudes across states, and even differ between predators. For example, in the central Indian state of Madhya Pradesh, the money payable for a head of livestock killed by a leopard is a quarter of the amount paid if the predator were a tiger. These measures need to be standardized.

(iii) Protect corridors: While the creation of forest corridors de nova remains a controversial subject, existing and historic forest corridors have been important for movement of wildlife between habitat patches. With increasing fragmentation, it is imperative that existing corridors be maintained, perhaps with the aid of reforestation in areas where the corridors have been 'worn thin' by grazing. This is one way to accommodate expanding tiger populations in sites with severely limited areas. Currently 30 % of the parks and 26 % of the sanctuaries are officially listed as connected with one another - more such corridors need to be given protection and/or restoration.

(iv) Human and livestock population control: Though clearly beyond the scope of any wildlife management scheme, these two factors remain the most insidious of threats to conservation of natural resources. Additionally, stall-feeding of existing cattle, where feasible, can keep them from indiscriminately roaming the forests: moreover such a husbandry scheme could meet some of the energy requirements of the villagers (by enabling biogas generation).

Funding sources for biological diversity and endangered species conservation are a critical concern and this has spawned several excellent reviews. Some of the schemes that might be appropriate for the case of the Indian tiger are:

(i) International conventions: WWF and IUCN, two international conservation programs have provided financial support for Project Tiger since its inception. Such funding should continue. The recently announced Rhinoceros and Tiger Conservation Act proposed to the US Congress this year seeks to earmark funds specifically for research and management projects aimed at these two species, and is a promising avenue to explore in the future.

(ii) Ecological tours: Most of the information available to visiting tourists is restricted to booklets on the area and/or checklists of fauna. Additional sources of revenue to be explored are the employment of trained bilingual naturalists that will organize nature trails and other such systematic exploration activities. These services exist only in some private resorts such as Tiger Tops in Nepal and small-scale private eco-tourism enterprises scattered across the Indian subcontinent. These services could be developed by the state Forest and Wildlife Departments on a larger scale.

(iii) Park fees: The current amounts charged are quite modest in comparison with the purchasing ability of tourists, many of whom come from countries with more powerful economies. India might do well to consider the model of Costa Rica in this respect, and allow tourism in parks to generate revenue.

Approaches that may not work in the Indian context

(i) Commercialization of wildlife hunting: This approach has met with success in countries like Zambia, where the Wildlife Conservation Revolving Fund has allowed sustainable harvest of elephants and channeled the proceedings into appropriate conservation venues. In theory, this approach has potential in the case of Project Tiger, where tiger densities have arisen beyond the carrying capacity of some parks and translocation is often inviable because of habitat fidelity of individuals. Moreover, there is an acknowledged market for tiger parts. Problems with this approach in India are regulating the take. Moreover, the idea of legalizing take (albeit regulated) will be quite abhorrent to ardent conservationists in India.

(ii) Charge for ecological services: Some authors have proposed levying fees on public goods and services such as high-quality water in forested watersheds. In a developing country like India rising inflation and ever-increasing fractions of populations below the poverty level make this an unfeasible option.

Conclusion

In the western world, a major ongoing debate addresses the inadequacy of single-species over biodiversity conservation efforts. In the case of Project Tiger, we have seen that the main problems arise not from focusing on a single species: it has been demonstrated that saving a large keystone species such as the tiger can conserve large areas of natural habitat and associated biota. Rather, the problem results from failure to consider the human-wildlife interface in protected areas, and to offer traditional forest-users alternatives instead of imposing blanket bans on forest entry.

Indeed, an interim WWF project report of 1981 declared

"(the) great lesson learned throughout the first decade of Project Tiger is a realization of the urgent need to restore productivity to the depleted multiple-use areas surrounding wildlife reserves through ecological development. This alone can bring about compatibility between the reserves and the neighbouring communities who are, at present, struggling for subsistence."

The clashes between human and wildlife interests in the middle 1980s in Ranthambore and other such parks underscore the consequences of this neglect. In some parks, the situation seems irredeemable. Only by working local needs into conservation efforts and by exploring creative means of making the wildlife pay for themselves can we retain any hope of ensuring amicable co-existence of humans and nature.

1969: Congress of the IUCN held in New Delhi placed the population at 2.500 and the species found its way into the Red Data Book.

1970: In India, legislation enacted banning tiger hunting and export of skins.

1972: WWF and IUCN funded Operation Tiger and subsequent nationwide census conducted by the Indian government estimated 1827 animals.

1972: The Indian Wildlife Protection Act declared it a protected species, with the caveat that an animal could be taken if it posed a threat to human life.

1972: WWF issued international appeal for funding.

1973: Project Tiger inaugurated at Corbett National Park, India.

1975: International trade in tiger products prohibited by CITES.

1977-1993: Number of Tiger Reserves multiply in India. Panna (M.P.) and Pench (Maharashtra) being the latest. Plight of Indravati and Nagarjunasagar Reserves becomes worse. Number of tigers (debateable always) dwindles however. Major losses at Ranthambore and Corbett Reserves ! Tiger census techniques and parameters questioned?

1994: US Congress introduced The Rhinoceros and Tiger Conservation Act of 1994.

http://www.cranes.org/Project_Tiger.htm - BlankTophttp://www.cranes.org/Project_Tiger.htm - BlankTop

5. Chipko Movement

Chipko means "to hug" in an Indian language. In 1730, a Jodhpur Maharaja ordered woodcutters to fetch wood from the Bishnoi region. Bishnois abhor killing – even of trees. Women and the elderly protected the trees by hugging them. 363 Bishnois were killed by the king's loggers before they gave up. Almost 250 years later, the saga was repeated when villagers from Gopeshwar, Uttar Pradesh confronted loggers from a sports goods factory in March 1973, who planned to consume the lovely lush forests on which their lives depended. The villagers rushed to the forests shouting "Chipko! Chipko!" and hugged the trees, daring the loggers to let their axes fall on their backs. These loggers were terrified by them and fled! Thus began one of the world's most famous non-violent conservation movements, the Chipko movement.

History

The forests of India are a critical resource for the subsistence of rural peoples throughout the country, but especially in hill and mountain areas, both because of their direct provision of food, fuel and fodder and because of their role in stabilizing soil and water resources. As these forests have been increasingly felled for commerce and industry, Indian villagers have sought to protect their livelihoods through the Gandhian method of satyagraha non-violent resistance. In the 1970s and 1980s this resistance to the destruction of forests spread throughout India and became organized and known as the Chipko Movement.

The first Chipko action took place spontaneously in April 1973 and over the next five years spread to many districts of the Himalaya in Uttar Pradesh. The name of the movement comes from a word meaning 'embrace': the villagers hug the trees, saving them by interposing their bodies between them and the contractors' axes. The Chipko protests in Uttar Pradesh achieved a major victory in 1980 with a 15-year ban on green felling in the Himalayan forests of that state by order of India's then Prime Minister, Indira Gandhi. Since then the movement has spread to Himachal Pradesh in the North, Kamataka in the South, Rajasthan in the West, Bihar in the East and to the Vindhyas in Central India. In addition to the 15-year ban in Uttar Pradesh, the movement has stopped clear felling in the Western Ghats and the Vindhyas and generated pressure for a natural resource policy which is more sensitive to people's needs and ecological requirements.

The Chipko Movement is the result of hundreds of decentralized and locally autonomous initiatives. Its leaders and activists are primarily village women, acting to save their means of subsistence and their communities. Men are involved too, however, and some of these have given wider leadership to the movement. Prominent Chipko figures include: Sunderlal Bahuguna, a Gandhian activist and philosopher, whose appeal to Mrs. Gandhi results in the green-felling ban and whose 5,000 kilometre trans-Himalaya foot march in 1981-83 was crucial in spreading the Chipko message. Bahuguna coined the Chipko slogan: 'ecology is permanent economy'.

Chandi Prasad Bhatt, one of the earliest Chipko activists, who fostered local-based industries based on the conservation and sustainable use of forest wealth for local benefit.

Dhoom Singh Negi, who, with Bachni Devi and many village women, first saved trees by hugging them in the 'Chipko embrace'. They coined the slogan: 'What do the forests bear? soil, water and pure air'.

Ghanasyam Raturi, the Chipko poet, whose songs echo throughout thc Himalaya of Uttar Pradesh.

Indu Tikekar, a doctor of philosophy, whose comparative religion have stressed the unity and oneness of life and put the Chipko Movement in this context.

A feature published by the United Nations Environment Programme reported the Chipko Movement thus: 'In effect the Chipko people are working a socio-economic revolution by winning control of their forest resources from the hands of a distant bureaucracy which is concerned with selling the forest for making urban-oriented products.'

"The solution of present-day problems lies in the re-establishment of a harmonious relationship between man and nature. To keep this relationship permanent we will have to digest the definition of real development: development is synonymous with culture. When we sublimate nature in a way that we achieve peace, happiness, prosperity and, ultimately, fulfillment along with satisfying our basic needs, we march towards culture." Sunderlal Bahuguna

Women Involvement

Role of women in the Chipko movement

In the Himalayan Mountains of India when the forests were logged excessively, the women were the first to recognize the relationship between deforestation and social and environmental impacts. The Chipko movement was a significant step forward in the fight to save Himalayan ecology and society as commercial logging was destroying both. A large number of women were actively involved in Chipko movement as they were the most affected by the deforestation. The Chipko movement is not only an environmental movement, but is a women's movement as well, for it was solely women who saved the Himalayan forests from being exploited by commercial logging companies.

The Chipko movement as a women's movement essentially began three decades ago during Gandhi's movement of non-violence, which attracted two young English women searching for a new way of life, to come to India. One of these was Madeleine Slade, the daughter of a British General, who was renamed Miraben, by Gandhi himself. She worked closely with him and realized that commercial exploitation was the reason why floods were occurring in the Himalayas. The second woman was Catherine Hillman, renamed Sarlaben. She realized that the British in India were out to destroy India's culture and self-sufficient village economy, and to further their colonial interests Sarlaben, who also worked with Gandhi, realized that the hill women of the Himalayas had great potential for social action.

Women in the hills of India were involved in many protests before the actual Chipko movement began. All of these earlier protests prepared the women for the Chipko movement, which ended up being a success because of the women's strength and many achievements. In Tehri Garhwal, in 1965, an anti-alcohol campaign was launched and was headed by mainly women. Finally, the government failed in its efforts in opening a liquor shop there and the movement spread to other areas where thousands of women would demonstrate in each area. This kind of participation gave them the confidence to organize dissent around protecting their forests. They had a genuine interest for sustenance activity based on forest

Another happening that shows the role of the women was in January of 1979, in Vadiargarh. Twenty-five hundred trees were marked for felling and the men of the village were bought off with bribes. Women from Kemar, one hundred kilometers away came and camped there. The women stood close to the marked trees to stop the loggers from felling trees. The women of the Chipko movement were very strong-willed, very creative and extremely empowered to protect the forests even if it meant giving up their husbands and possibly their lives. The women of the Chipko movement not only protected the forests and their society, but the movement added to the world's consciousness of environmental issues.

One of the latest Chipko actions was directed against the state policy of social forestry. In February of 1988, in the Chamba district, thousands of eucalyptus saplings were uprooted in a forest department nursery. This was a protest against the Forest Department for it's failure to plant trees suitable for fuel and fodder, as the eucalyptus tree is not an ecologically sensible tree because it does not protect the soil or the villages from landslides. Chipko has an active reforestation program, which stresses the ecological dependency of the local people upon the forests and the need to sustain the forest environment. This is yet another success that the women of the Chipko movement achieved, and continue to maintain until the present.

Chipko continues the traditional realm of tree hugging, but has undertaken more project-oriented work in close collaboration with the local government. Women are still the ones who fight against the state because women are the most involved in agriculture and they continue to link deforestation to environmental problems more easily than men do. Furthermore, men have more contact with the government and therefore have more respect and fear for the government than women have. Also, for poor men, the prospect of more hotels, shops, schools and infrastructure makes them believe their incomes will be raised. Women, on the other hand, who provide subsistence goods, which are necessary for their village survival, wish to maintain their status quo by retaining the traditional ecosystem.

The Chipko movement was an important inspiration to other women's movements. The role of the woman in this moment is unquestionable. They were the first to recognize the environmental problem with deforestation and the ones who absolutely disagreed with commercial logging and development. As the sole providers of their families with clean water and fuel and fodder, the women of the Himalayas were the most directly affected, and hence, the strongest fighters in the protection of the forests. As a women's movement, the Chipko movement has ultimately led to further women's movements worldwide, and continues to fight for proper forestry policies. Women within India have a stronger voice than ever and have gained a political status that many women can be inspired by.

The following questions are taken for examination:

1. Is Chipko a movement rooted in economic conflicts over mountain forests or guided by ideas of deep ecology?
2. Is Chipko a social movement based on gender collaboration or a 'feminist movement' based on gender conflicts?
3. Has anyone in the Chipko movement actually hugged trees at the risk of her/his life and not for waiting photographers? These points will be taken up below for some elaboration.

1. Is Chipko a movement rooted in economic conflicts over mountain forests or guided by ideas of deep ecology?

Documented evidences from the movement sources do not indicate any influences of the brand of thinking known as 'deep ecology'. Dependable historical account of this widely written about movement is, surprisingly, scanty. Among the early writers on the history of the movement, Bandyopadhyay (1992) as well as Guha (1989) have not indicated any link with 'deep ecology'. On 24 June 1973, the first successful resistance to forest felling at the Mandal forests was based on economics and aimed at obtaining higher allotment of trees for felling to the Dasholi Gram Swarajya Sangh (DGSS), a local Gandhian organisation. On 26 March 1974, the more vociferous yet non-violent resistance at the Reni forests was triggered off by the news of auction of some local forests for felling to a sports-goods company from the plains. The contract system for forest felling allowed rich contractors from the plains make large profits from felling in the mountain forests. The basic theme of the movement as opposition to this practice is precisely expressed in the following lines from a famous poem by Raturi, the folk-poet of the movement:

Embrace the trees in the forests
And save them from being felled!

Save the treasure of our mountains
From being looted away from us!!

The movement got its initial start in the conflicts over mountain forests between the economic interests of the mountain communities and the economies of the plains. However, this fundamental basis of the movement got substantially reduced with the contract system of felling being stopped and the establishment of the public sector Forest Development Corporation. The felling were then onwards undertaken with the help of local village cooperatives.

Reference in the literature is frequently made of an environmental branch of the movement, which called for a total ban on commercial felling in the whole Garhwal and Kumaon Himalaya. This part of the movement is reported to have originated in the Tehri-Garhwal region, particularly the Henwal valley region, and is identified with the slogan:

What do the forests bear? Soil, water and pure air!!

The slogan is an excellent and simple summarization of the ecological importance of the mountain forests, especially in the Himalayan context. Many academic analysts, including the present author, had unhesitatingly accepted the slogan, when first informed about it. However, with the passage of time, several questions on the representative character and origin of this slogan have emerged. Notwithstanding the significant role played by the women of Henwal valley region in the protection of mountain forests, many women in the Garhwal and Kumaon region do not find the slogan as very realistic. Can the women in the mountain villages who spend several hours each day in the forests struggling to collect daily fuelwood and green fodder, ever forget to include fuelwood and green fodder in the list of important forest products, they ask. The convoluted argument that firewood and green fodder can grow only when there is soil, water and pure air, and hence they are secondary, appears too distant, theoretical and urban in the face of the hard struggle for survival in the rural mountain villages.

Naturally, the slogan has impressed urban environmentalists the world over but, for the women in the mountain villages who struggle to keep the cooking fire running and the domestic cattle well-fed at home, the slogan is an abstract one, at best a reflection of half-truth of their lives. This point indicates why the ecological message of the Chipko movement has impressed environmentalists in the urban areas and the countries of the North, much more than those in the mountainous hinterlands in the South. However, there is also a positive side to it. Much of the success of the movement in getting tacit political support lies in this capacity of the leadership of the movement to mobilize the vocal and urban environmentalists. Thus, in line with the distinction made by Guha (1989), the Chipko Movement has the private face of a quintessential peasant movement and a public face of one of the most celebrated environmental movements of the world. In answering the main question raised above, Chipko has its roots in the hard economic struggle for survival, while its face has been tactically decorated by some 'deep ecological' terms.

2. Is Chipko a social movement based on gender collaboration or a feminist movement based on gender conflicts?

In the early literature on Chipko no serious questions were raised about the movement being based on gender conflict. There was no lack of recognition of the fact the issue of forests in the Garhwal and Kumaon Himalaya touches the women much more intensely, than the men. The presence of large number of women in the forest action at Reni, and the largescale participation of the village women have led to some analysts claiming Chipko to be a 'women's movement'. Guha (1989) has answered these questions in a substantive manner showing the location of Chipko in the tradition of social movements of the region. However, inspite of that, Shiva (1992), identified Chipko as 'a women's movement', though no activist woman from the movement has made any such claim. The acutely subjective nature of such claims and the confusions they generate can be explained by a closer look at the way the incidence of the protest led by Gaura Devi in 1974 is seen from the ecofeminist viewpoint. As Guha (1989) describes,

Reni's importance in the saga of Chipko andolan (movement) is twofold. It was the first occasion on which women participated in any major way, this participation, moreover, coming in the absence of their own menfolk and DGSS activists.

Guha has elaborated on how the officials made a clever move to get the menfolk and the DGSS activists away from the villages around Reni forests, so that felling could be undertaken without resistance. The forest officials were concerned about the resistance to forest felling by both men and women. As Gaura Devi, the woman leader of the forest action at Reni explained (Guha 1989):

It was not a question of planned organisation of the women for the movement, rather it happened spontaneously. Our men were out of the village so we had to come forward and protect the trees.

The above statement clearly establishes the nature of the movement as a joint struggle based on gender collaboration. Thus, while the men in the concerned villages were diverted by a clever official move, the women took up the mantle of resistance. Interestingly, Shiva's (1992) description of the same incidence, from an ecofeminist viewpoint merely says:

A group of village women led by one Gaura Devi hugged trees, challenging the brute power of hired sawyers, about to cut down the trees for a sports goods company. The above statement suffers from reductionist drawbacks and distortion of facts. Due to the reductionist view, Shiva is unable to see the Reni action in a holistic perspective. Thus, the link between the steps taken by Gaura Devi and the contrived absence of the men in the village has been missed in her analysis. Referring to the contrived absence of the men folk of the village, Guha (1989) describes the same incidence in the following words:

Gaura Devi quickly mobilized the other housewives and went to the forest. Pleading with the laborers not to start the felling operations, the women initially met with abuse and threats. When the women refused to budge, the men were eventually forced to retire....As such, even at the level of participation Chipko can hardly be said to constitute a women's movement.

Gaura Devi herself did not mention any incidence of having led the women to embrace trees, as has been projected by Shiva (1992). This is historically incorrect. In the ecofeminist literature on Chipko, the women of Garhwal and Kumaon have often been described as opponents of change and mere carriers of tradition. Similarly, the men folk are described as rapacious agents of economic development and change. Realistic, holistic and painstaking research results by scholars in the same region have, fortunately, provided a different picture (see for example Mehta 1996). More recently, such myths have been more effectively exploded by the leading roles played by the women of Garhwal and Kumaon in the popular movement demanding a new and development oriented state in this mountain region.

Notwithstanding sensationalist writings, the women activists of the Chipko movement have considered that the movement has strengthened itself from gender collaboration against the inappropriate management practices for the mountain forests. Women have played significant roles in the movement, just as their male counterparts. There is no reason for seeing the Chipko movement as based on gender conflicts..

3. Has anyone in the Chipko movement actually embraced trees at the risk of her/his life and not for waiting photographers?

A common impression exists all over the world, except in the villages of Garhwal and Kumaon, that large number of people, especially women, have been embracing trees to prevent their felling. While the media has played an important role in spreading the positive message of the movement, some journalists have failed miserably to maintain minimum professional standards and have created serious confusions at the international level on the above question. Examples of such unprofessional reporting is given below:

In a magazine Sanctuary, Shiva (1992) declared that 'one Gaura Devi' led a group of village women to hug trees. A number of researchers had discussed the Reni action with Gaura Devi. However, there is no documented support to the claim of Shiva. She was neither present at the spot in Reni, nor she refers to any discussion with Gaura Devi. There has been a media created confusion on the issue of who embraced the trees in Chipko Movement. This has also disturbed the activists of the movement. The spreading of misinformation is taken to comical heights by a Malaysian journalist Fong (1996) who, in an article in The Star wrote that :

Her (Vandana Shiva's) name is synonymous with the Chipko Movement (Chipko means embrace) in India, an active anti-logging movement in the 70s and early 80s. To stem environmental destruction, Vandana (Shiva) led thousands of women to embrace (literally) the trees in the Himalayan mountains in their bid to stop logging activities.

In the characteristic style of sensationalist journalism, Fong (1996) does not provide any date, place, forest area, or villages associated with the incidence he reports. Nor he mentions one name out of the thousands of women that Shiva, reportedly, had led somewhere in the Himalayan mountains. The activists of the Chipko movement were, on one hand, amused at the totally comical nature of Fong's claim. On the other hand, in a letter of protest to the editor of The Star, they wrote (Jardhari et al. 1996):

The interview is based on false claims of Vandana Shiva and has angered many.......The real activists are so simple that they do not know why Vandana Shiva is reportedly publishing wrong claims about Chipko in the foreign press. We should all stand up against this new green exploitation of the people's simplicity and courage by clever, greedy and selfish persons like Vandana Shiva.

Contrary to all the unfounded greenish journalistic attempts in the international media, to garner the glory of the Chipko Movement, there has so far been only one reported clear instance of actual use of the method of embracing trees, and that too by a male activist. In the year 1977, Dhoom Singh Negi, a courageous and less known Gandhian activist from the village Pipleth, successfully prevented felling by embracing trees in the Salet forest area in the Garhwal Himalaya, as has been reported by Shiva and Bandyopadhyay (1986). In all other instances of Chipko movement, resistance was expressed in other non-violent forms. In most cases, the presence of a large number of angry villagers was enough to discourage the contractors from trying to fell trees.

All photographs of 'Chipko Actions' represent enactments. When the only reported incidence of embracing trees to protect them from felling occurred in Salet forests in the Garhwal Himalaya, and human life was at risk, there was no photographer around in the remote mountain forests.

This text is now brought to an end with a tribute to Dhoom Singh Negi, the little known man of strong commitments who embraced trees against falling axes in the Salet forests. Many courageous activists, men and women of determination, have brought 'Chipko' from the stage of a possible instrument of struggle to the stage of a trend setting achievement. Individuals like Dhoom Singh Negi are busy working in their small and remote Himalayan villages for the cause of sustainable human development. On the occasion of the completion of a quarter century since the mountain women's action at Reni forests in 1974, this article is a tribute to all of them.

What is the importance of the woods?

The Information and Public Relations, Government of Uttar Pradesh, Lucknow, INDIA lists that handicraft, food, processing, textile, electrical equipment, khadi, leather, sports good, toys carpet, and garments as major export items. Brassware, carpet, perfumes, silk, handlooms, and electrical automobile industries contribute to the eocnomy. The state has 312, 182 units in small sector involving invesment of (Rupees=RS) Rs28.275 billion with a number of 1,942 in medium and heavy industries in which Rs281.73 billion is invested. It also listed that 20% of Uttar Pradesh's GDP is contributed by the manufacturing sector as compared to 27.5% of India's. India is highly dependent on labor-intensive products for exports.

Products	*1994*	*1995*	*1996*	*1997*	*1998*
Wood in Rough Square D	-	-	1,678	603	NA
Wood Simply worked	243	294	1,151	482	NA
Wood Manufactures N.E.S.	5,360	7195	7,059	7,624	NA
Fruit/Veg Juices	1,681	3,202	899	2,037	NA
Spices	149,166	179,939	252,965	285,332	NA
Pearls/Precious Stones	4,060,449	4,745,985	4,175,691	4,475,467	NA

The movement moves...

In Uttar Pradesh, this movement achieved a major victory in 1980, which came with a 15-year ban on green felling in the Himalayan forests by order of India's then Prime Minister, Ms. Indira Gandhi. It also stopped clear felling in the Western Ghats and the Vindhyas and generated pressure for a natural resources policy, which is more sensitive to people's needs and ecological requirements. Then the movement spread to Himachal Pradesh in the North, Karnataka in the South, Rajasthan in the West, Bihar in the East and to the Vindhyas in Central India.

Conclusion

After seeing the scenario of the struggle between man and environment I remember this poem:

On cold nights I am

the heat of your hearth,
I screen you from the sun
with friendly shade
I give people fruits and flowers
As you thirst, my fruits refresh you
I am the beam that holds your house,
The board of your table,
the bed you lie on
The timber that builds your boat
and from which you get furniture.
I am the hands of your hoe,
And the door of your homestead
The wood of your cradle and the shell
of your coffin.

References

http://www.upinfo.org/index1.html

http://www.TED Case Study.htm

Shiva V. (1992) 'The Chipko Earth Charter' Sanctuary 12(3):44-49.

6. India – Environmental (Protection) Act, 198605/23/1986

THE ENVIRONMENT (PROTECTION) ACT, 1986

No. 29 OF 1986

[23rd May, 1986.]

An Act to provide for the protection and improvement of environment and for matters connected there with:

WHEREAS the decisions were taken at the United Nations Conference on the Human Environment held at Stockholm in June, 1972, in which India participated, to take appropriate steps for the protection and improvement of human environment;

AND WHEREAS it is considered necessary further to implement the decisions aforesaid in so far as they relate to the protection and improvement of environment and the prevention of hazards to human beings, other living creatures, plants and property;

BE it enacted by Parliament in the Thirty-seventh Year of the Republic of India as follows:-

CHAPTER I
PRELIMINARY
1.SHORT TITLE, EXTENT AND COMMENCEMENT

(1) This Act may be called the Environment (Protection) Act, 1986. (2) It extends to the whole of India.

(3) It shall come into force on such date as the Central Government may, by notification in the Official Gazette, appoint and different dates may be appointed for different provisions of this Act and for different areas.[1]

2.DEFINITIONS

In this Act, unless the context otherwise requires,—

(a) "Environment" includes water, air and land and the inter-relationship which exists among and between water, air and land, and human beings, other living creatures, plants, micro-organism and property;

(b) "Environmental pollutant" means any solid, liquid or gaseous substance present in such concentration as may be, or tend to be, injurious to environment;

(c) "Environmental pollution" means the presence in the environment of any environmental pollutant;

(d) "Handling", in relation to any substance, means the manufacture, processing, treatment, package, storage, transportation, use, collection, destruction, conversion, offering for sale, transfer or the like of such substance;

(e) "Hazardous substance" means any substance or preparation which, by reason of its chemical or Physico-chemical properties or handling, is liable to cause harm to human beings, other living creatures, plant, micro-organism, property or the environment;

(f) "Occupier", in relation to any factory or premises, means a person who has, control over the affairs of the factory or the premises and includes in relation to any substance, the person in possession of the substance;

(g) "Prescribed" means prescribed by rules made under this Act.

CHAPTER II

GENERAL POWERS OF THE CENTRAL GOVERNMENT

3. POWER OF CENTRAL GOVERNMENT TO TAKE MEASURES TO PROTECT AND IMPROVE ENVIRONMENT

(1) Subject to the provisions of this Act, the Central Government, shall have the power to take all such measures as it deems necessary or expedient for the purpose of protecting and improving the quality of the environment and preventing controlling and abating environmental pollution.

(2) In particular, and without prejudice to the generality of the provisions of sub-section (1), such measures may include measures with respect to all or any of the following matters, namely:—

(i) Co-ordination of actions by the State Governments, officers and other authorities—

(a) under this Act, or the rules made there under, or

(b) Under any other law for the time being in force which is relatable to the objects of this Act;

(ii) Planning and execution of a nation-wide programme for the prevention, control and abatement of environmental pollution;

(iii) Laying down standards for the quality of environment in its various aspects;

(iv) Laying down standards for emission or discharge of environmental pollutants from various sources whatsoever: Provided that different standards for emission or discharge may be laid down under this clause from different sources having regard to the quality or composition of the emission or discharge of environmental pollutants from such sources;

(v) Restriction of areas in which any industries, operations or processes or class of industries, operations or processes shall not be carried out or shall be carried out subject to certain safeguards;

(vi) Laying down procedures and safeguards for the prevention of accidents which may cause environmental pollution and remedial measures for such accidents;

(vii) Laying down procedures and safeguards for the handling of hazardous substances;

(viii) Examination of such manufacturing processes, materials and substances as are likely to cause environmental pollution;

(ix) Carrying out and sponsoring investigations and research relating to problems of environmental pollution;

(x) Inspection of any premises, plant, equipment, machinery, manufacturing or other processes, materials or substances and giving, by order, of such directions to such authorities, officers or persons as it may consider necessary to take steps for the prevention, control and abatement of environmental pollution;

(xi) Establishment or recognition of environmental laboratories and institutes to carry out the functions entrusted to such environmental laboratories and institutes under this Act;

(xii) Collection and dissemination of information in respect of matters relating to environmental pollution;

(xiii) Preparation of manuals, codes or guides relating to the prevention, control and abatement of environmental pollution;

(xiv) Such other matters as the Central Government deems necessary or expedient for the purpose of securing the effective implementation of the provisions of this Act. (3) The Central Government may, if it considers it necessary or expedient so to do for the purpose of this Act, by order, published in the Official Gazette, constitute an authority or authorities by such name or names as may be specified in the order for the purpose of exercising and performing such of the powers and functions (including the power to issue directions under section 5) of the Central Government under this Act and for taking measures with respect to such of the matters referred to in sub-section (2) as may be mentioned in the order and subject to the supervision and control of the Central Government and the provisions of such order, such authority or authorities may exercise and powers or perform the functions or take the measures so mentioned in the order as if such authority or authorities had been empowered by this Act to exercise those powers or perform those functions or take such measures.

4. APPOINTMENT OF OFFICERS AND THEIR POWERS AND FUNCTIONS

(1) Without prejudice to the provisions of sub-section (3) of section 3, the Central Government may appoint officers with such designation as it thinks fit for the purposes of this Act and may

entrust to them such of the powers and functions under this Act as it may deem fit.

(2) The officers appointed under sub-section (1) shall be subject to the general control and direction of the Central Government or, if so directed by that Government, also of the authority or authorities, if any, constituted under sub- section (3) of section 3 or of any other authority or officer.

5. POWER TO GIVE DIRECTIONS

Notwithstanding anything contained in any other law but subject to the provisions of this Act, the Central Government may, in the exercise of its powers and performance of its functions under this Act, issue directions in writing to any person, officer or any authority and such person, officer or authority shall be bound to comply with such directions.[3]

Explanation—For the avoidance of doubts, it is hereby declared that the power to issue directions under this section includes the power to direct—

(a) The closure, prohibition or regulation of any industry, operation or process; or

(b) Stoppage or regulation of the supply of electricity or water or any other service.

6. RULES TO REGULATE ENVIRONMENTAL POLLUTION

(1) The Central Government may, by notification in the Official Gazette, make rules in respect of all or any of the matters referred to in section 3.

(2) In particular, and without prejudice to the generality of the foregoing power, such rules may provide for all or any of the following matters, namely:—

(a) the standards of quality of air, water or soil for various areas and purposes;[4]

(b) the maximum allowable limits of concentration of various environmental pollutants (including noise) for different areas;

(c) the procedures and safeguards for the handling of hazardous substances;[5]

(d) the prohibition and restrictions on the handling of hazardous substances in different areas;[6]

(e) the prohibition and restriction on the location of industries and the carrying on process and operations in different areas;[7]

(f) the procedures and safeguards for the prevention of accidents which may cause environmental pollution and for providing for remedial measures for such accidents.[8]

CHAPTER III
PREVENTION, CONTROL, AND ABATEMENT OF ENVIRONMENTAL POLLUTION

7. PERSONS CARRYING ON INDUSTRY OPERATION, ETC., NOT TO ALLOW EMISSION OR DISCHARGE OF ENVIRONMENTAL POLLUTANTS IN EXCESS OF THE STANDARDS

No person carrying on any industry, operation or process shall discharge or emit or permit to be discharged or emit any environmental pollutants in excess of such standards as may be prescribed.[9]

8. PERSONS HANDLING HAZARDOUS SUBSTANCES TO COMPLY WITH PROCEDURAL SAFEGUARDS

No person shall handle or cause to be handled any hazardous substance except in accordance with such procedure and after complying with such safeguards as may be prescribed.[10]

9. FURNISHING OF INFORMATION TO AUTHORITIES AND AGENCIES IN CERTAIN CASES

(1) Where the discharge of any environmental pollutant in excess of the prescribed standards occurs or is apprehended to occur due to any accident or other unforeseen act or event, the person responsible for such discharge and the person in charge of the place at which such discharge occurs or is apprehended to occur shall be bound to prevent or mitigate the environmental pollution caused as a result of such discharge and shall also forthwith—

(a) intimate the fact of such occurrence or apprehension of such occurrence; and

(b) be bound, if called upon, to render all assistance, to such authorities or agencies as may be prescribed.[11]

(2) On receipt of information with respect to the fact or apprehension on any occurrence of the nature referred to in sub-section (1), whether through intimation under that sub-section or otherwise, the authorities or agencies referred to in sub-section (1) shall, as early as practicable, cause such remedial measures to be taken as necessary to prevent or mitigate the environmental pollution. (3) The expenses, if any, incurred by any authority or agency with respect to the remedial measures referred to in sub-section (2), together with interest (at such reasonable rate as the Government may, by order, fix) from the date when a demand for the expenses is made until it is paid, may be recovered by such authority or agency from the person concerned as arrears of land revenue or of public demand.

10. POWERS OF ENTRY AND INSPECTION

(1) Subject to the provisions of this section, any person empowered by the Central Government in this behalf[12] shall have a right to enter, at all reasonable times with such assistance as he considers necessary, any place—

(a) for the purpose of performing any of the functions of the Central Government entrusted to him;

(b) for the purpose of determining whether and if so in what manner, any such functions are to be performed or whether any provisions of this Act or the rules made there under or any notice, order, direction or authorization served, made, given or granted under this Act is being or has been complied with;

(c) for the purpose of examining and testing any equipment, industrial plant, record, register, document or any other material object or for conducting a search of any building in which he has reason to believe that an offence under this Act or the rules made there under has been or is being or is about to be committed and for seizing any such equipment, industrial plant, record, register, document or other material object if he has reason to believe that it may furnish evidence of the commission of an offence punishable under this Act or the rules made there under or that such seizure is necessary to prevent or mitigate environmental pollution.

(2) Every person carrying on any industry, operation or process of handling any hazardous substance shall be bound to

render all assistance to the person empowered by the Central Government under sub-section (1) for carrying out the functions under that sub-section and if he fails to do so without any reasonable cause or excuse, he shall be guilty of an offence under this Act.

(3) If any person willfully delays or obstructs any persons empowered by the Central Government under sub-section (1) in the performance of his functions, he shall be guilty of an offence under this Act.

(4) The provisions of the Code of Criminal Procedure, 1973, or, in relation to the State of Jammu and Kashmir, or an area in which that Code is not in force, the provisions of any corresponding law in force in that State or area shall, so far as may be, apply to any search or seizures under this section as they apply to any search or seizure made under the authority of a warrant issued under section 94 of the said Code or as the case may be, under the corresponding provision of the said law.

11. POWER TO TAKE SAMPLE AND PROCEDURE TO BE FOLLOWED IN CONNECTION THEREWITH

(1) The Central Government or any officer empowered by it in this behalf,[13] shall have power to take, for the purpose of analysis, samples of air, water, soil or other substance from any factory, premises or other place in such manner as may be prescribed.[14]
(2) The result of any analysis of a sample taken under sub-section (1) shall not be admissible in evidence in any legal proceeding unless the provisions of sub-sections (3) and (4) are complied with.

(3) Subject to the provisions of sub-section (4), the person taking the sample under sub-section (1) shall—

(a) serve on the occupier or his agent or person in charge of the place, a notice, then and there, in such form as may be prescribed, of his intention to have it so analysed;

(b) in the presence of the occupier of his agent or person, collect a sample for analysis;

(c) cause the sample to be placed in a container or containers which shall be marked and sealed and shall also be signed both by the person taking the sample and the occupier or his agent or person;

(d) send without delay, the container or the containers to the laboratory established or recognized by the Central Government under section 12.

(4) When a sample is taken for analysis under sub-section (1) and the person taking the sample serves on the occupier or his agent or person, a notice under clause (a) of sub-section (3), then,—

(a) in a case where the occupier, his agent or person willfully absents himself, the person taking the sample shall collect the sample for analysis to be placed in a container or containers which shall be marked and sealed and shall also be signed by the person taking the sample, and

(b) in a case where the occupier or his agent or person present at the time of taking the sample refuses to sign the marked and sealed container or containers of the sample as required under clause (c) of sub-section (3), the marked and sealed container or containers shall be signed by the person taking the samples, and the container or containers shall be sent without delay by the person taking the sample for analysis to the laboratory established or recognized under section 12 and such person shall inform the Government Analyst appointed or recognized under section 12 in writing, about the willful absence of the occupier or his agent or person, or, as the case may be, his refusal to sign the container or containers.

12. ENVIRONMENTAL LABORATORIES

(1) The Central Government[15] may, by notification in the Official Gazette,—

(a) establish one or more environmental laboratories;

(b) recognize one or more laboratories or institutes as environmental laboratories to carry out the functions entrusted to an environmental laboratory under this Act.[16]

(2) The Central Government may, by notification in the Official Gazette, make rules specifying—

(a) The functions of the environmental laboratory;[17]

(b) The procedure for the submission to the said laboratory of samples of air, water, soil or other substance for analysis or tests, the form of the laboratory report thereon and the fees payable for such report;[18]

(c) Such other matters as may be necessary or expedient to enable that laboratory to carry out its functions.

13. GOVERNMENT ANALYSTS

The Central Government may by notification in the Official Gazette, appoint or recognize such persons as it thinks fit and having the prescribed qualifications[19] to be Government Analysts for the purpose of analysis of samples of air, water, soil or other substance sent for analysis to any environmental laboratory established or recognized under sub-section (1) of section 12.

14. REPORTS OF GOVERNMENT ANALYSTS

Any document purporting to be a report signed by a Government analyst may be used as evidence of the facts stated therein in any proceeding under this Act.

15. PENALTY FOR CONTRAVENTION OF THE PROVISIONS OF THE ACT AND THE RULES, ORDERS AND DIRECTIONS

(1) Whoever fails to comply with or contravenes any of the provisions of this Act, or the rules made or orders or directions issued there under, shall, in respect of each such failure or contravention, be punishable with imprisonment for a term which may extend to five years with fine which may extend to one lakh rupees, or with both, and in case the failure or contravention continues, with additional fine which may extend to five thousand rupees for every day during which such failure or contravention continues after the conviction for the first such failure or contravention.

(2) If the failure or contravention referred to in sub-section (1) continues beyond a period of one year after the date of conviction, the offender shall be punishable with imprisonment for a term which may extend to seven years.

16. OFFENCES BY COMPANIES

(1) Where any offence under this Act has been committed by a company, every person who, at the time the offence was committed, was directly in charge of, and was responsible to, the company for the conduct of the business of the company, as well

as the company, shall be deemed to be guilty of the offence and shall be liable to be proceeded against and punished accordingly:

Provided that nothing contained in this sub-section shall render any such person liable to any punishment provided in this Act, if he proves that the offence was committed without his knowledge or that he exercised all due diligence to prevent the commission of such offence.

(2) Notwithstanding anything contained in sub-section (1), where an offence under this Act has been committed by a company and it is proved that the offence has been committed with the consent or connivance of, or is attributable to any neglect on the part of, any director, manager, secretary or other officer of the company, such director, manager, secretary or other officer shall also deemed to be guilty of that offence and shall be liable to be proceeded against and punished accordingly.

Explanation—For the purpose of this section,—

(a) "company" means any body corporate and includes a firm or other association of individuals;

(b) "director", in relation to a firm, means a partner in the firm.

17. OFFENCES BY GOVERNMENT DEPARTMENTS

(1) Where an offence under this Act has been committed by any Department of Government, the Head of the Department shall be deemed to be guilty of the offence and shall be liable to be proceeded against and punished accordingly. Provided that nothing contained in this section shall render such Head of the Department liable to any punishment if he proves that the offence was committed without his knowledge or that he exercise all due diligence to prevent the commission of such offence.

(2) Notwithstanding anything contained in sub-section (1), where an offence under this Act has been committed by a Department of Government and it is proved that the offence has been committed with the consent or connivance of, or is attributable to any neglect on the part of, any officer, other than the Head of the Department, such officer shall also be deemed to be guilty of that offence and shall be liable to be proceeded against and punished accordingly.

CHAPTER IV
MISCELLANEOUS
18. PROTECTION OF ACTION TAKEN IN GOOD FAITH

No suit, prosecution or other legal proceeding shall lie against the Government or any officer or other employee of the Government or any authority constituted under this Act or any member, officer or other employee of such authority in respect of anything which is done or intended to be done in good faith in pursuance of this Act or the rules made or orders or directions issued there under.

19. COGNIZANCE OF OFFENCES

No court shall take cognizance of any offence under this Act except on a complaint made by—

(a) the Central Government or any authority or officer authorized in this behalf by that Government,[20] or

(b) any person who has given notice of not less than sixty days, in the manner prescribed, of the alleged offence and of his intention to make a complaint, to the Central Government or the authority or officer authorized as aforesaid.

20. INFORMATION, REPORTS OR RETURNS

The Central Government may, in relation to its function under this Act, from time to time, require any person, officer, State Government or other authority to furnish to it or any prescribed authority or officer any reports, returns, statistics, accounts and other information and such person, officer, State Government or other authority shall be bound to do so.

21. MEMBERS, OFFICERS AND EMPLOYEES OF THE AUTHORITY CONSTITUTED UNDER SECTION 3 TO BE PUBLIC SERVANTS

All the members of the authority, constituted, if any, under section 3 and all officers and other employees of such authority when acting or purporting to act in pursuance of any provisions of this Act or the rules made or orders or directions issued thereunder shall be deemed to be public servants within the meaning of section 21 of the Indian Penal Code (45 of 1860).

22. BAR OF JURISDICTION

No civil court shall have jurisdiction to entertain any suit or proceeding in respect of anything done, action taken or order or direction issued by the Central Government or any other authority or officer in pursuance of any power conferred by or in relation to its or his functions under this Act.

23. POWERS TO DELEGATE

Without prejudice to the provisions of sub-section (3) of section 3, the Central Government may, by notification in the Official Gazette, delegate, subject to such conditions and limitations as may be specified in the notifications, such of its powers and functions under this Act [except the powers to constitute an authority under sub-section (3) of section 3 and to make rules under section 25] as it may deem necessary or expedient, to any officer, State Government or other authority.

24. EFFECT OF OTHER LAWS

(1) Subject to the provisions of sub-section (2), the provisions of this Act and the rules or orders made therein shall have effect notwithstanding anything inconsistent therewith contained in any enactment other than this Act.

(2) Where any act or omission constitutes an offence punishable under this Act and also under any other Act then the offender found guilty of such offence shall be liable to be punished under the other Act and not under this Act.

25. POWER TO MAKE RULES

(1) The Central Government may, by notification in the Official Gazette, make rules for carrying out the purposes of this Act.

(2) In particular, and without prejudice to the generality of the foregoing power, such rules may provide for all or any of the following matters, namely—

(a) the standards in excess of which environmental pollutants shall not be discharged or emitted under section 7;[21]

(b) the procedure in accordance with and the safeguards in compliance with which hazardous substances shall be handled or caused to be handled under section 8;[22]

(c) the authorities or agencies to which intimation of the fact of occurrence or apprehension of occurrence of the discharge of any environmental pollutant in excess of the prescribed standards shall be given and to whom all assistance shall be bound to be rendered under sub-section (1) of section 9;[23]

(d) the manner in which samples of air, water, soil or other substance for the purpose of analysis shall be taken under sub-section (1) of section 11;[24]

(e) the form in which notice of intention to have a sample analyzed shall be served under clause (a) of sub section (3) of section 11;[25] (f) the functions of the environmental laboratories,[26] the procedure for the submission to such laboratories of samples of air, water, soil and other substances for analysis or test;[27] the form of laboratory report; the fees payable for such report and other matters to enable such laboratories to carry out their functions under sub-section (2) of section 12;

(g) the qualifications of Government Analyst appointed or recognized for the purpose of analysis of samples of air, water, soil or other substances under section 13;[28]

(h) the manner in which notice of the offence and of the intention to make a complaint to the Central Government shall be given under clause (b) of section 19;[29]

(I) the authority of officer to whom any reports, returns, statistics, accounts and other information shall be furnished under section 20;

(j) any other matter which is required to be, or may be, prescribed.

26. RULES MADE UNDER THIS ACT TO BE LAID BEFORE PARLIAMENT

Every rule made under this Act shall be laid, as soon as may be after it is made, before each House of Parliament, while it is in session, for a total period of thirty days which may be comprised in one session or in two or more successive sessions, and if, before the expiry of the session immediately following the session or the successive sessions aforesaid, both Houses agree in making any modification in the rule or both Houses agree that the rule should not be made, the rule shall thereafter have effect only in such modified form or be of no effect, as the case may be; so, however, that any such modification or annulment shall be without prejudice to the validity of anything previously done under that rule.

Bibliography

Ambast, R.S., (1985) "Plant Ecology", Banaras Hindu University, Banaras.

Amin Geeta, (1996) "An Analysis of standard IV environment studies textbook prepared by Sandhan and Lok Jumbish". M. Ed Dissertation at CASE, The Maharaja Sayajirao University of Baroda, Baroda.

Anil Kumar De, Arnab Kumar De., (2004) "Environmental Education" New Age International (P) Limited Publishers, New Delhi.

Baker, (1988) Development of environmental value inventory 1978 Quoted in sterling publishers, Agarwal Y.P., (ed.) Research in Emerging fields of education, published by Sterling Publishers, New Delhi.

Bharat Bhusan (1997) "Environmental Issues 'Problems and policy Perspectives: Paradigms for 21st century" paper presented at the National Seminar on Environmental Education at Shimla 16-18 Oct. 1997.

Catherine Preetha, (2000) "A study on the role of NGO in imparting environmental awareness in Vadodara" City M. Ed Dissertation at CASE, The Maharaja Sayajirao University of Baroda, Baroda.

Chandola R.P.,(1995) Environment and Life published by RBSA Publishers, Jaipur.

David Huges Evans., (1977) Environmental education key issues of the future. Published by Pergamon Press Limited, U. K.

Dorathy C Andrews (1987) "Analysis of Elementary school curriculum on environment in the social environment perspectives". M. Ed Dissertation at CASE, The Maharaja Sayajirao University of Baroda, Baroda.

Gill J. S., Environmental Education in the school Curriculum Developed by the NCERT, Pub. by National Council of Educational Research and Training, New Delhi.

Gupta Santosh., (1997) "Observation : Starting a Process of self learning published in the Green Teacher published by Center of Environmental Education", Ahmedabad.

Gupta, V. K.,(1995) "Teaching and Learning of Science and Technology" pub. by Vikas publishing house pvt. Ltd. New Delhi.

Harsha Sundaram (1987) "An Exploration into the out of school resources in Baroda for effective organization of curricular experience in environment students at elementary school". M. Ed Dissertation at CASE, The Maharaja Sayajirao University of Baroda, Baroda.

- http://gurukul.ucc.american.edu/ted/chipko.htm
- http://projecttiger.nic.in/whyistigersad.htm
- http://projecttiger.nic.in/whyshouldwesavetiger.htm
- http://projecttiger.nic.in/yearofcreation.htm
- http://www.airweb.org.nz/tiger/project5.html
- http://www.iucn.org/en/about/
- http://www.sanctuaryasia.com/projecttiger/index.php
- http://www.TEDcasestudy.htm
- http://www.upinfo.org/index1.html
- http://www.wildlywise.com/projecttiger.htm
- http://www.womenexcel.com/ecowatch/chipkomove.htm

Jean Grambs, (1963) William J Iverson, Franklin K. Patterson, Modern methods in secondary Education pub. by holt, Rienhart and Winston. New York.

John Huckle and Stephen Sterling Ed (1996) "Education for sustainabilty" pub. by Earth scan Publication Ltd. London.

Jonathan Collett and Stephen Karakashian (1996) "Greening the College Curriculum" A guide to Environmental Teaching in Liberal Arts pub by Island press Washington DC.

Kaptan Sonal (2001) "Effectiveness of cartoons and comics based learning material (CCBLM) for teaching of Environmental Science in Std. II" M. Ed Dissertation at CASE, The Maharaja Sayajirao University of Baroda, Baroda.

Karkara G. S.(2000) "Environmental law" published by Central Law Publications Allahabad.

Khosoo T.N.,(1986) Environmental Priorities in India and sustainable development, New Delhi. Indian Science Congress Association.

Leaonard H Clark and Irving S Starr (1981) " Secondary and middle school teaching methods" pub. by Mac millan publishing co., in New York.

Narendra Vaidya (1971) "Thc Impact of Science Teaching" pub by Oxford and IBH publishing house Co. New Delhi.

Nayar Usha, Mangalgiri Anjana, (1988) "Environmental education" Training of teacher educators curriculum developers and educational planners and administrators. Pub by UNESCO UNEP international environment education and NIEPA New Delhi.

NCERT (2000) "Biology" Textbook for class XI pub. by Gujarat state board of Textbook , Gandhinagar.

NCERT (2003) "Science and technology" A textbook for class X pub. by NCERT, New Delhi.

NCERT (2003) "Science And Technology" Textbook for Class IX pub. by NCERT New Delhi.

NCERT (2003). "Science" Textbook for class VIII, pub. by NCERT New Delhi.

NCERT. (1989) "Biology" textbook, standard XII part II, pub. by NCERT New Delhi.

NPE (1986) "National Policy on Education", Ministry of human resource development Government of India, New Delhi.

Odum, Eugene P., (1971) Fundamental of Ecology, Philadelphia, W. B. Saunders company 1971.

Pai Sudhakar Ganesh (1981) "Preparation and tryout of curriculum in environmental studies leading to life long education for college students". Unpublished Ph.D thesis at CASE, The Maharaja Sayajirao University of Baroda, Baroda.

Pandya Jyoti, M., (1999) "A study of environmental attitude among B. Ed students teachers at the MSU of Baroda". M. Ed Dissertation at CASE, The Maharaja Sayajirao University of Baroda, Baroda.

Pandey V.C., (2005) "Environmental Education" Isha books. New Delhi.

Pandit Kameshwar., (1997) "Environmental Issues in different Socio- Geographical Context". Paper presented in National

Seminar on Environmental Education in Shimla on 16-18 October.

Panneerselvam, A., and Ramakrishnan M., (1996) "Environmental Science Education", published by sterling private limited New Delhi

Perry, Jones and Hammersley., (1974) The Teachers hand book for Environmental Studies, pub by Blanford press, London.

Powar K. B., (1994) "Environmental Challenges and the Universities" Assocaition of Indain Universities, New Delhi.

Praharaj. B. (1990) "Environmental knowledge, Environmental Attitude and perception regarding environmental education among pre service and in service secondary school leaders" unpublished Ph.D thesis of CASE MSU. Baroda.

Rao V.K., Reddy R.S., (2003) "Environmental Education" Commonwealth publishers, New Delhi.

Richardson S. John ., (1951) " Methods and materials for teaching General and physical science" . MC Graw Hill Book Company Inc. London.

Sharma D. V. Ed. (1995) Towards quality secondary Education Agenda for 21st century pub by Council of boards of school Education in India (COBSE) Vikas publishing house pvt. Ltd. New Delhi.

Sharma R. C, (1996) "Modern Science Teaching", published by Dhanpatrai and Sons, New Delhi.

Sharma R. C., (1981) "Environmental Education", published by metropolitan printers New Delhi,

Sharma Y. P., (1997) "Environmental Education and Role of mass media" paper presented in the National seminar on Environmental Education in Shimla on 16-18 October.

Stapp Willam B., (1982) An Instructional Program Approach to environmental education k-12 published in world views on science education edited by U-N Wanchoo Oxford and IBH publishing Co, New Delhi.

Susan Drake Swith (Ed.) (1998) " Valuing the Global Environment : Actions and Investments for a 21st century pub by GEF Global Environment Facility Washington D.C.

Tharian Abey K., (1996) "Development of a multimedia Package for environment awareness among VII standard students in the context of Baroda". M. Ed Dissertation at CASE, The Maharaja Sayajirao University of Baroda, Baroda.

Tomar Archana (1997) "Education for Environmental Awareness" Pub. In The Progress of Education Vol. LXXI No 11 June Pune.

Tomar Archana, (1998) "An intervention to improve the quality of instruction in environmental science for primary level school children", Unpublished Ph.D thesis at CASE, The Maharaja Sayajirao University of Baroda, Baroda.

Trivedi. P.R., (2004) "Environmental Education", APH publishing corporation, New Delhi.

UNESCO (1990) "Source book in Environmental Education for secondary school teachers" pub by UNESCO Principal Regional office for Asia and the Pacific Bangkok.

WWF (2000) "Teacher Training Workshop for Environmental Education" organized by Gujarat state office WWF for Nature India. 26th and 27th Feb, 2000.

- www.augius.com
- www.edugreen.com
- www healthandenergy.com
- www.iisd.org/50/comm/commbd/desd/do7
- www.markshep.com

Index

M

N

Z